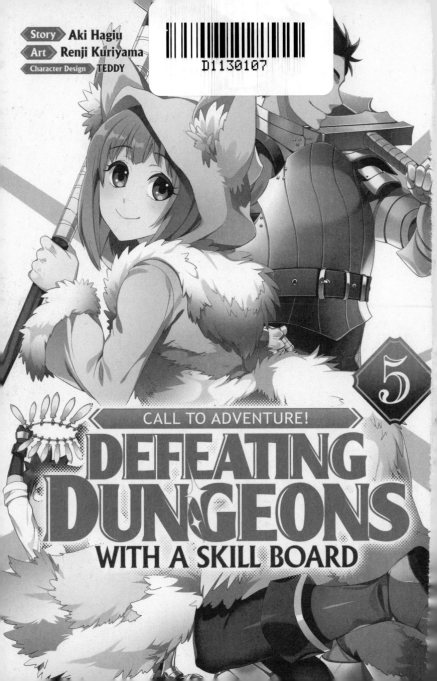

Story Aki Hagiu
Art Renji Kuriyama
Character Design TEDDY

D1130107

5

CALL TO ADVENTURE!

DEFEATING DUNGEONS

WITH A SKILL BOARD

5

CONTENTS

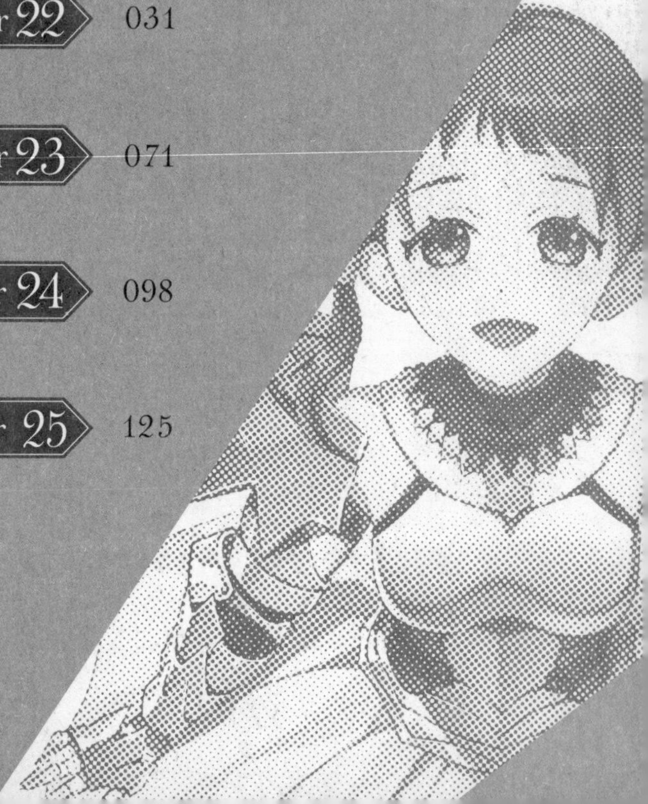

Chapter 21

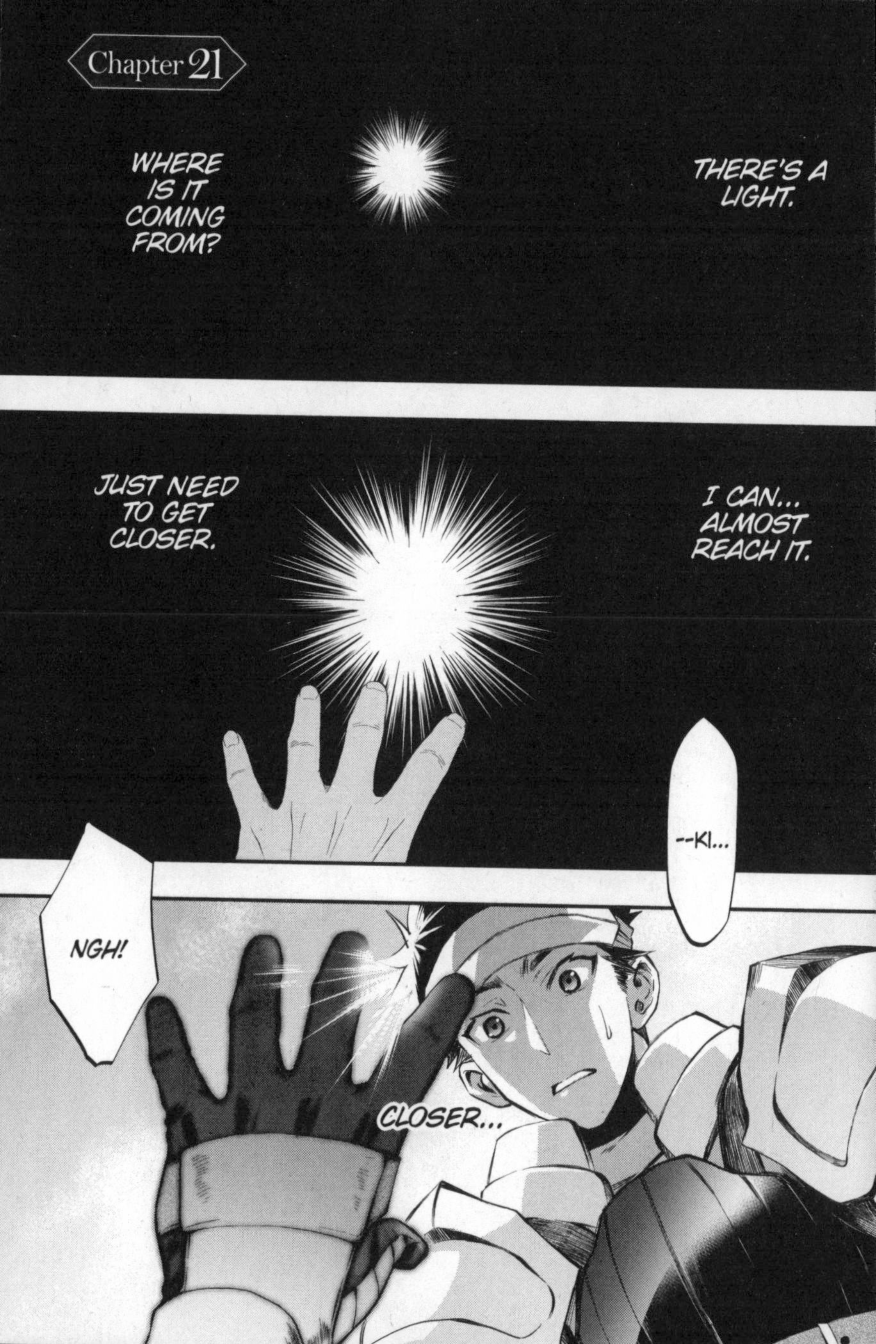
THERE'S A LIGHT.
WHERE IS IT COMING FROM?
I CAN... ALMOST REACH IT.
JUST NEED TO GET CLOSER.
--KI...
NGH!
CLOSER...

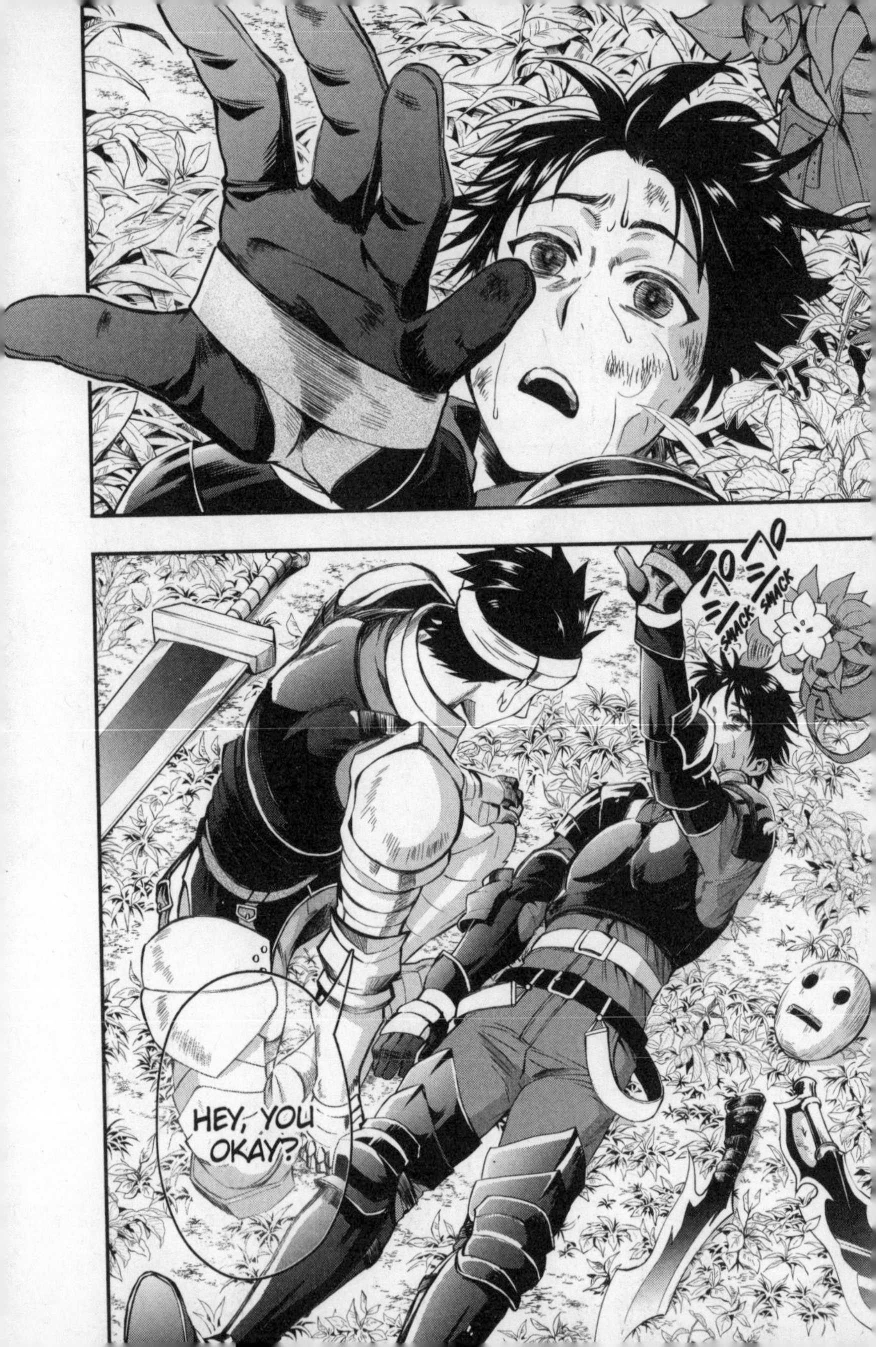
SMACK SMACK
HEY, YOU OKAY?

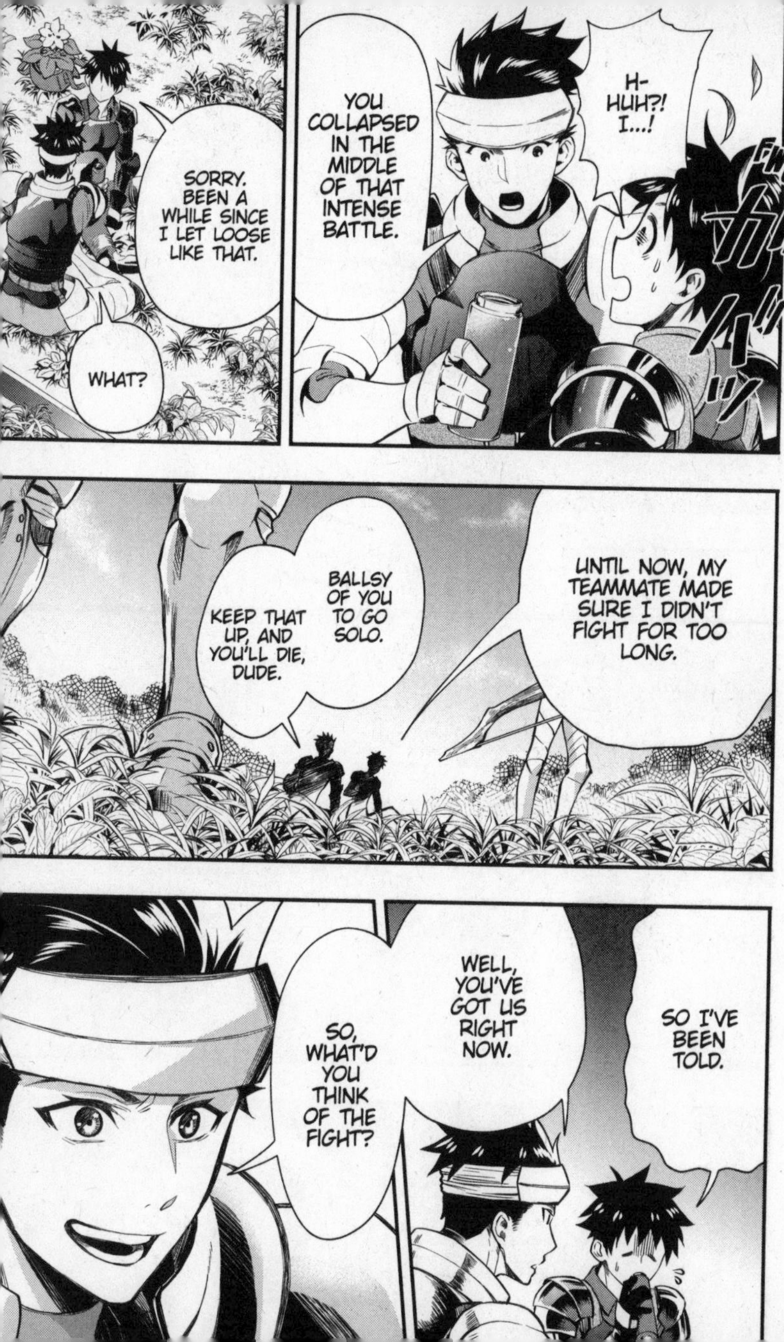
H-HUH?! I...!
FWUP
YOU COLLAPSED IN THE MIDDLE OF THAT INTENSE BATTLE.
SORRY. BEEN A WHILE SINCE I LET LOOSE LIKE THAT.
WHAT?
UNTIL NOW, MY TEAMMATE MADE SURE I DIDN'T FIGHT FOR TOO LONG.
BALLSY OF YOU TO GO SOLO.
KEEP THAT UP, AND YOU'LL DIE, DUDE.
SO I'VE BEEN TOLD.
WELL, YOU'VE GOT US RIGHT NOW.
SO, WHAT'D YOU THINK OF THE FIGHT?

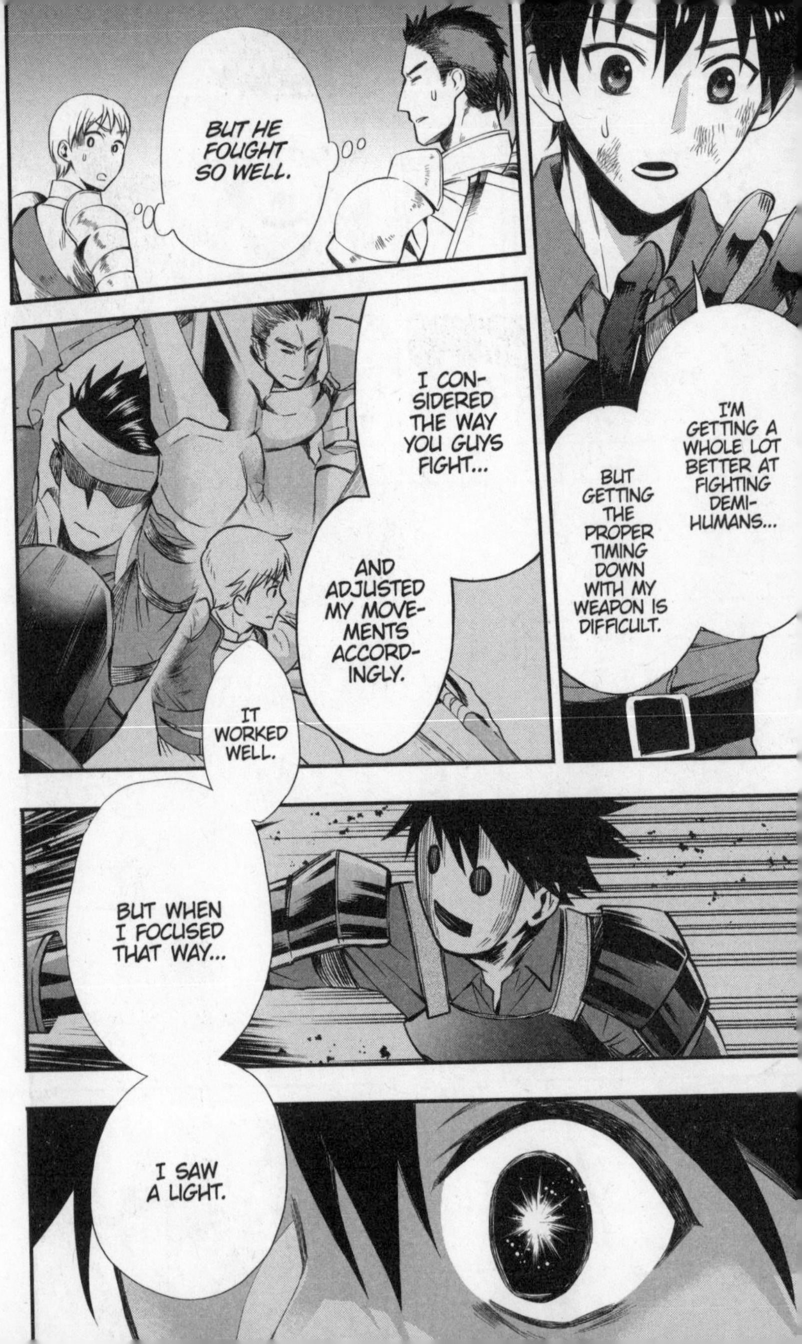
I'M GETTING A WHOLE LOT BETTER AT FIGHTING DEMI-HUMANS...
BUT GETTING THE PROPER TIMING DOWN WITH MY WEAPON IS DIFFICULT.
BUT HE FOUGHT SO WELL.
I CONSIDERED THE WAY YOU GUYS FIGHT...
AND ADJUSTED MY MOVEMENTS ACCORDINGLY.
IT WORKED WELL.
BUT WHEN I FOCUSED THAT WAY...
I SAW A LIGHT.

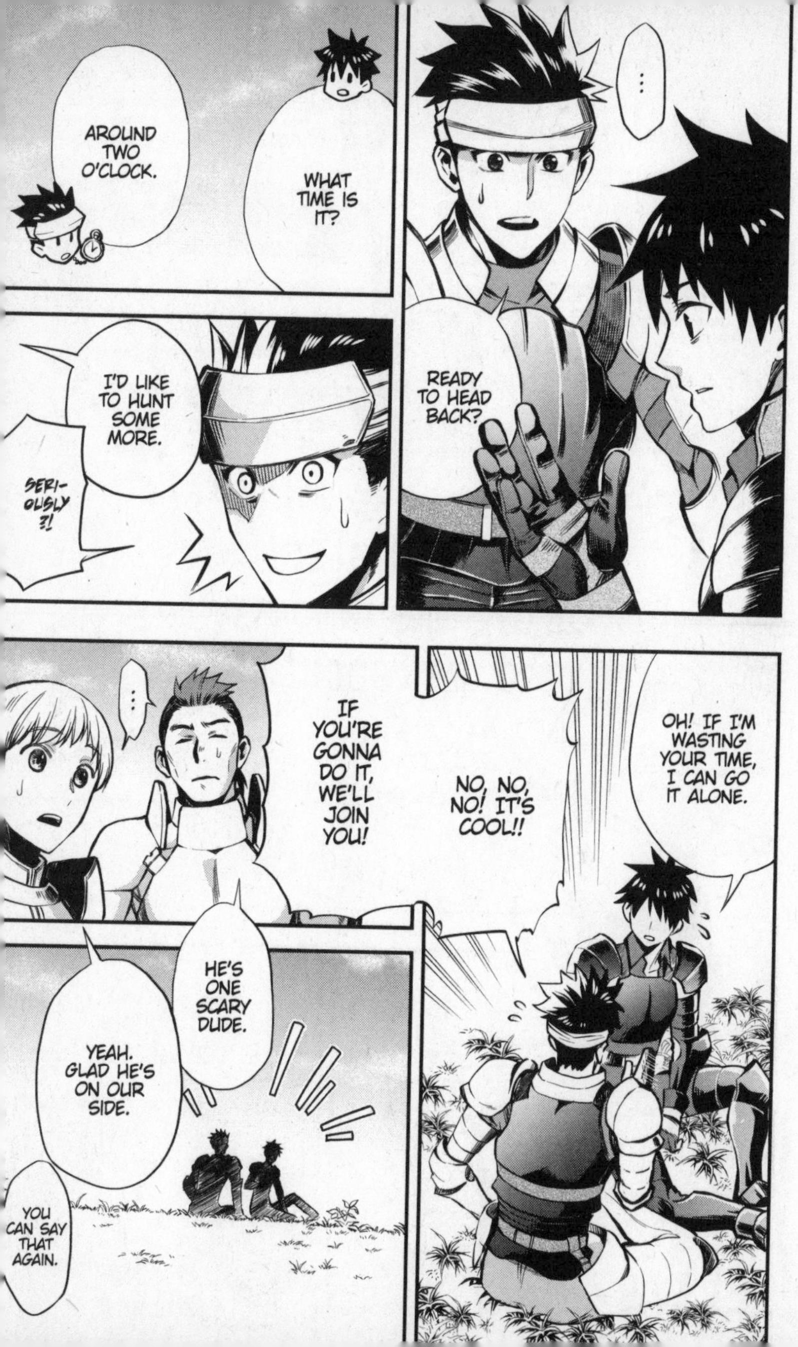
…
READY TO HEAD BACK?
WHAT TIME IS IT?
AROUND TWO O'CLOCK.
I'D LIKE TO HUNT SOME MORE.
SERI-OUSLY?!
OH! IF I'M WASTING YOUR TIME, I CAN GO IT ALONE.
NO, NO, NO! IT'S COOL!!
…
IF YOU'RE GONNA DO IT, WE'LL JOIN YOU!
HE'S ONE SCARY DUDE.
YEAH. GLAD HE'S ON OUR SIDE.
YOU CAN SAY THAT AGAIN.

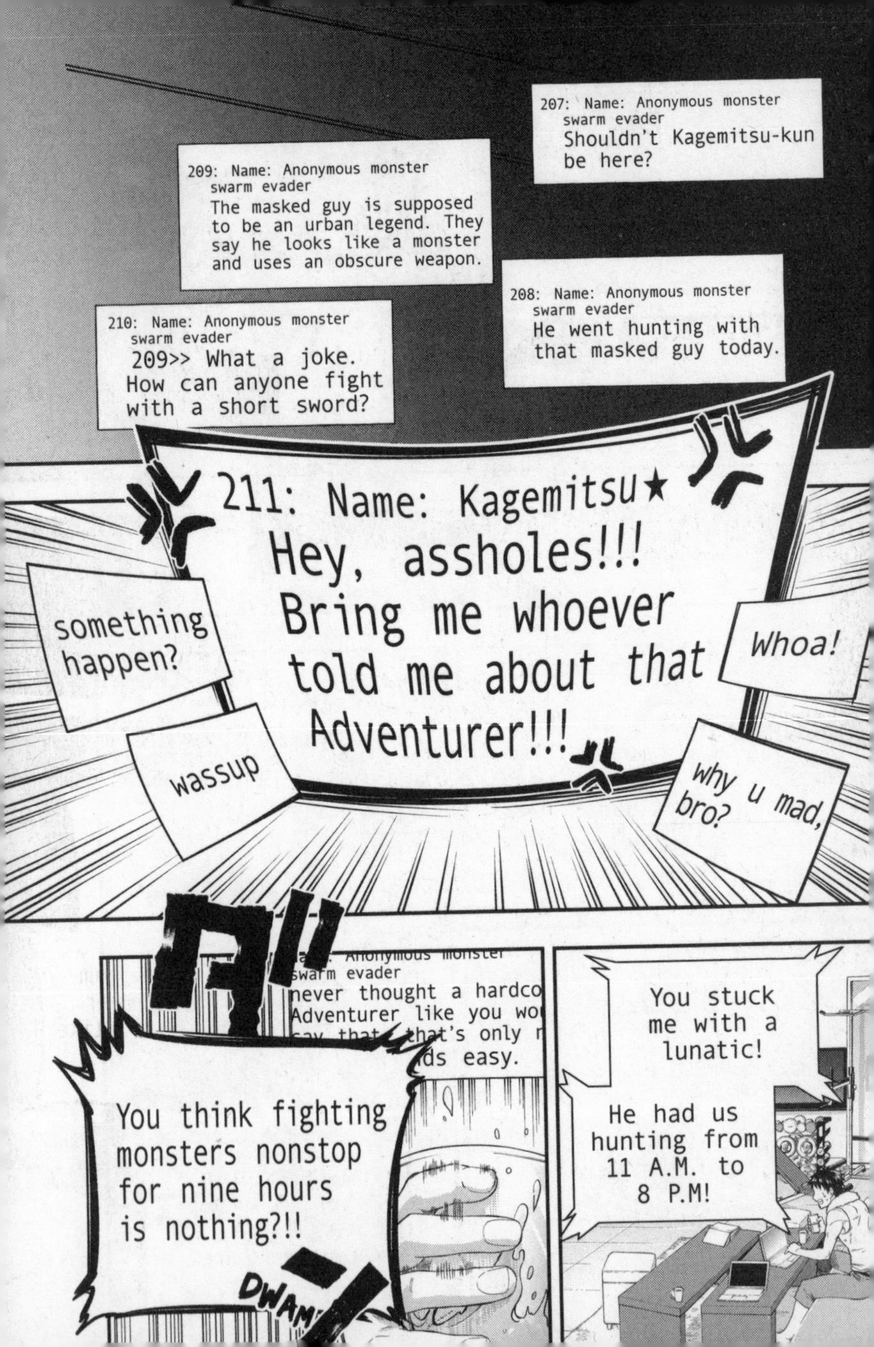
207: Name: Anonymous monster swarm evader
Shouldn't Kagemitsu-kun be here?
208: Name: Anonymous monster swarm evader
He went hunting with that masked guy today.
209: Name: Anonymous monster swarm evader
The masked guy is supposed to be an urban legend. They say he looks like a monster and uses an obscure weapon.
210: Name: Anonymous monster swarm evader
209>> What a joke. How can anyone fight with a short sword?
211: Name: Kagemitsu★
Hey, assholes!!! Bring me whoever told me about *that* Adventurer!!!
Whoa!
something happen?
why u mad, bro?
wassup
swarm evader
never thought a hardco
Adventurer like you wo
ds easy.
You think fighting monsters nonstop for nine hours is nothing?!!
DWAM
You stuck me with a lunatic!
He had us hunting from 11 A.M. to 8 P.M!

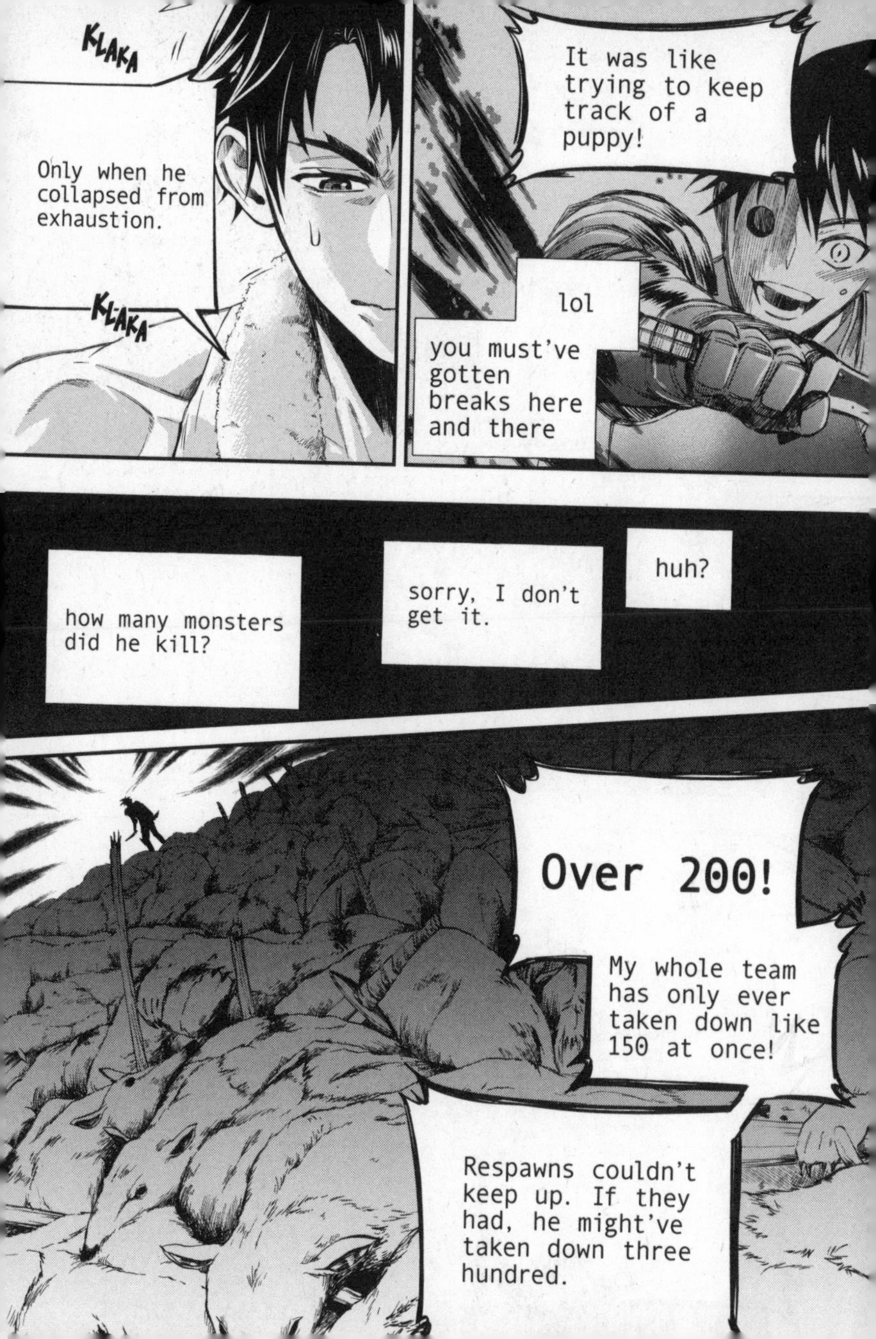
It was like trying to keep track of a puppy!
lol
you must've gotten breaks here and there
KLAKA
Only when he collapsed from exhaustion.
KLAKA
huh?
sorry, I don't get it.
how many monsters did he kill?
Over 200!
My whole team has only ever taken down like 150 at once!
Respawns couldn't keep up. If they had, he might've taken down three hundred.

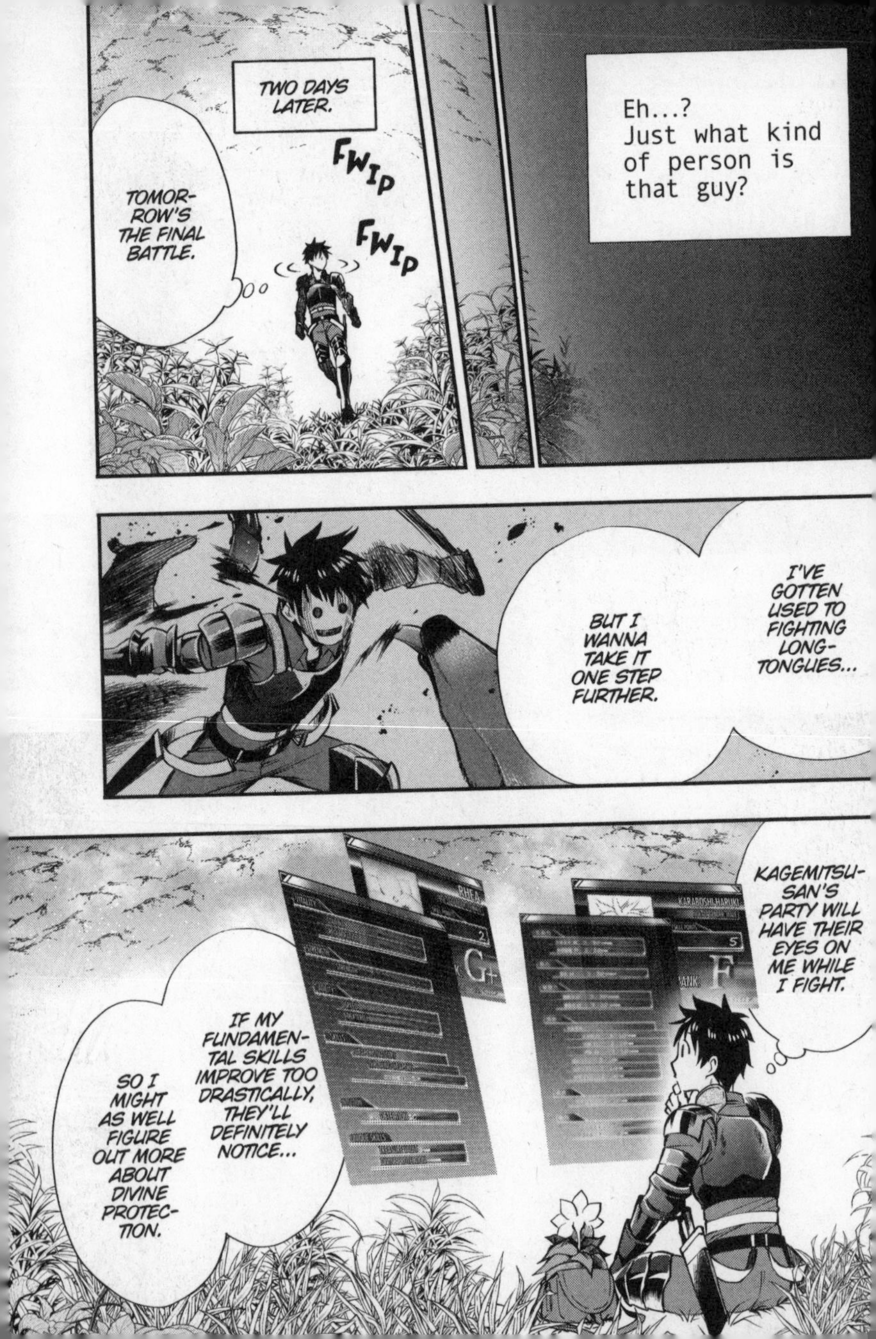
Eh...?
Just what kind of person is that guy?
TWO DAYS LATER.
FWIP
FWIP
TOMORROW'S THE FINAL BATTLE.
I'VE GOTTEN USED TO FIGHTING LONG-TONGUES...
BUT I WANNA TAKE IT ONE STEP FURTHER.
KAGEMITSU-SAN'S PARTY WILL HAVE THEIR EYES ON ME WHILE I FIGHT.
IF MY FUNDAMENTAL SKILLS IMPROVE TOO DRASTICALLY, THEY'LL DEFINITELY NOTICE...
SO I MIGHT AS WELL FIGURE OUT MORE ABOUT DIVINE PROTECTION.

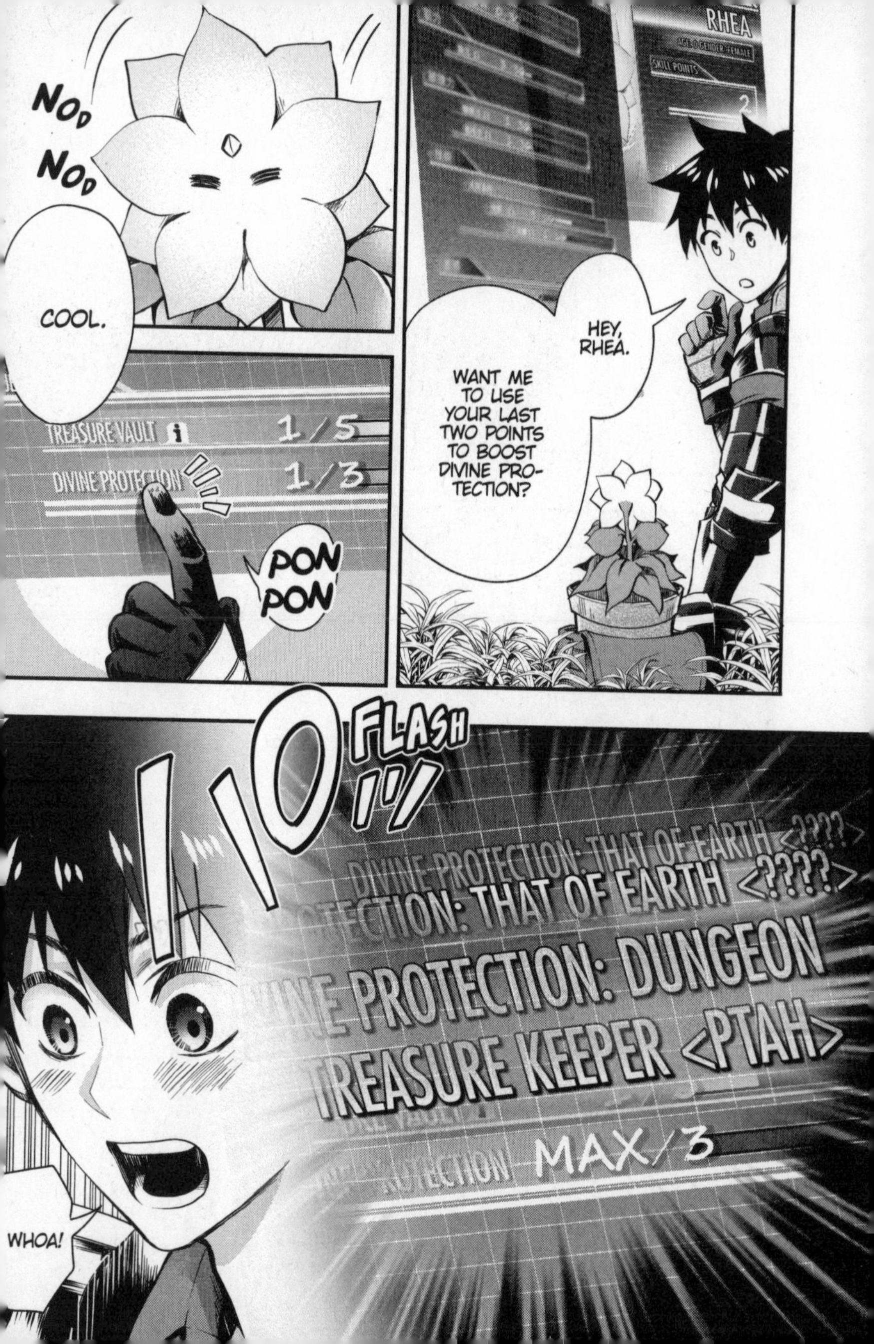
RHEA
AGE 0 GENDER: FEMALE
SKILL POINTS
2
HEY, RHEA.
WANT ME TO USE YOUR LAST TWO POINTS TO BOOST DIVINE PROTECTION?
NOD NOD
COOL.
TREASURE VAULT 1/5
DIVINE PROTECTION 1/3
PON PON
FLASH
DIVINE PROTECTION: THAT OF EARTH <????>
PROTECTION: THAT OF EARTH <????>
DIVINE PROTECTION: DUNGEON TREASURE KEEPER <PTAH>
MAX/3
WHOA!

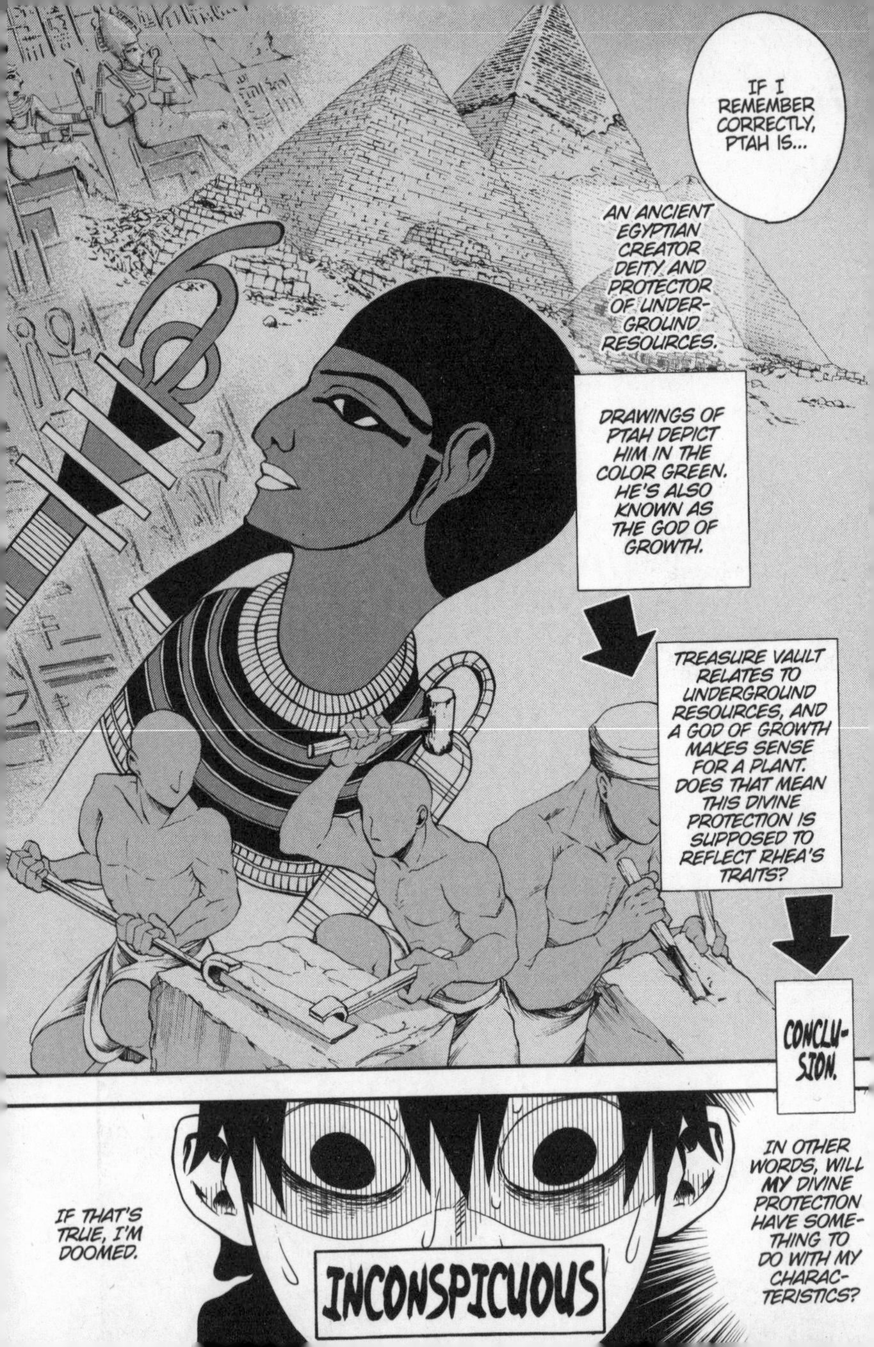
IF I REMEMBER CORRECTLY, PTAH IS...
AN ANCIENT EGYPTIAN CREATOR DEITY AND PROTECTOR OF UNDER-GROUND RESOURCES.
DRAWINGS OF PTAH DEPICT HIM IN THE COLOR GREEN. HE'S ALSO KNOWN AS THE GOD OF GROWTH.
TREASURE VAULT RELATES TO UNDERGROUND RESOURCES, AND A GOD OF GROWTH MAKES SENSE FOR A PLANT. DOES THAT MEAN THIS DIVINE PROTECTION IS SUPPOSED TO REFLECT RHEA'S TRAITS?
CONCLU-SION.
IN OTHER WORDS, WILL MY DIVINE PROTECTION HAVE SOME-THING TO DO WITH MY CHARAC-TERISTICS?
INCONSPICUOUS
IF THAT'S TRUE, I'M DOOMED.

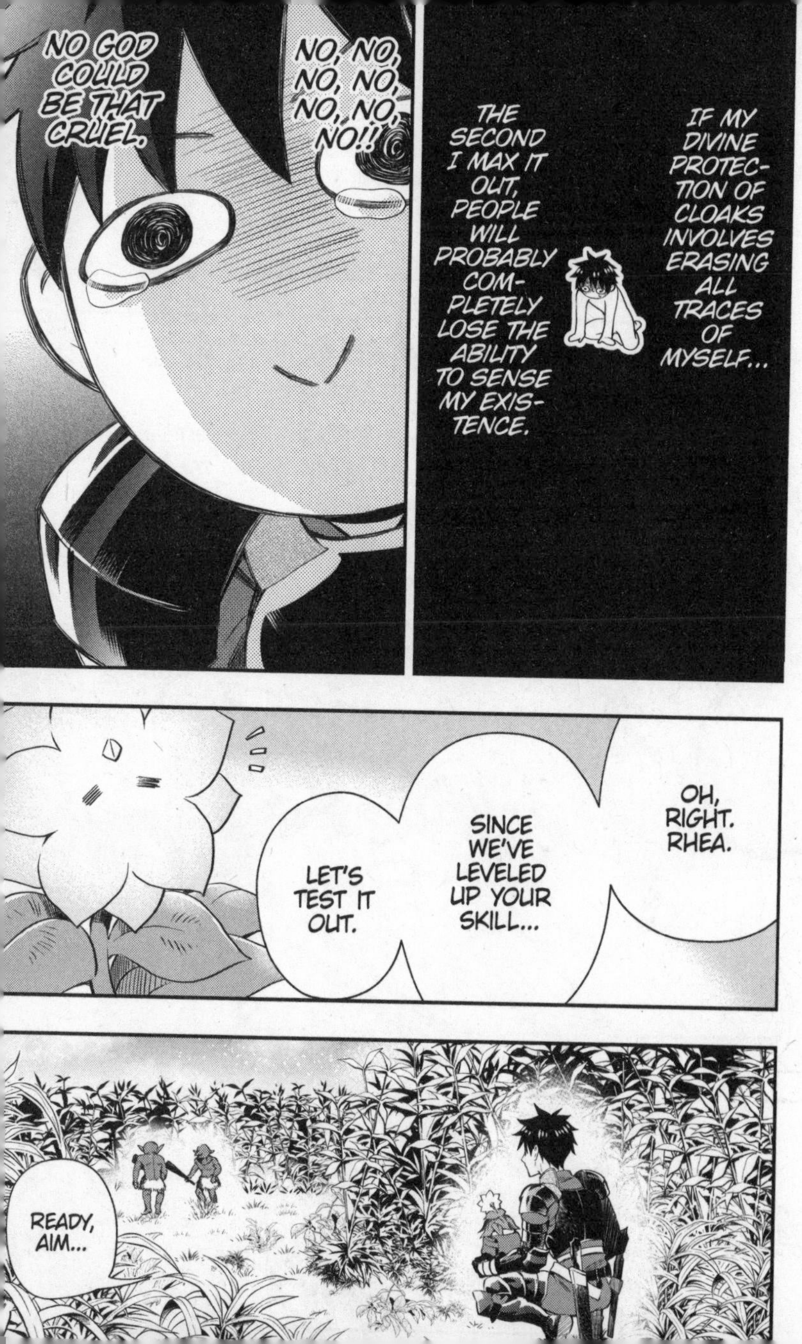
IF MY DIVINE PROTECTION OF CLOAKS INVOLVES ERASING ALL TRACES OF MYSELF...
THE SECOND I MAX IT OUT, PEOPLE WILL PROBABLY COMPLETELY LOSE THE ABILITY TO SENSE MY EXISTENCE.
NO, NO, NO, NO, NO, NO, NO!!
NO GOD COULD BE THAT CRUEL.
OH, RIGHT. RHEA.
SINCE WE'VE LEVELED UP YOUR SKILL...
LET'S TEST IT OUT.
READY, AIM...

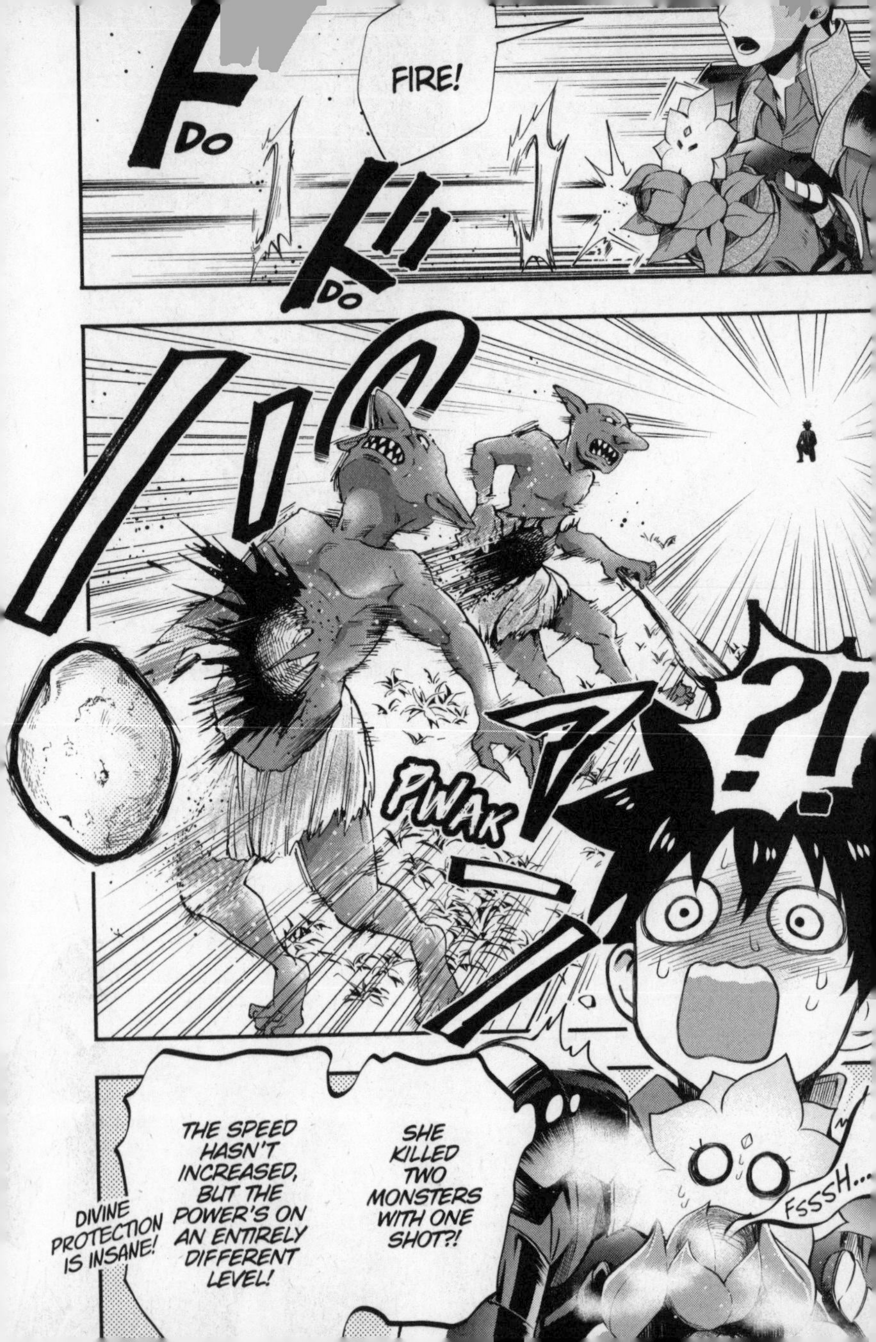
FIRE!
DO
DO
?!
PWAK
FSSSH...
SHE KILLED TWO MONSTERS WITH ONE SHOT?!
THE SPEED HASN'T INCREASED, BUT THE POWER'S ON AN ENTIRELY DIFFERENT LEVEL!
DIVINE PROTECTION IS INSANE!

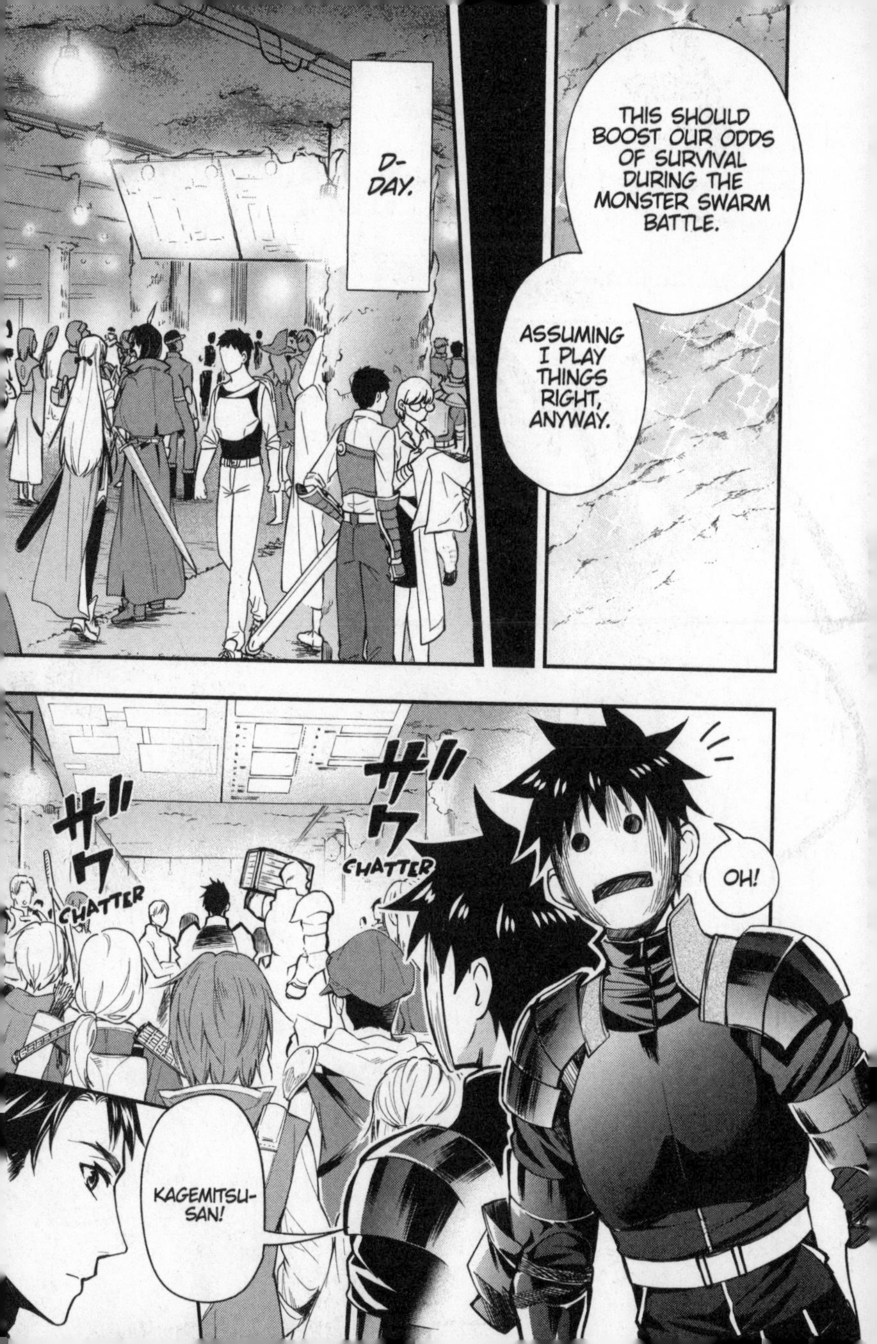

THIS SHOULD BOOST OUR ODDS OF SURVIVAL DURING THE MONSTER SWARM BATTLE.
ASSUMING I PLAY THINGS RIGHT, ANYWAY.
D-DAY.
OH!
ザワ
CHATTER
ザワ
CHATTER
KAGEMITSU-SAN!

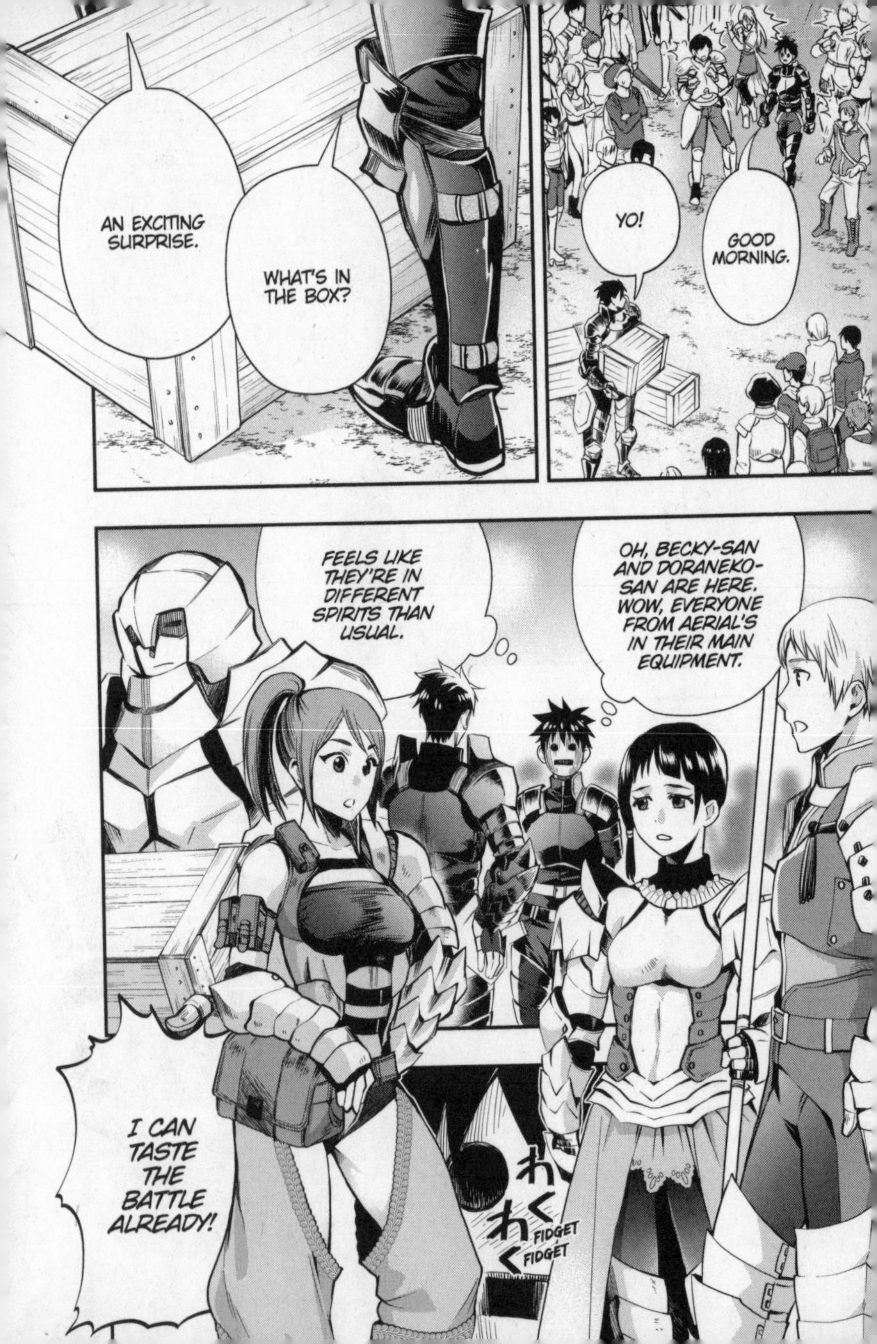
GOOD MORNING.
YO!
WHAT'S IN THE BOX?
AN EXCITING SURPRISE.
OH, BECKY-SAN AND DORANEKO-SAN ARE HERE. WOW, EVERYONE FROM AERIAL'S IN THEIR MAIN EQUIPMENT.
FEELS LIKE THEY'RE IN DIFFERENT SPIRITS THAN USUAL.
わくわく
FIDGET FIDGET
I CAN TASTE THE BATTLE ALREADY!

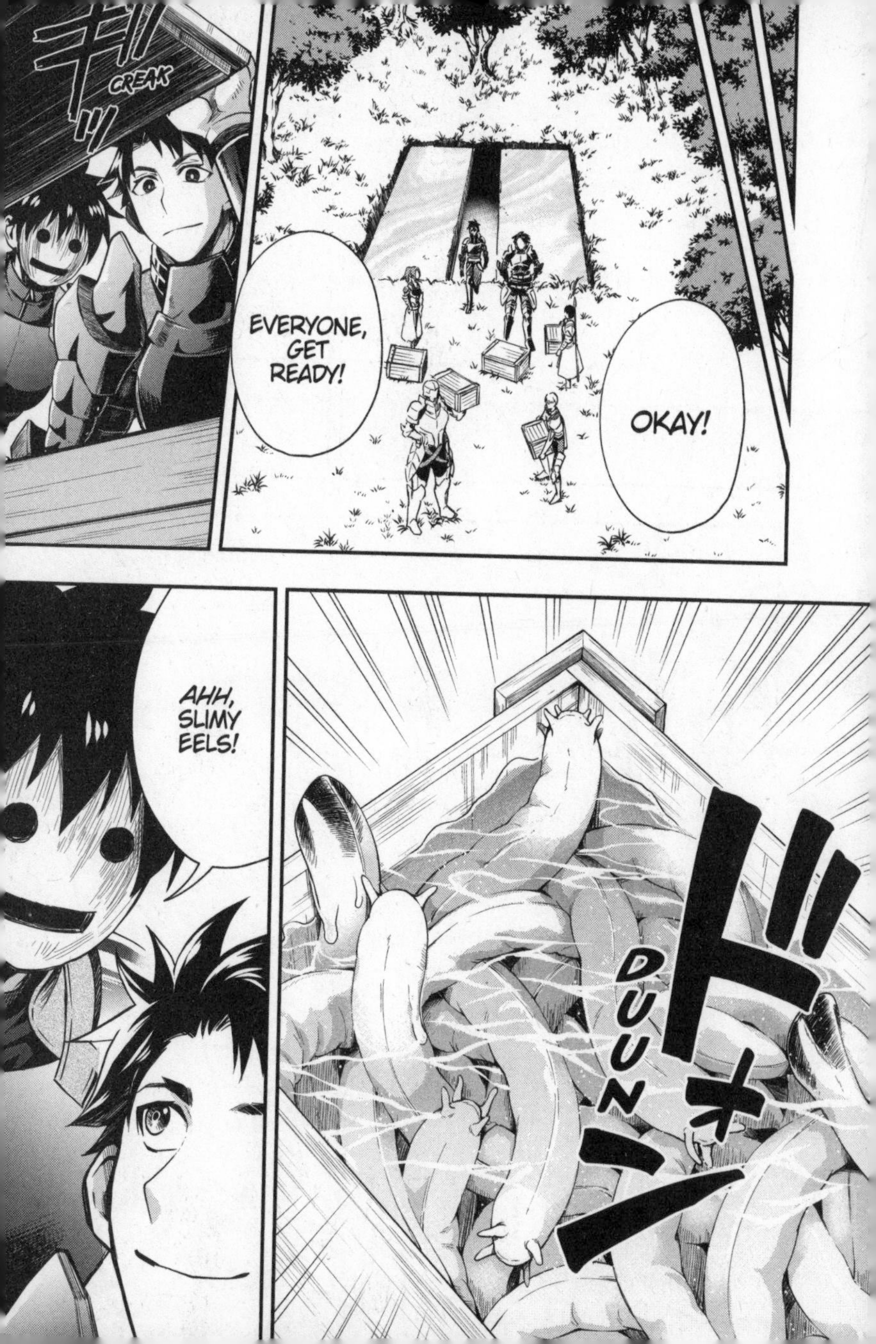
EVERYONE, GET READY!
OKAY!
CREAK
DUUN
AHH, SLIMY EELS!

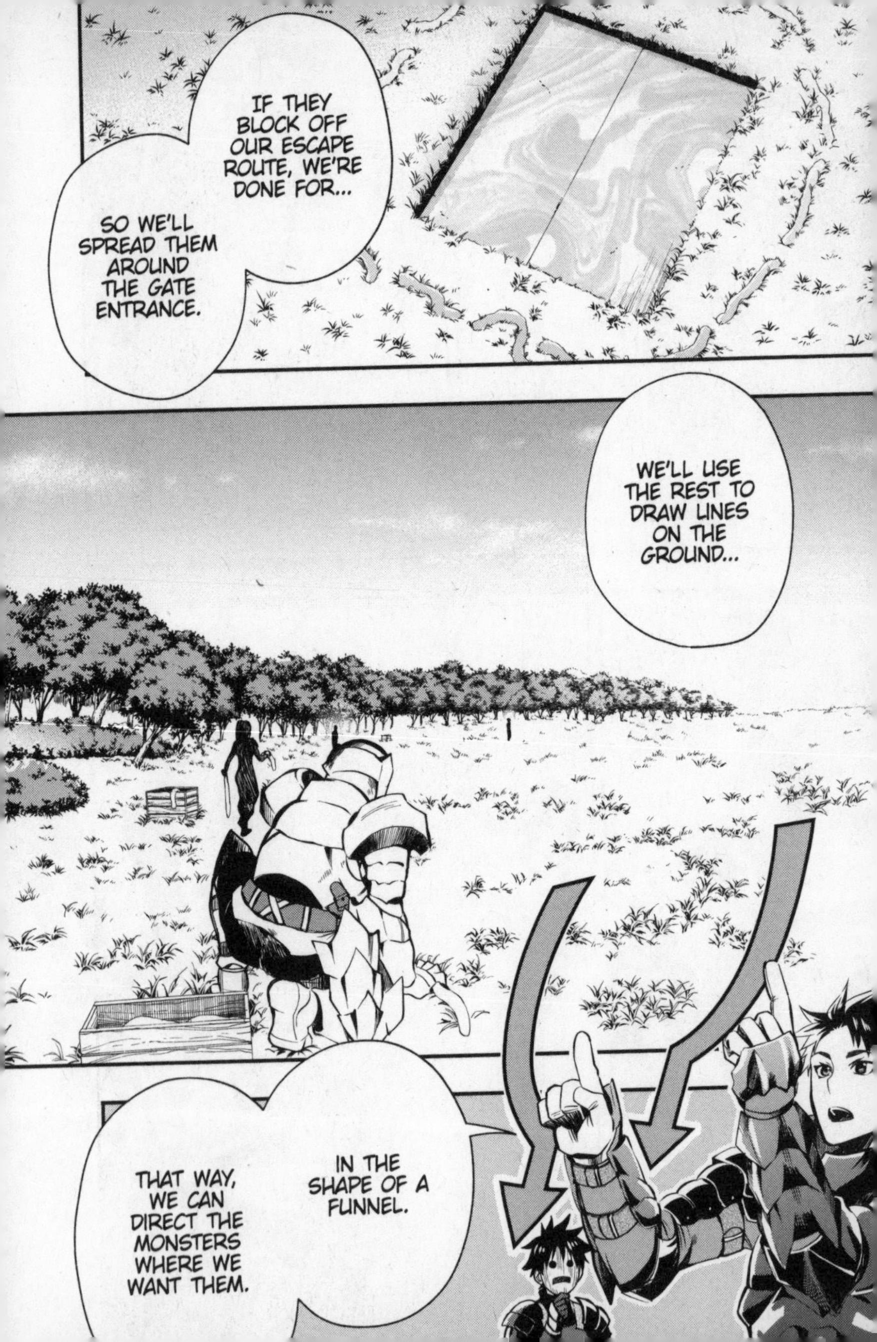
IF THEY BLOCK OFF OUR ESCAPE ROUTE, WE'RE DONE FOR...
SO WE'LL SPREAD THEM AROUND THE GATE ENTRANCE.
WE'LL USE THE REST TO DRAW LINES ON THE GROUND...
IN THE SHAPE OF A FUNNEL.
THAT WAY, WE CAN DIRECT THE MONSTERS WHERE WE WANT THEM.

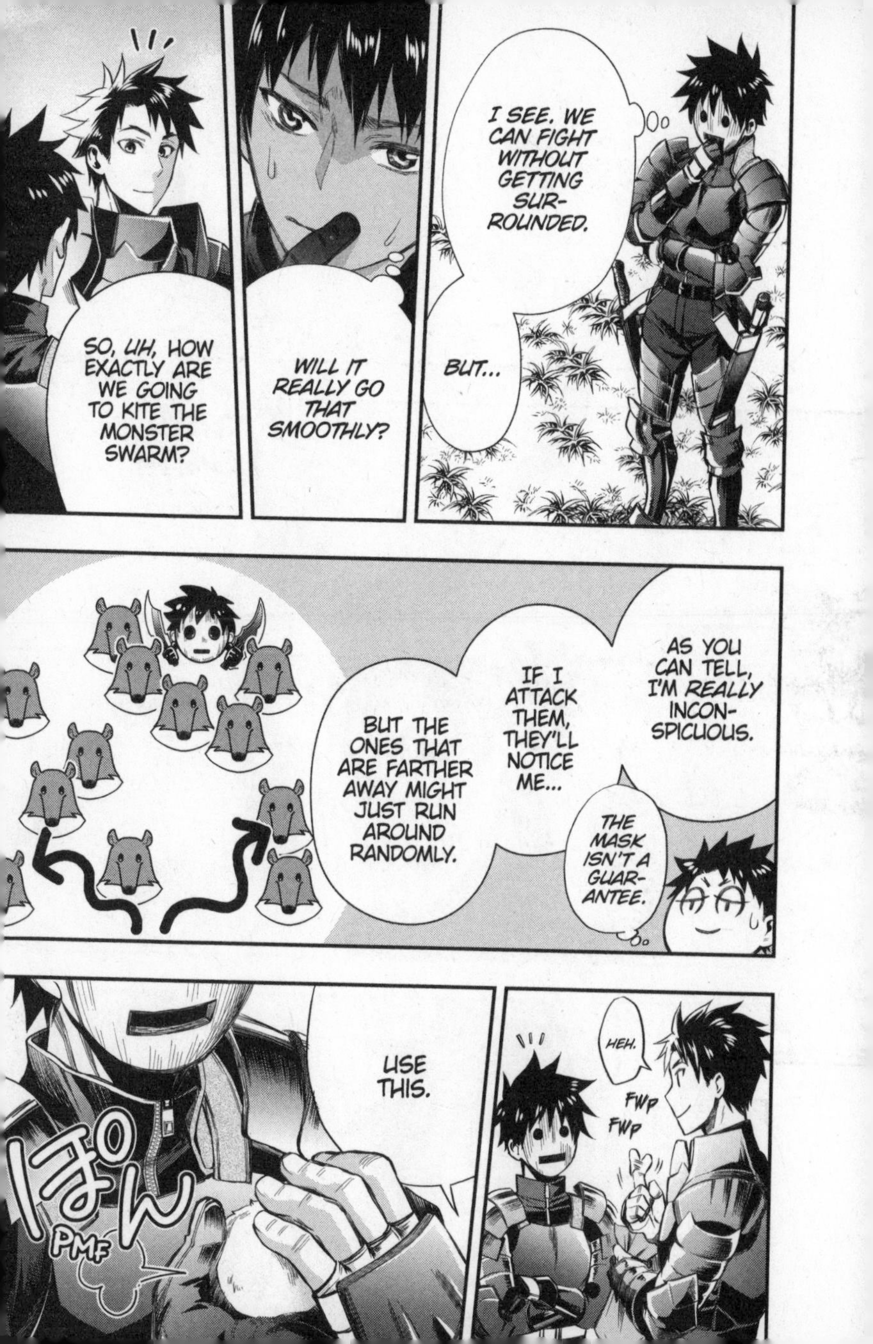
I SEE. WE CAN FIGHT WITHOUT GETTING SUR-ROUNDED.
BUT...
WILL IT REALLY GO THAT SMOOTHLY?
SO, UH, HOW EXACTLY ARE WE GOING TO KITE THE MONSTER SWARM?
AS YOU CAN TELL, I'M REALLY INCON-SPICUOUS.
THE MASK ISN'T A GUAR-ANTEE.
IF I ATTACK THEM, THEY'LL NOTICE ME...
BUT THE ONES THAT ARE FARTHER AWAY MIGHT JUST RUN AROUND RANDOMLY.
HEH.
FWP
FWP
USE THIS.
ぽん
PMF

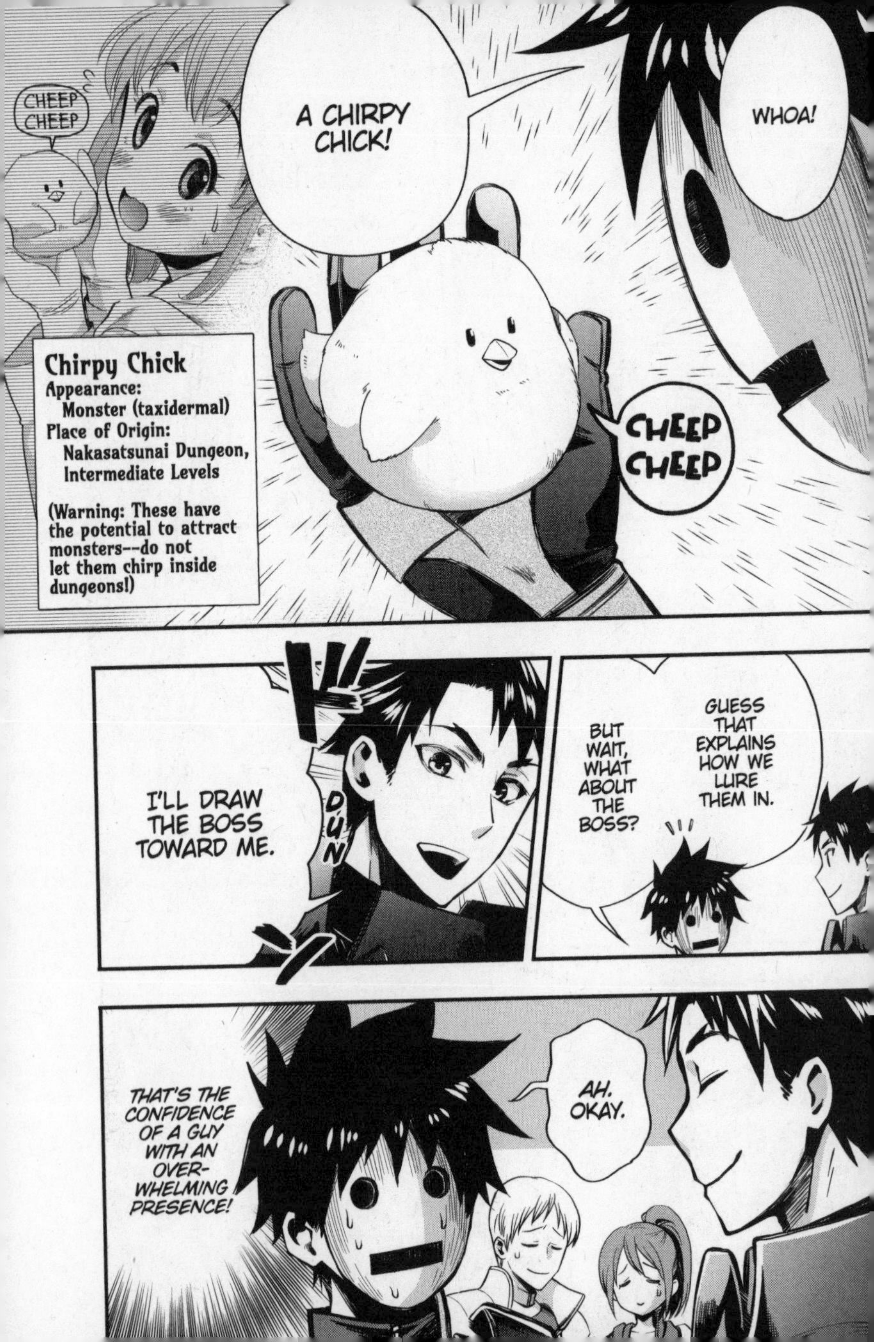
WHOA!
A CHIRPY CHICK!
CHEEP CHEEP
CHEEP CHEEP
Chirpy Chick
Appearance:
Monster (taxidermal)
Place of Origin:
Nakasatsunai Dungeon, Intermediate Levels
(Warning: These have the potential to attract monsters--do not let them chirp inside dungeons!)
GUESS THAT EXPLAINS HOW WE LURE THEM IN.
BUT WAIT, WHAT ABOUT THE BOSS?
I'LL DRAW THE BOSS TOWARD ME.
DUN
AH. OKAY.
THAT'S THE CONFIDENCE OF A GUY WITH AN OVER-WHELMING PRESENCE!

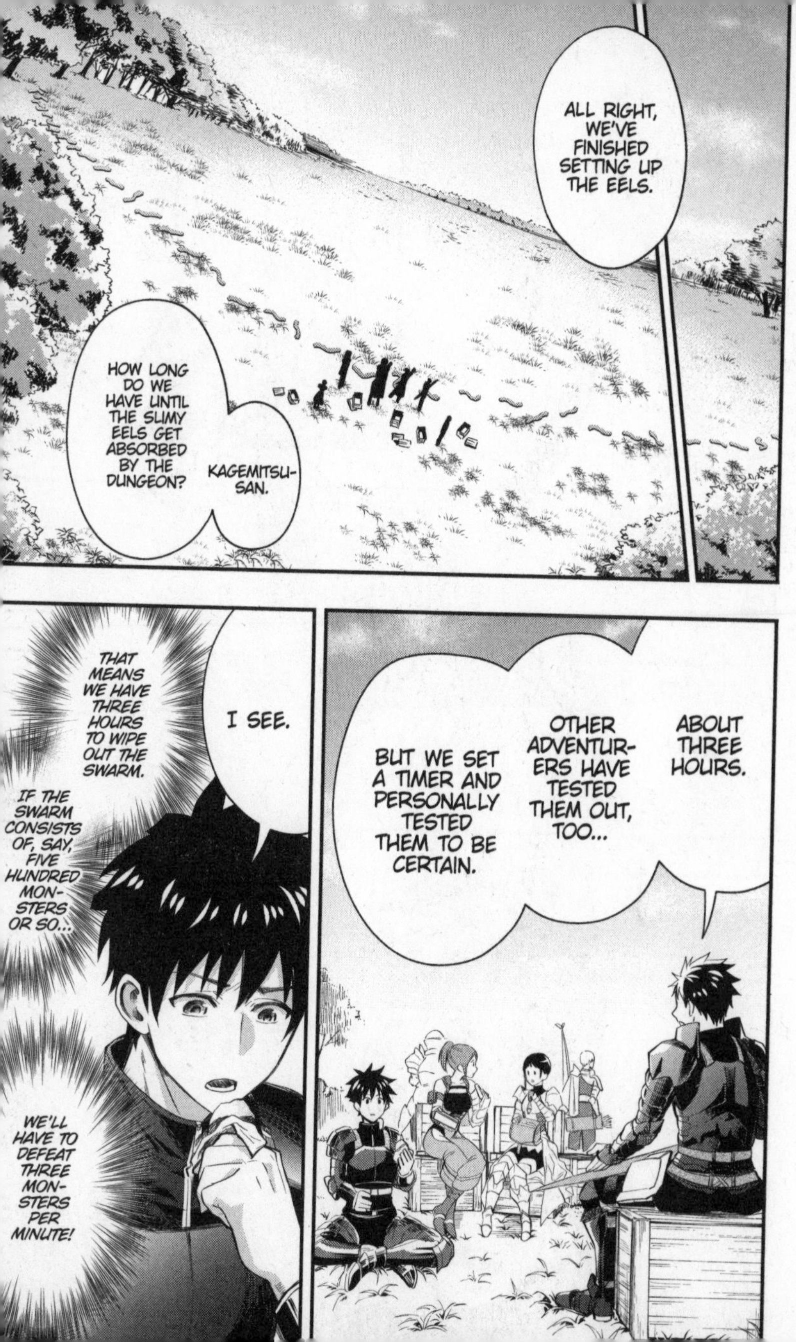
ALL RIGHT, WE'VE FINISHED SETTING UP THE EELS.
HOW LONG DO WE HAVE UNTIL THE SLIMY EELS GET ABSORBED BY THE DUNGEON?
KAGEMITSU-SAN.
ABOUT THREE HOURS.
OTHER ADVENTURERS HAVE TESTED THEM OUT, TOO...
BUT WE SET A TIMER AND PERSONALLY TESTED THEM TO BE CERTAIN.
I SEE.
THAT MEANS WE HAVE THREE HOURS TO WIPE OUT THE SWARM.
IF THE SWARM CONSISTS OF, SAY, FIVE HUNDRED MONSTERS OR SO...
WE'LL HAVE TO DEFEAT THREE MONSTERS PER MINUTE!

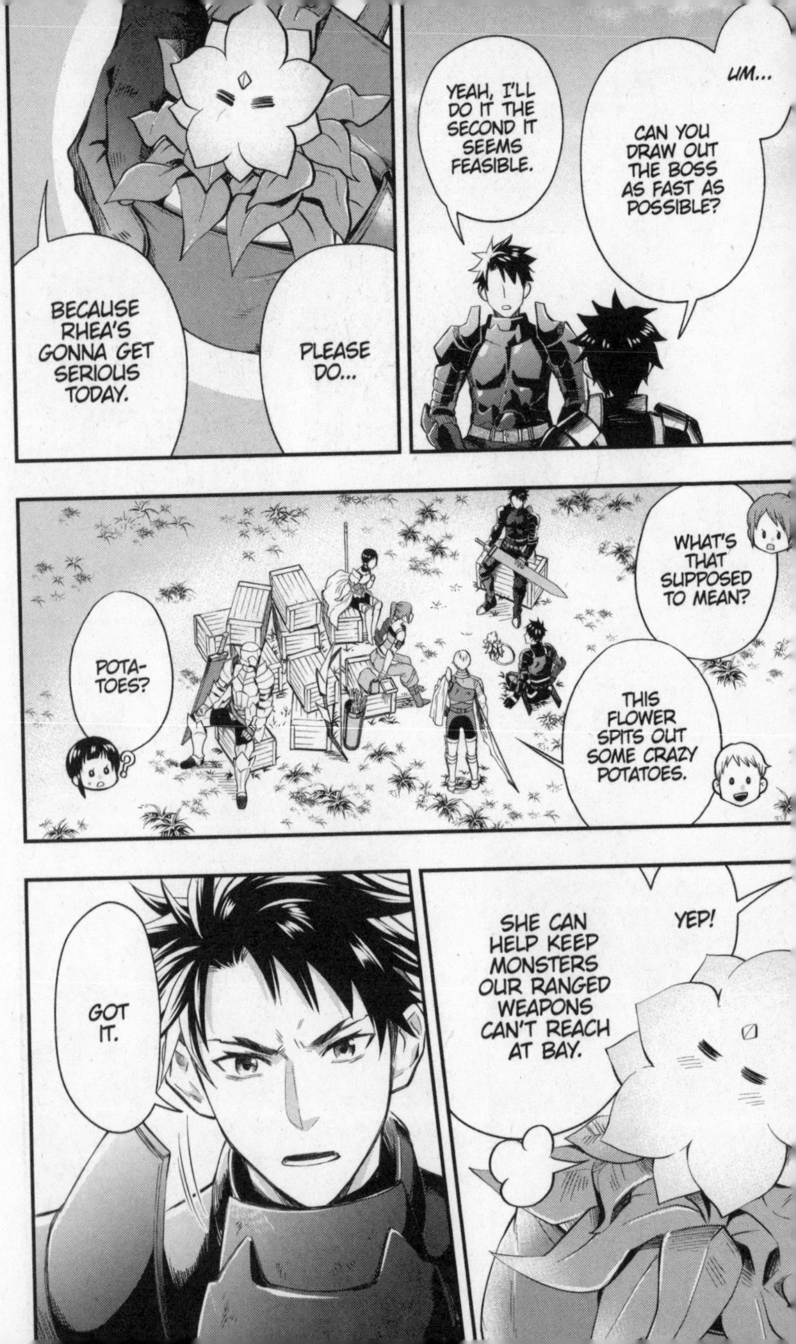
UM...
CAN YOU DRAW OUT THE BOSS AS FAST AS POSSIBLE?
YEAH, I'LL DO IT THE SECOND IT SEEMS FEASIBLE.
PLEASE DO...
BECAUSE RHEA'S GONNA GET SERIOUS TODAY.
WHAT'S THAT SUPPOSED TO MEAN?
THIS FLOWER SPITS OUT SOME CRAZY POTATOES.
POTA-TOES?
YEP!
SHE CAN HELP KEEP MONSTERS OUR RANGED WEAPONS CAN'T REACH AT BAY.
GOT IT.

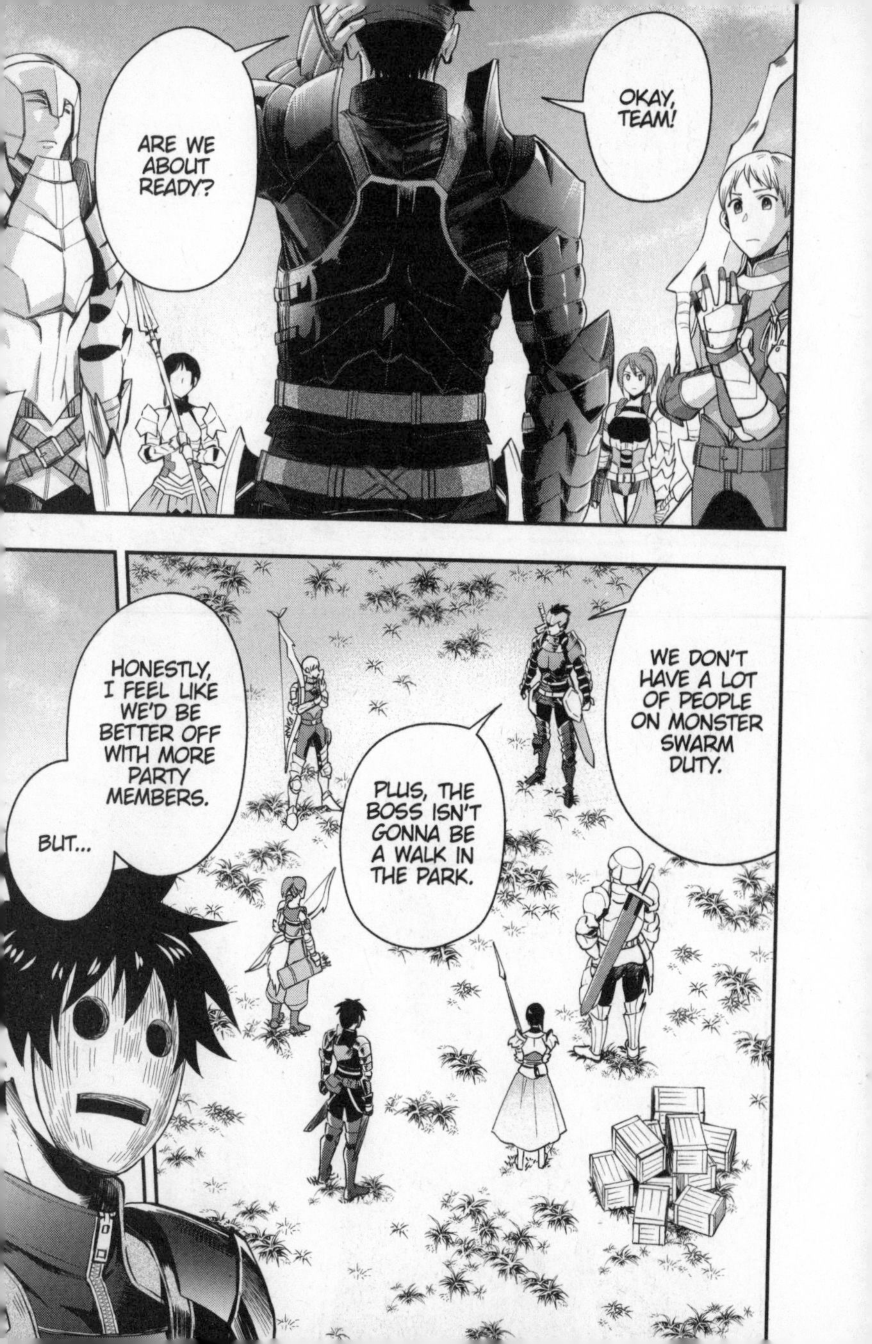
OKAY, TEAM!
ARE WE ABOUT READY?
WE DON'T HAVE A LOT OF PEOPLE ON MONSTER SWARM DUTY.
PLUS, THE BOSS ISN'T GONNA BE A WALK IN THE PARK.
HONESTLY, I FEEL LIKE WE'D BE BETTER OFF WITH MORE PARTY MEMBERS.
BUT...

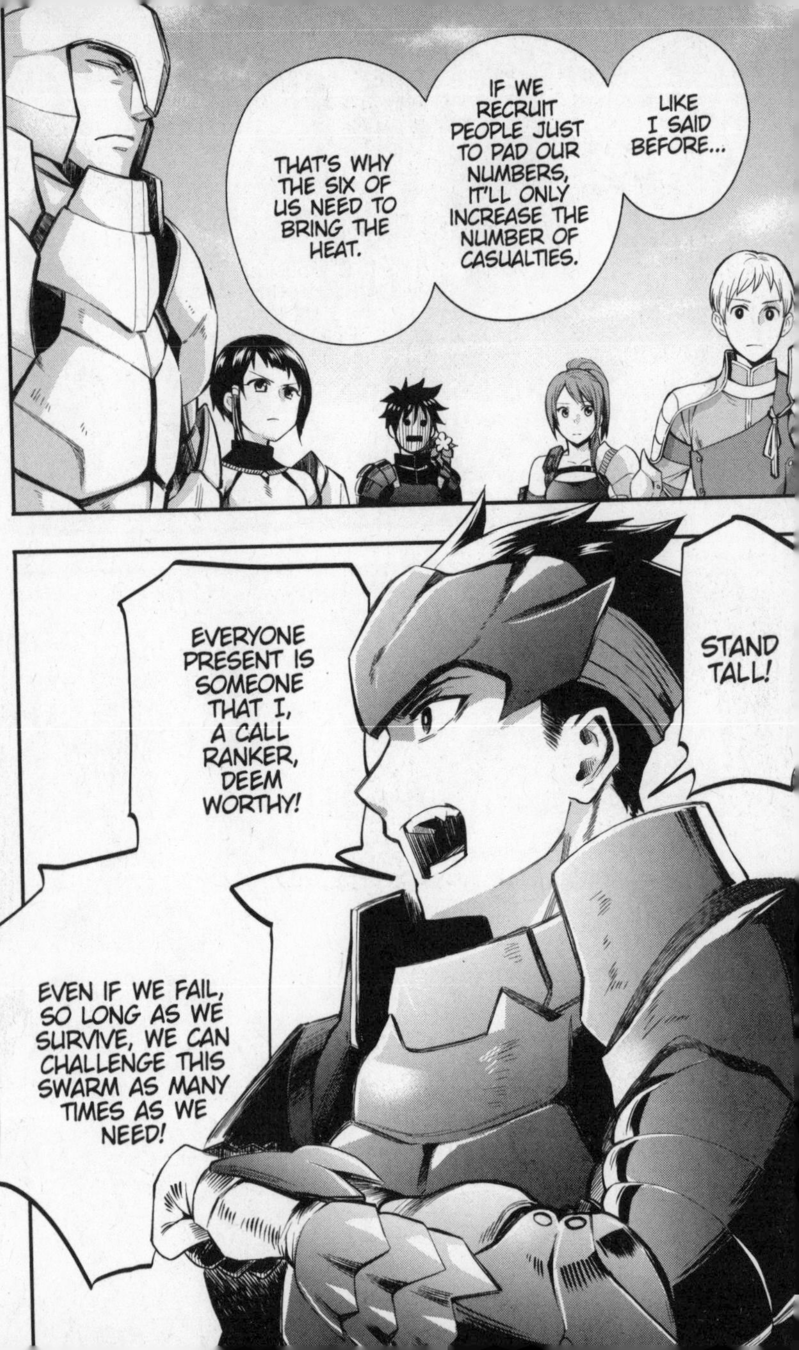
LIKE I SAID BEFORE...
IF WE RECRUIT PEOPLE JUST TO PAD OUR NUMBERS, IT'LL ONLY INCREASE THE NUMBER OF CASUALTIES.
THAT'S WHY THE SIX OF US NEED TO BRING THE HEAT.
STAND TALL!
EVERYONE PRESENT IS SOMEONE THAT I, A CALL RANKER, DEEM WORTHY!
EVEN IF WE FAIL, SO LONG AS WE SURVIVE, WE CAN CHALLENGE THIS SWARM AS MANY TIMES AS WE NEED!

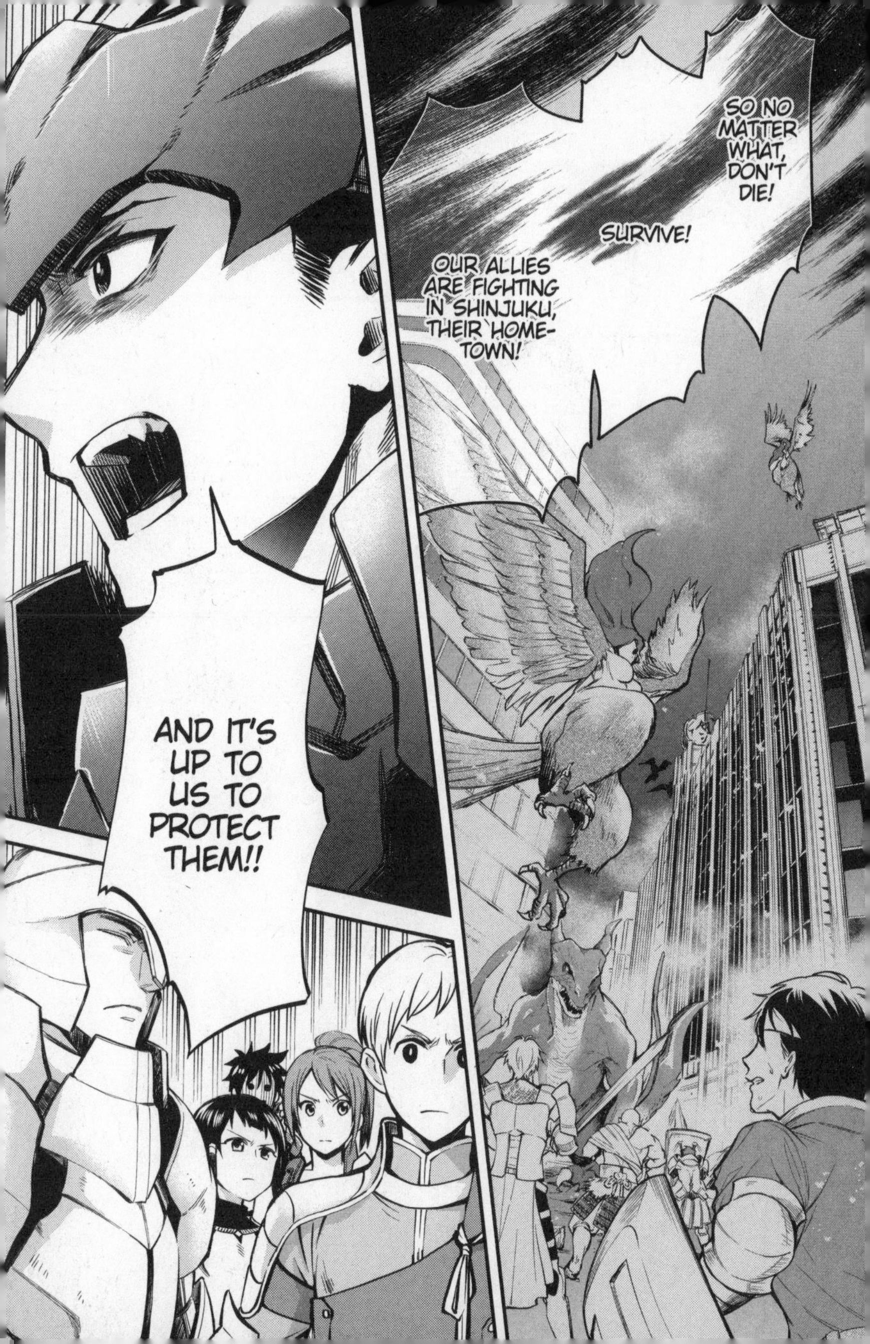
SO NO MATTER WHAT, DON'T DIE!
SURVIVE!
OUR ALLIES ARE FIGHTING IN SHINJUKU, THEIR HOME-TOWN!
AND IT'S UP TO US TO PROTECT THEM!!

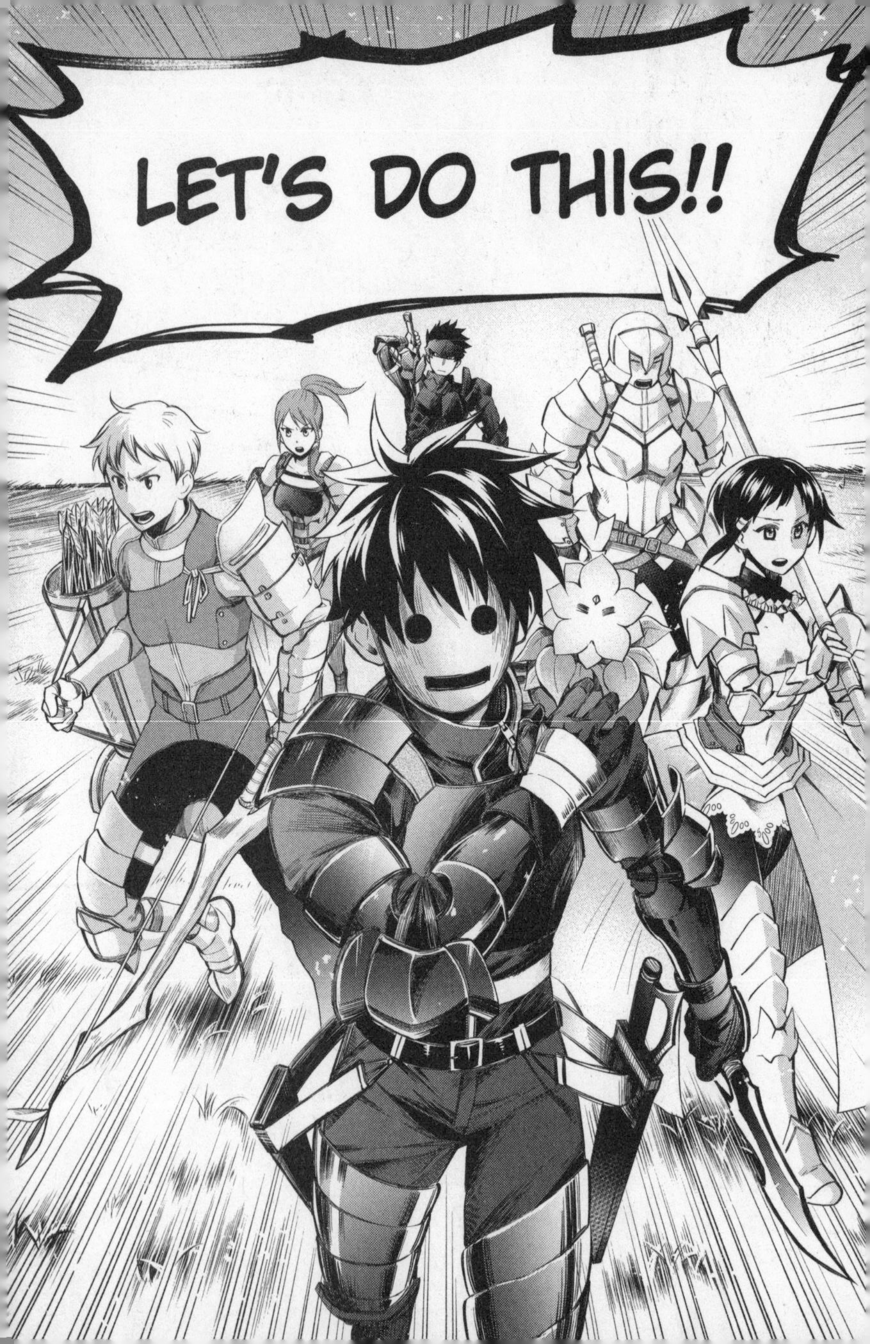
LET'S DO THIS!!

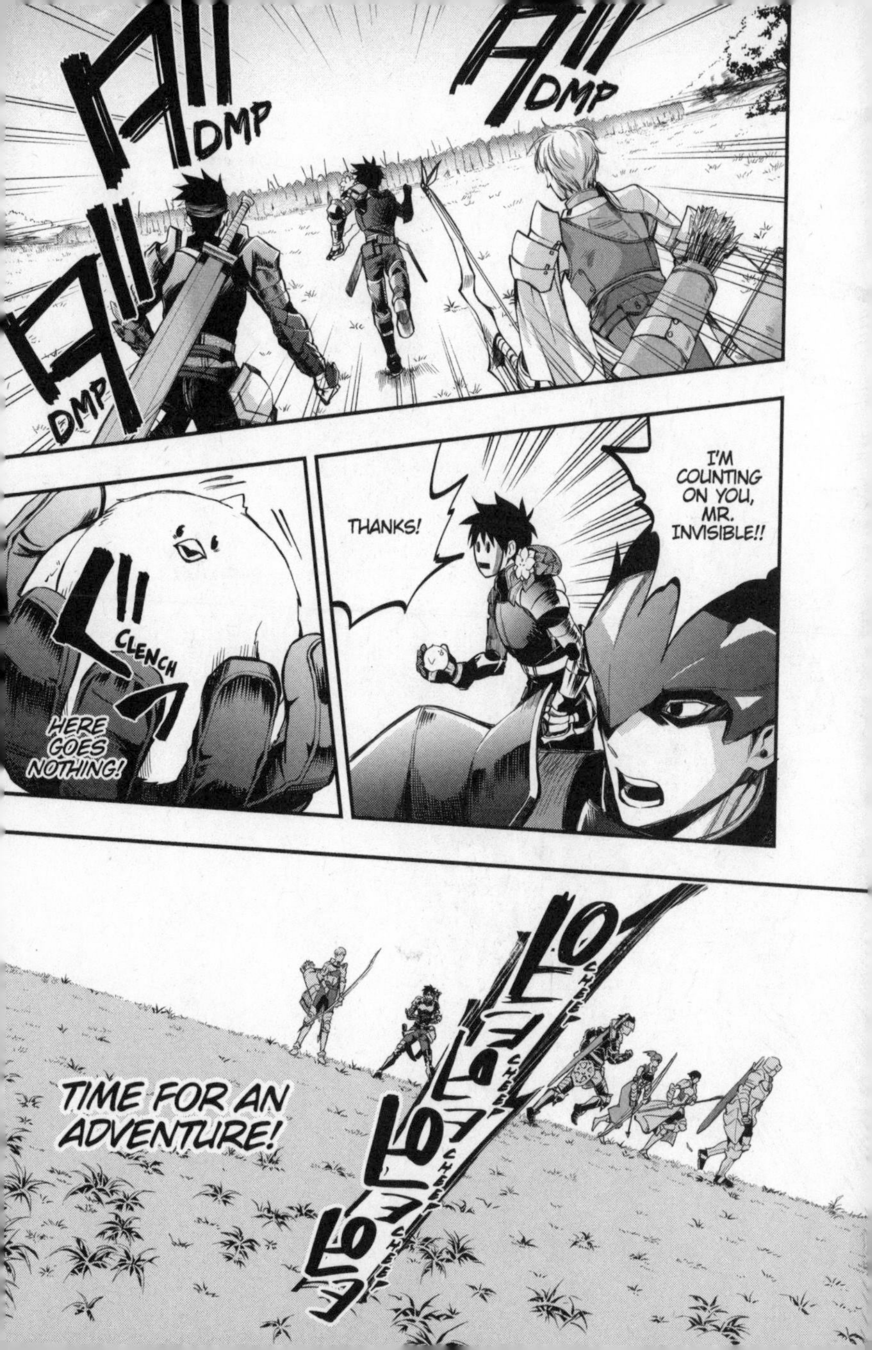
DMP
DMP
DMP
I'M COUNTING ON YOU, MR. INVISIBLE!!
THANKS!
CLENCH
HERE GOES NOTHING!
CHEEP
CHEEP
CHEEP
CHEEP
TIME FOR AN ADVENTURE!

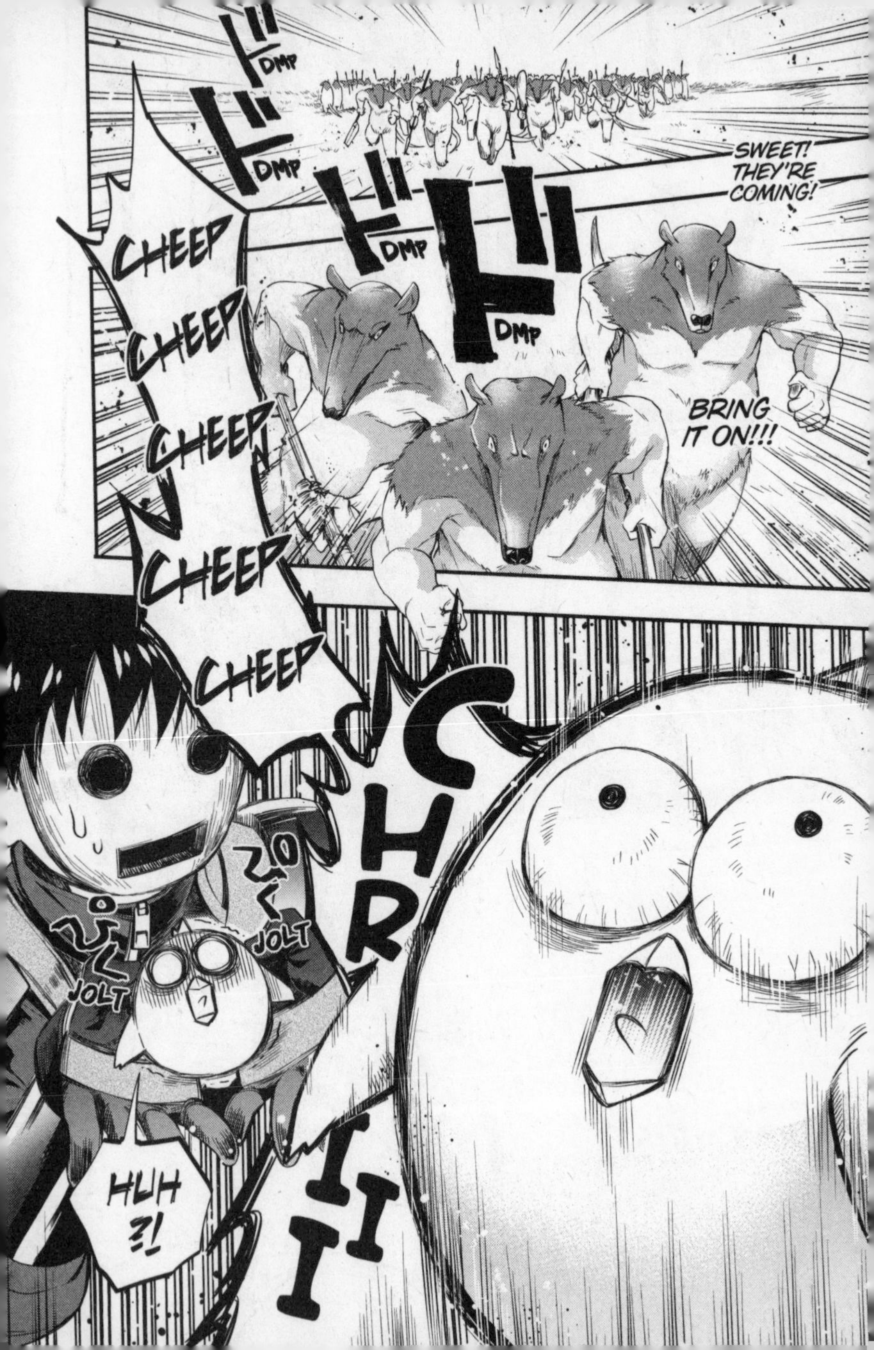
SWEET! THEY'RE COMING!
BRING IT ON!!!
ド DMP
ド DMP
ド DMP
ド DMP
CHEEP
CHEEP
CHEEP
CHEEP
CHEEP
CHRIII
JOLT
JOLT
HUH ?!

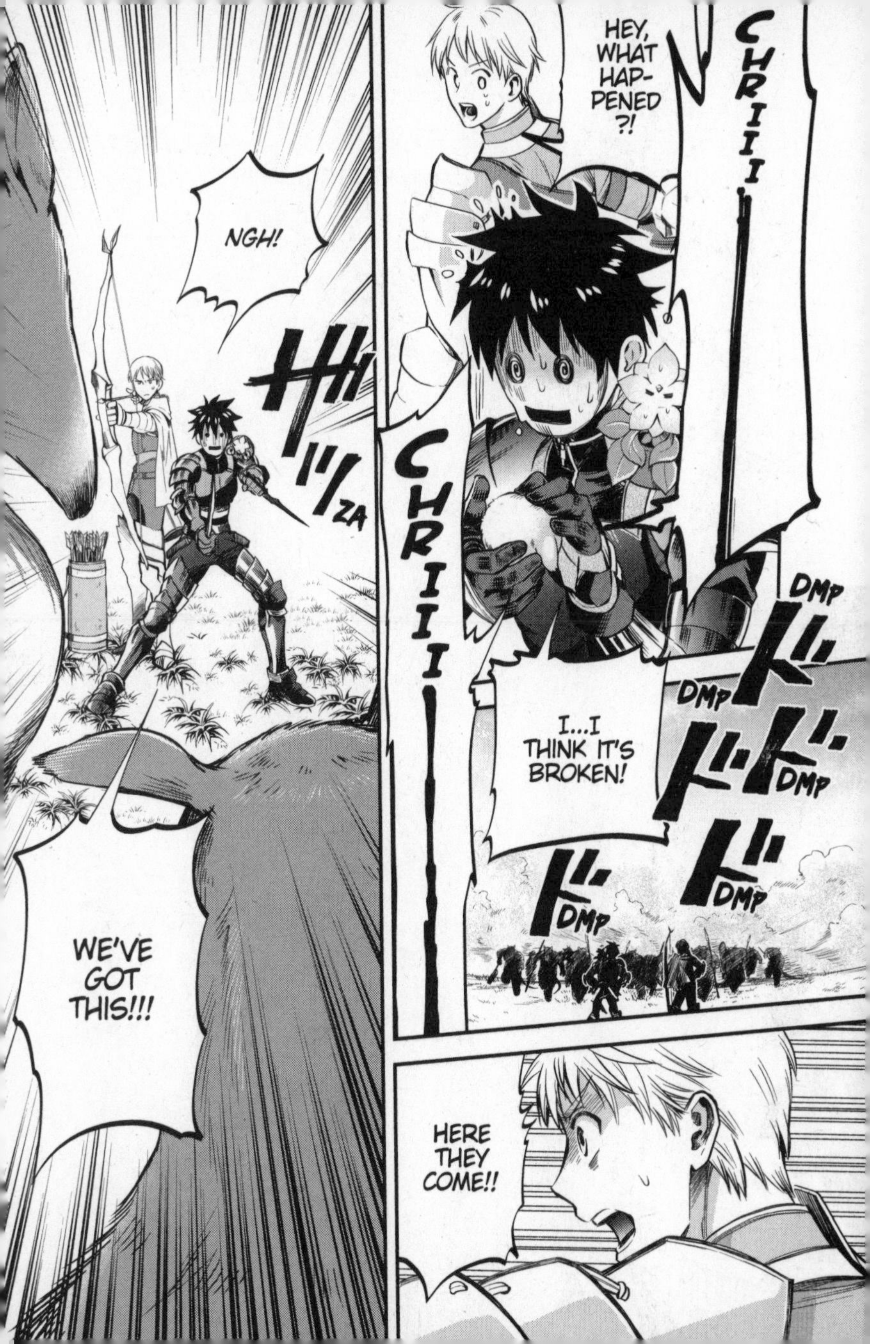
CHRIIII
HEY, WHAT HAP-PENED?!
CHRIIII
I...I THINK IT'S BROKEN!
DMP
DMP
DMP
DMP
DMP
HERE THEY COME!!
NGH!
ZA
WE'VE GOT THIS!!!

CALL TO ADVENTURE!

DEFEATING DUNGEONS

WITH A SKILL BOARD

5

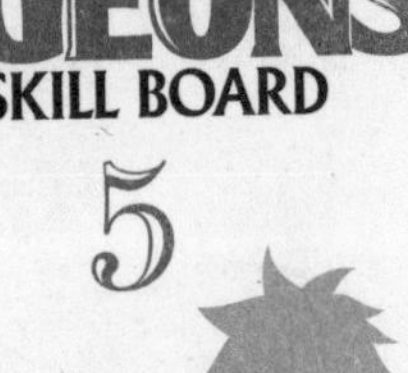

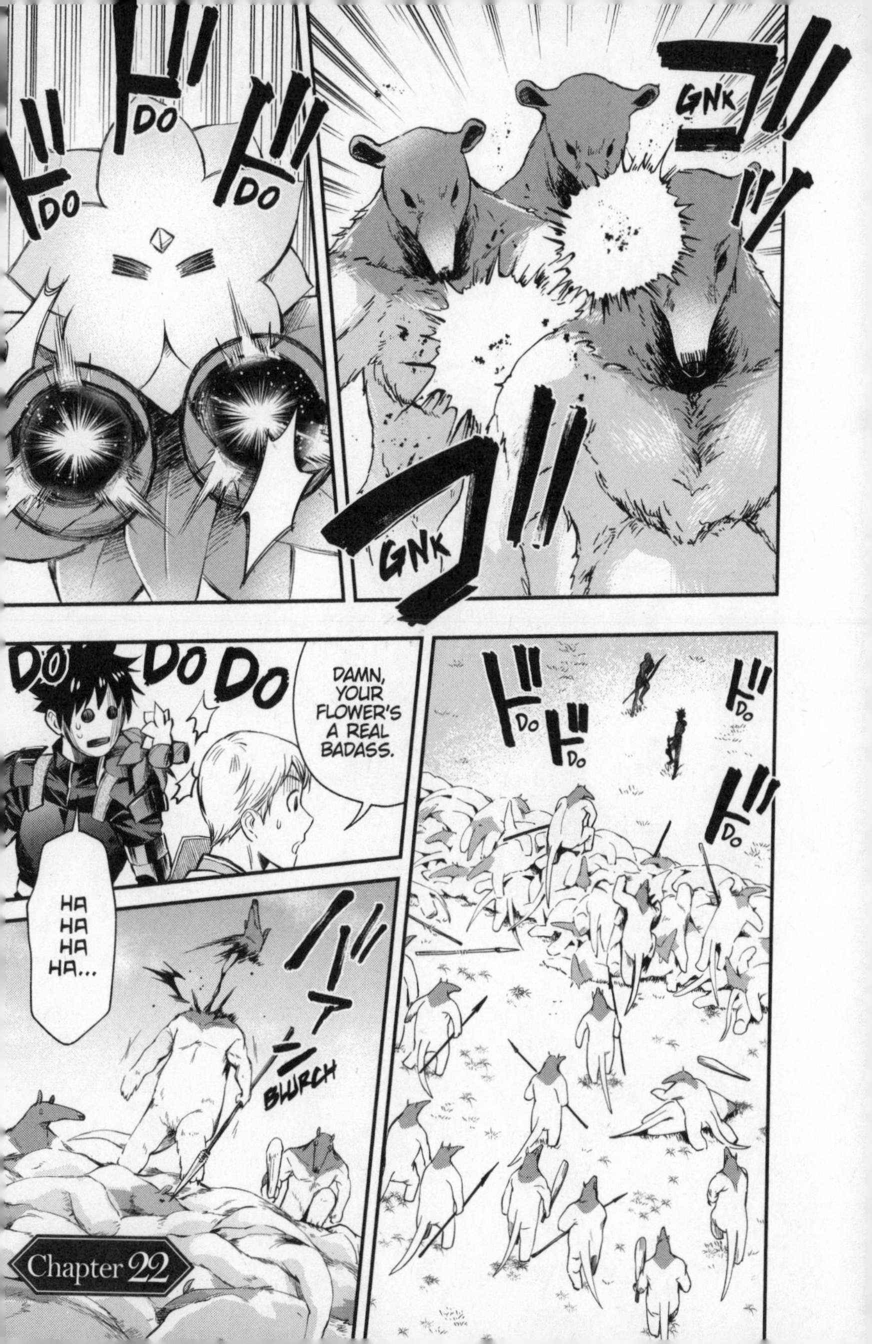
GNK
GNK
DO
DO
DO
DO
DO
DO
DO
DO
DO DO DO
DAMN, YOUR FLOWER'S A REAL BADASS.
HA HA HA HA...
BLURCH
Chapter 22

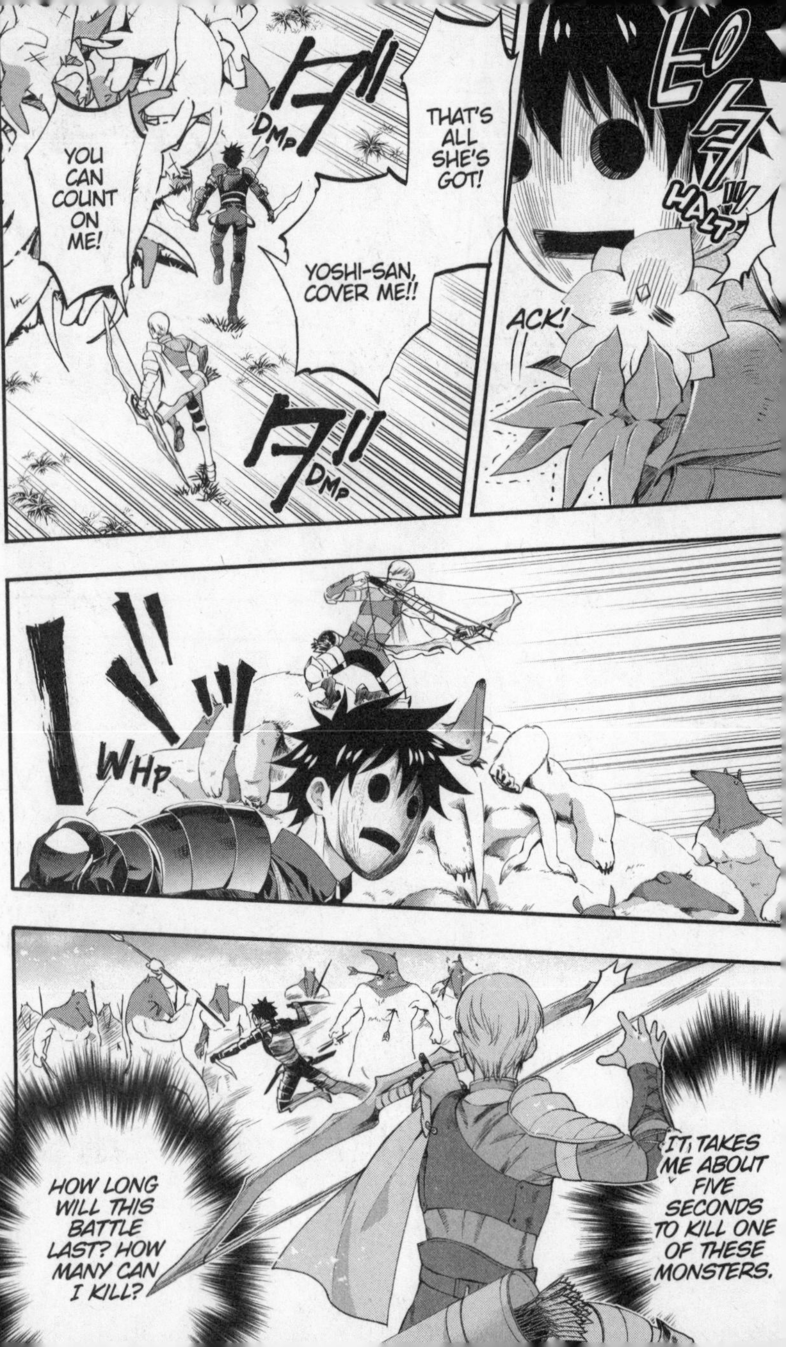
HALT!!
ACK!
THAT'S ALL SHE'S GOT!
YOSHI-SAN, COVER ME!!
DMP
YOU CAN COUNT ON ME!
DMP
WHP
IT TAKES ME ABOUT FIVE SECONDS TO KILL ONE OF THESE MONSTERS.
HOW LONG WILL THIS BATTLE LAST? HOW MANY CAN I KILL?

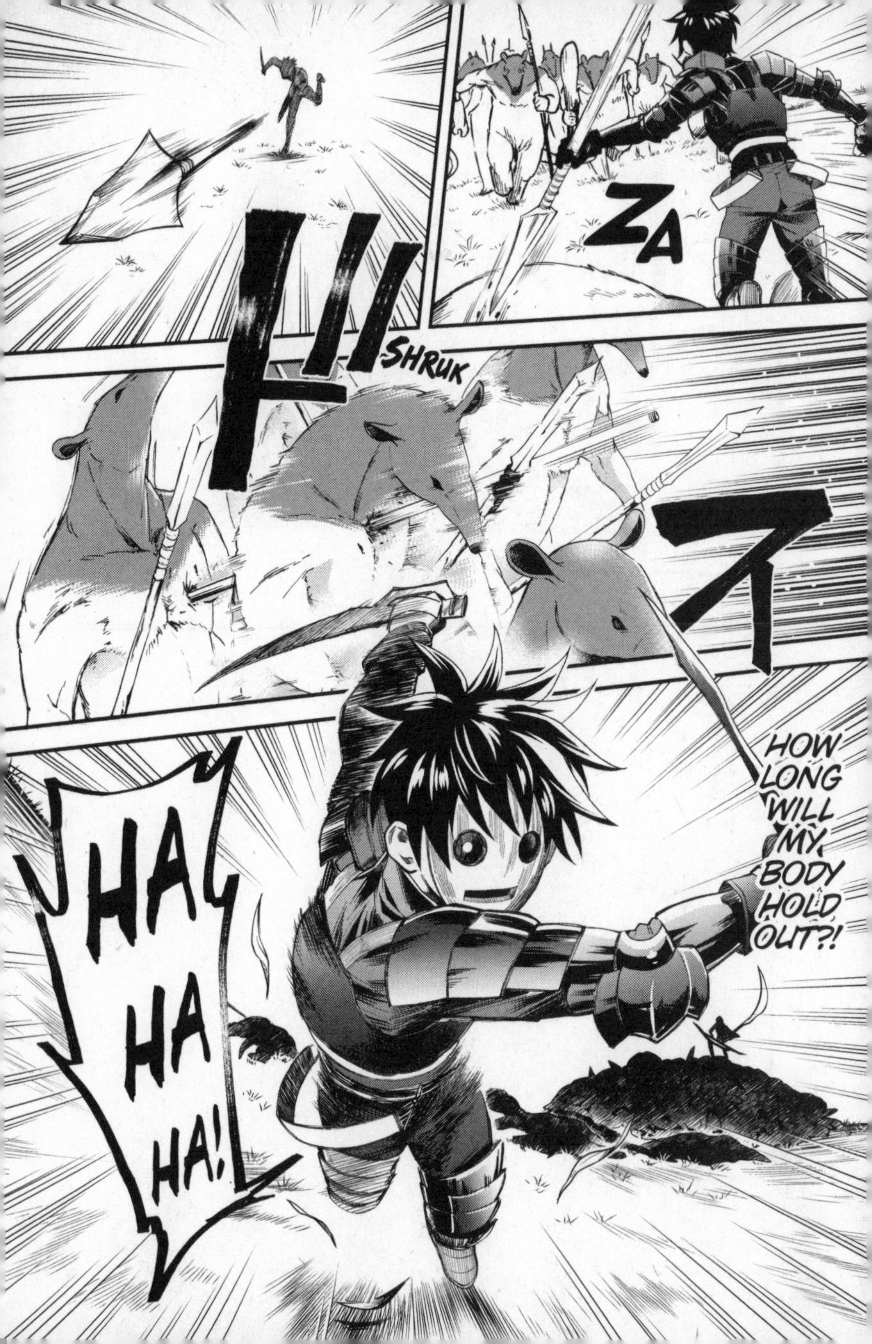
ZA
SHRUK
HOW LONG WILL MY BODY HOLD OUT?!
HA HA HA!

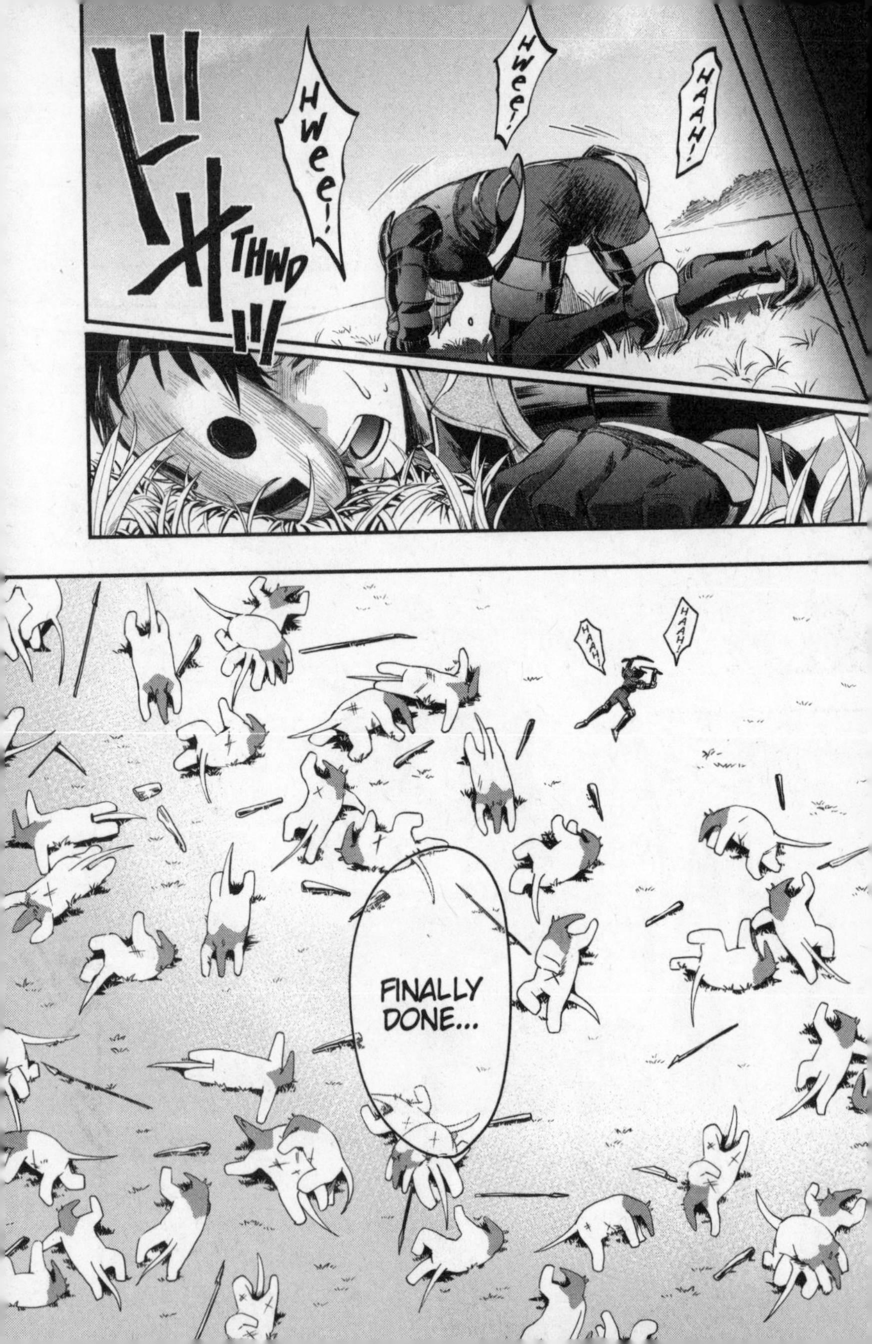
HAAH!
Hwee!
Hwee!
THWD
HAAH!
HAAH!
FINALLY DONE...

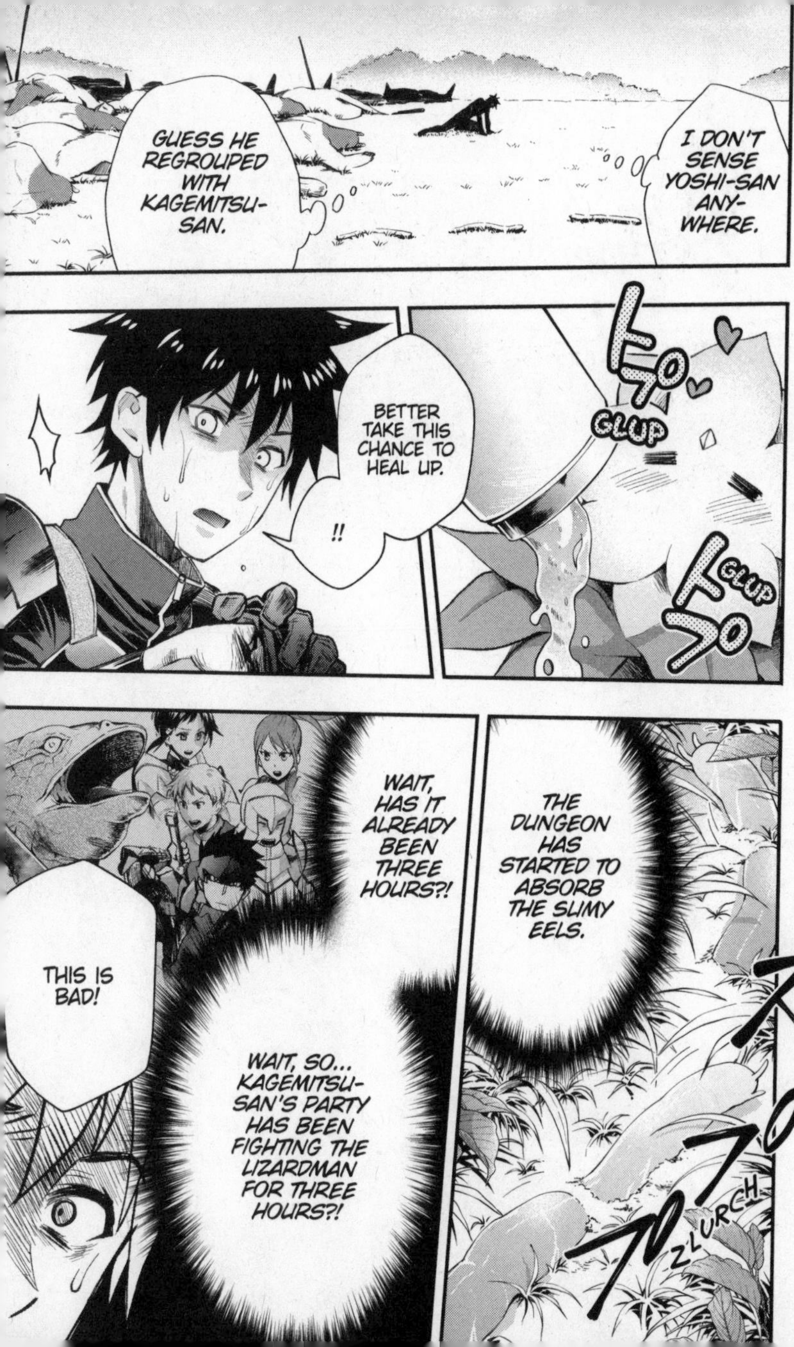

I DON'T SENSE YOSHI-SAN ANY-WHERE.
GUESS HE REGROUPED WITH KAGEMITSU-SAN.
GLUP
GLUP
BETTER TAKE THIS CHANCE TO HEAL UP.
!!
THE DUNGEON HAS STARTED TO ABSORB THE SLIMY EELS.
ZLURCH
WAIT, HAS IT ALREADY BEEN THREE HOURS?!
THIS IS BAD!
WAIT, SO... KAGEMITSU-SAN'S PARTY HAS BEEN FIGHTING THE LIZARDMAN FOR THREE HOURS?!

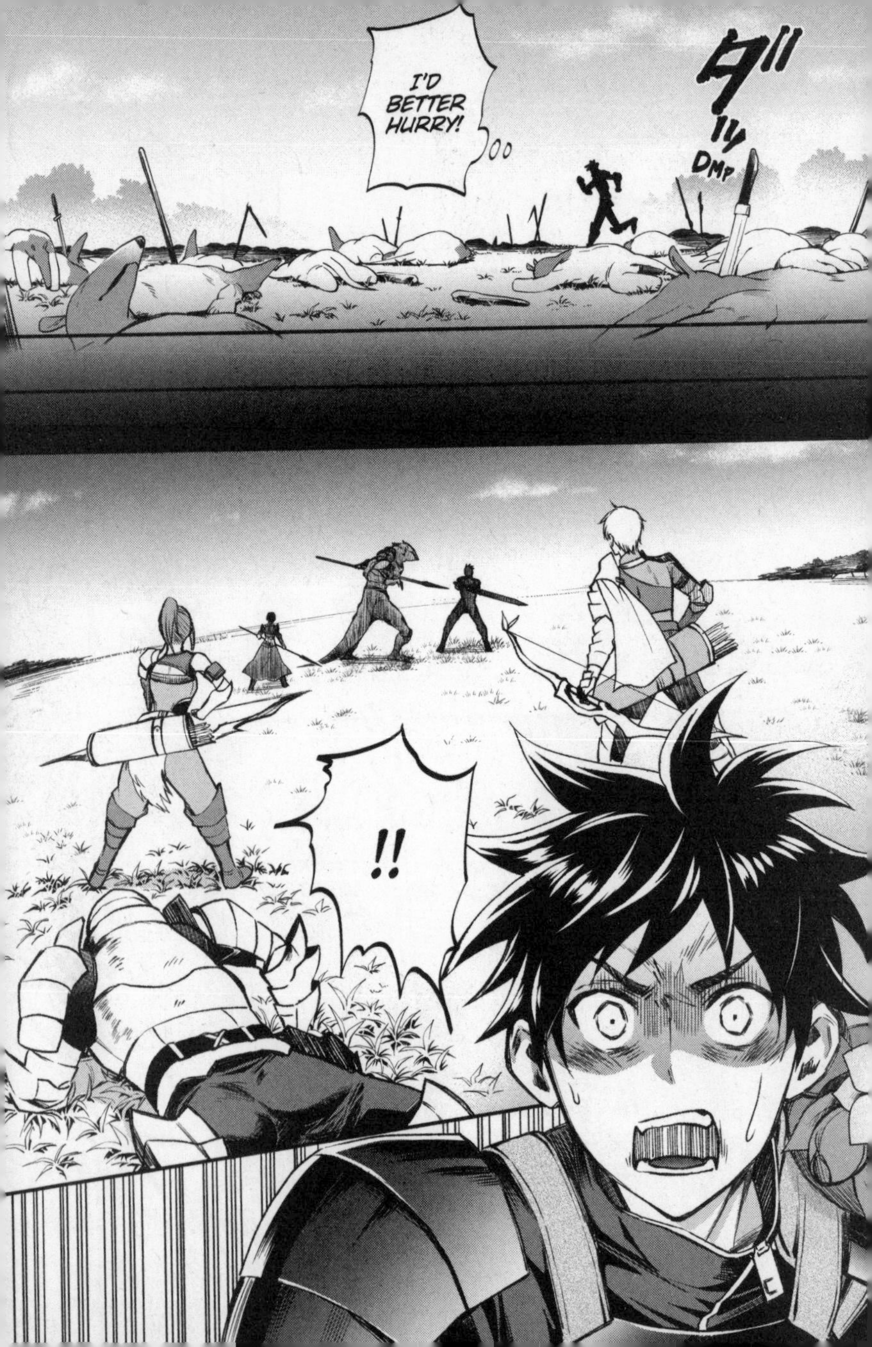

ダッ
DMP
I'D BETTER HURRY!
!!

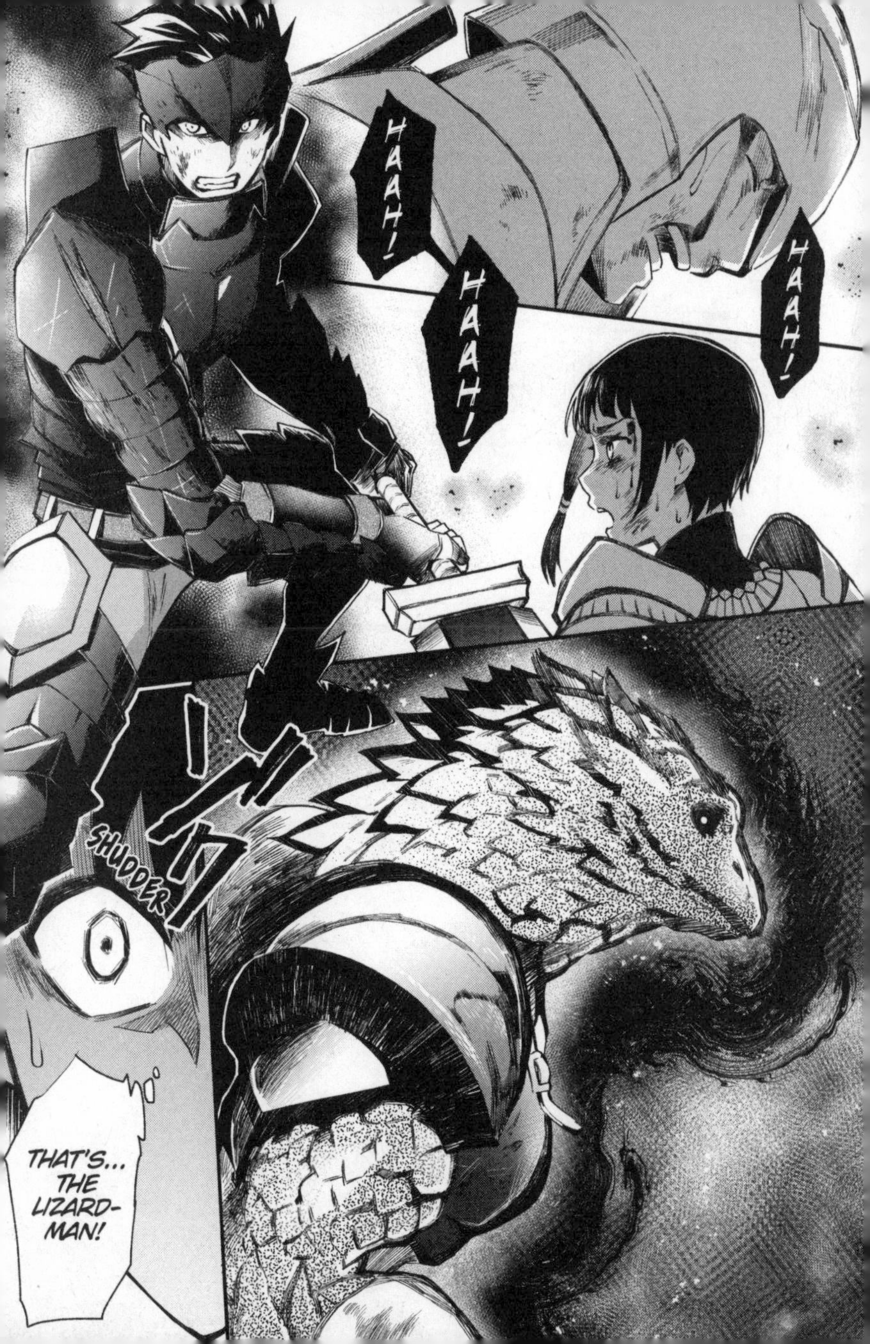
HAAAH!
HAAAH!
HAAAH!
SHUDDER
THAT'S... THE LIZARD-MAN!

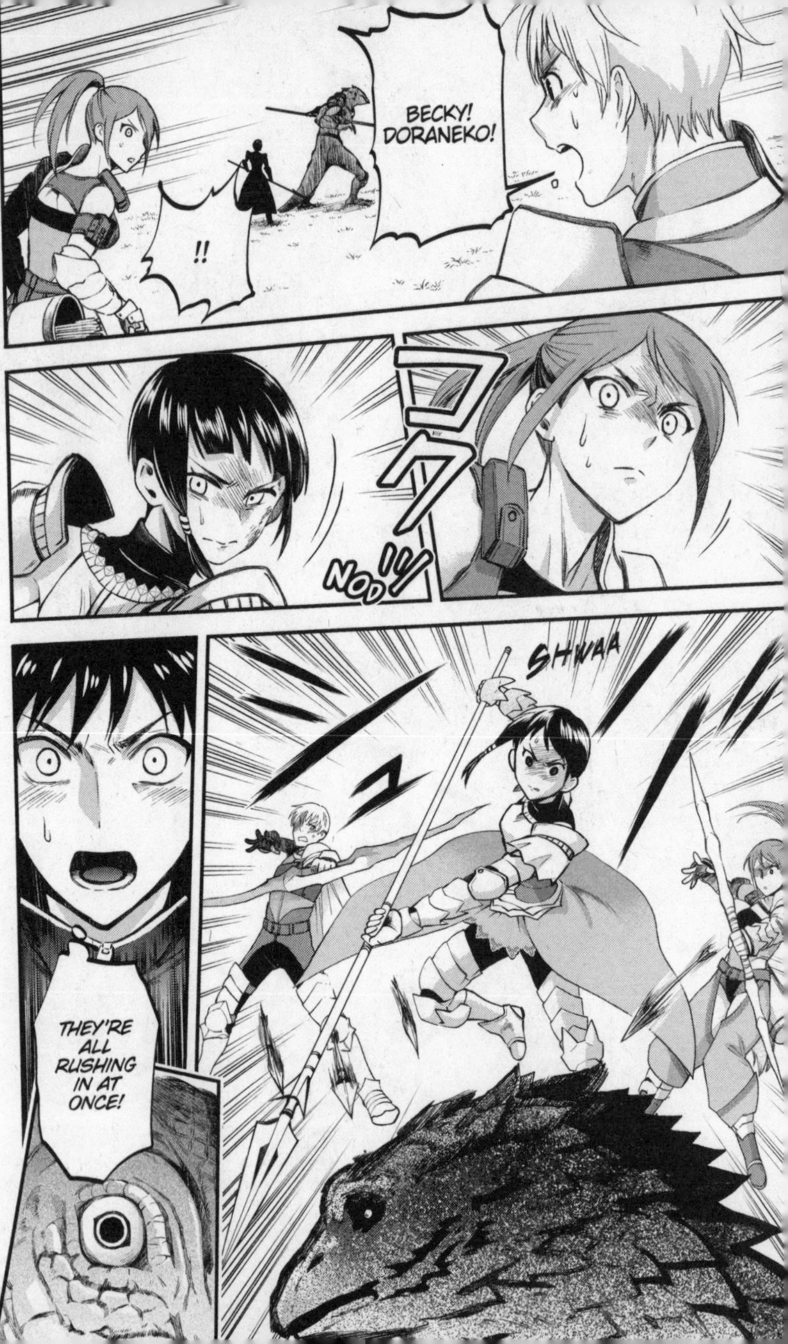
BECKY! DORANEKO!
!!
NOD
SHWAA
THEY'RE ALL RUSHING IN AT ONCE!

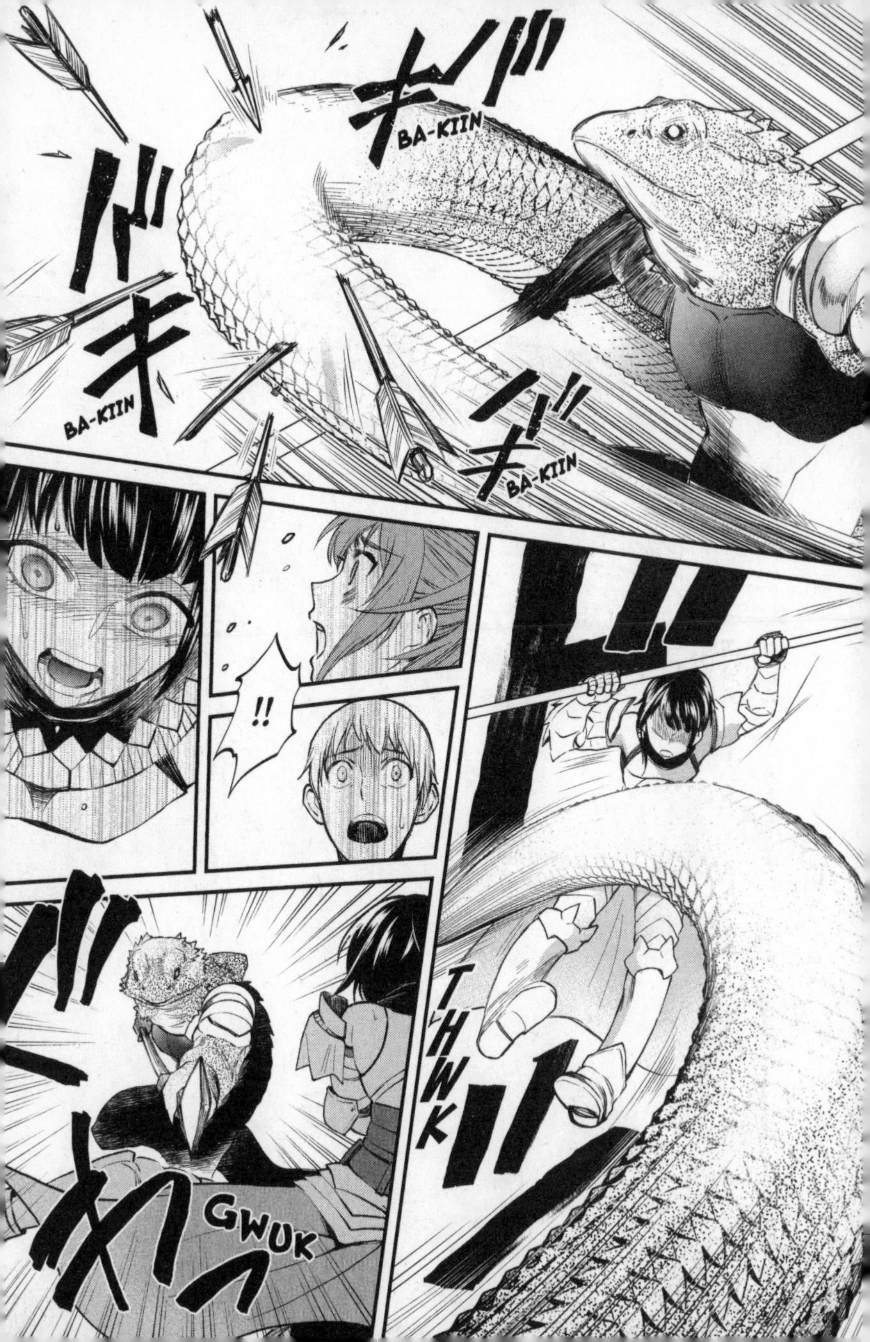
BA-KIIN
BA-KIIN
BA-KIIN
!!
THWK
GWUK

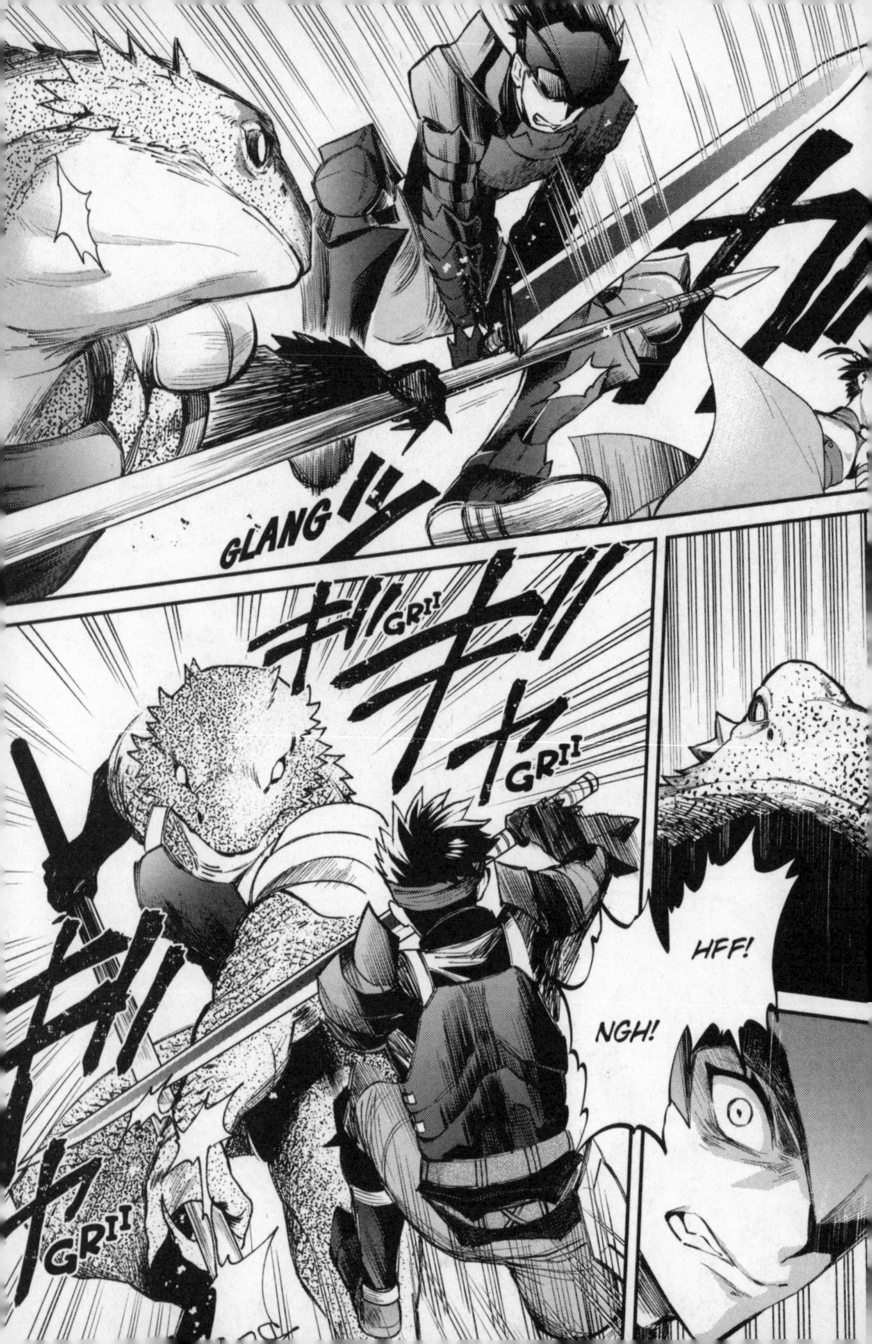
GLANG
HFF!
GRII
GRII
NGH!
GRII

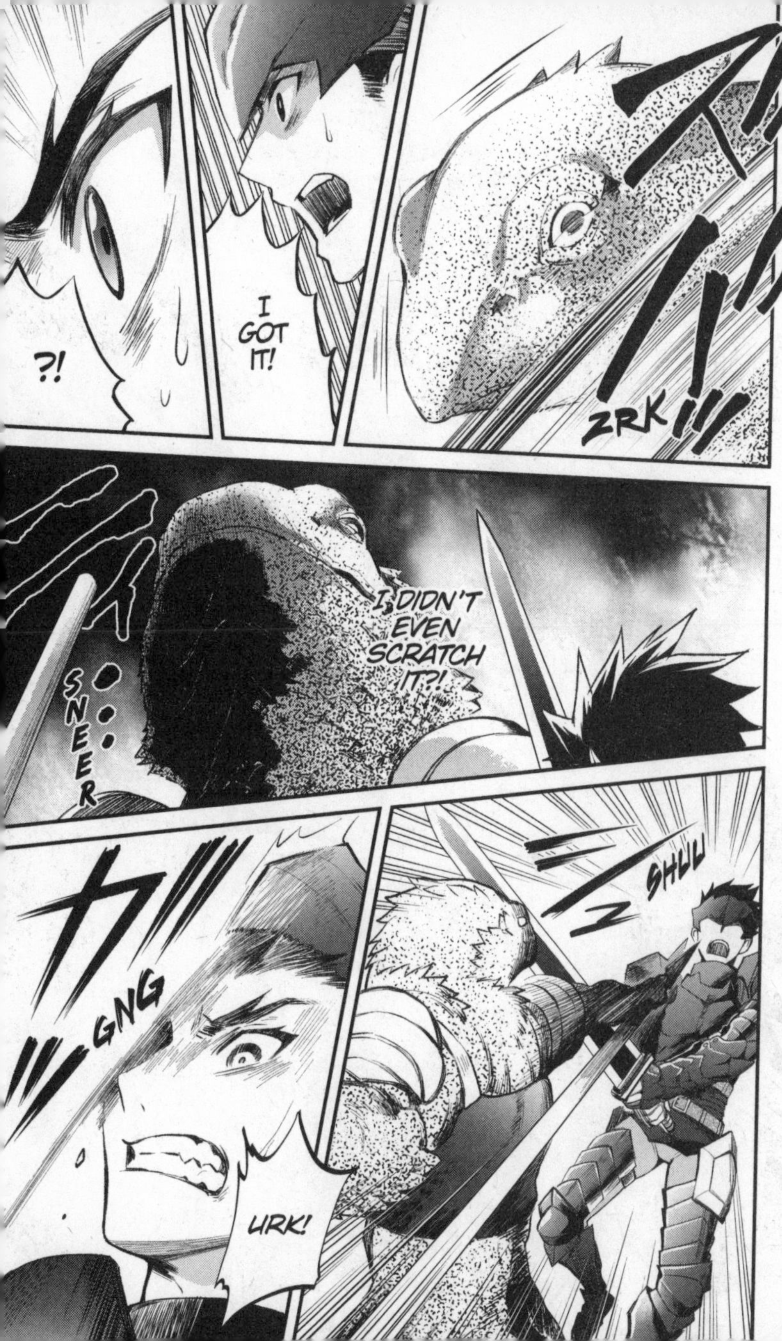
ZRK
I GOT IT!
?!
I DIDN'T EVEN SCRATCH IT?!
SNEER...
SHUU
GNG
URK!

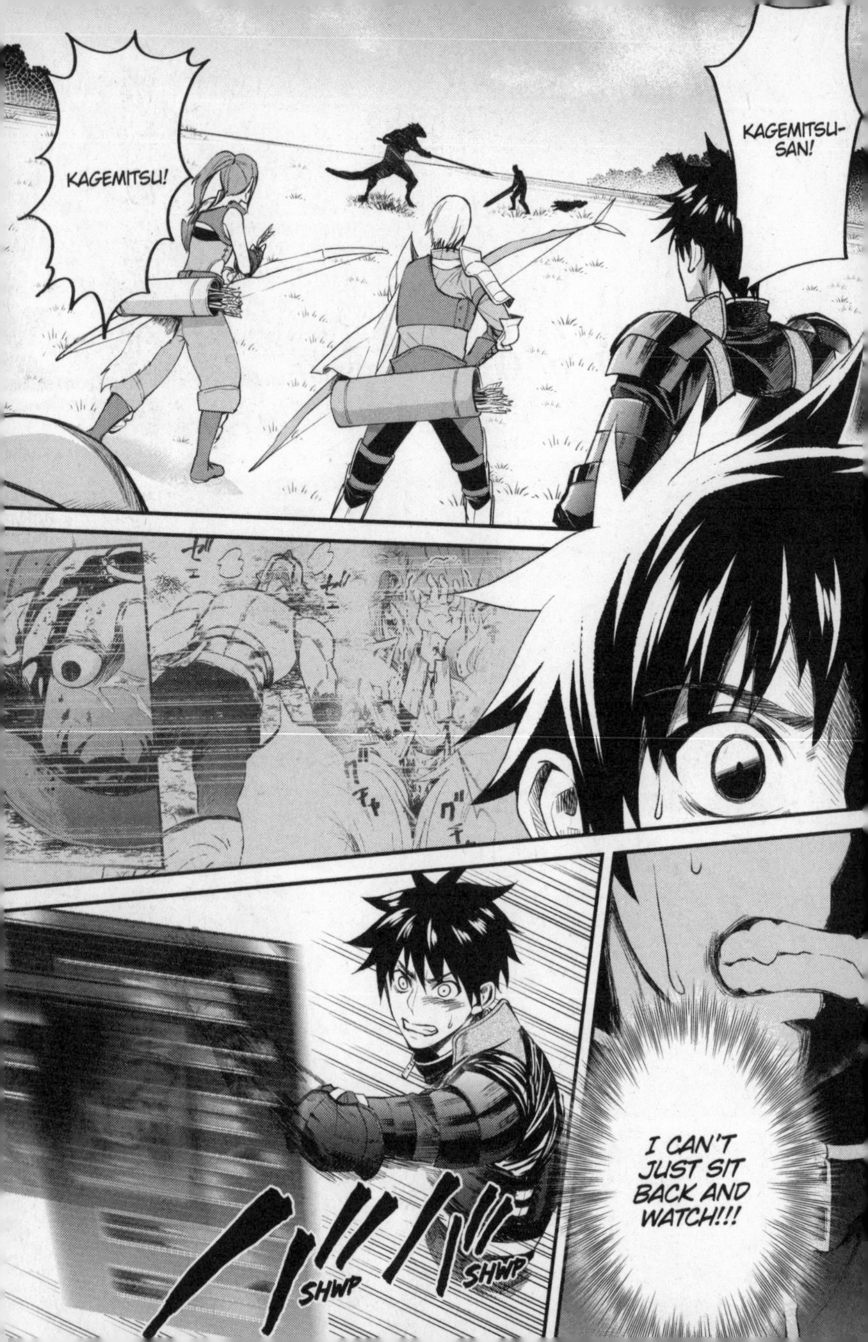
KAGEMITSU-SAN!
KAGEMITSU!
I CAN'T JUST SIT BACK AND WATCH!!!
SHWP
SHWP

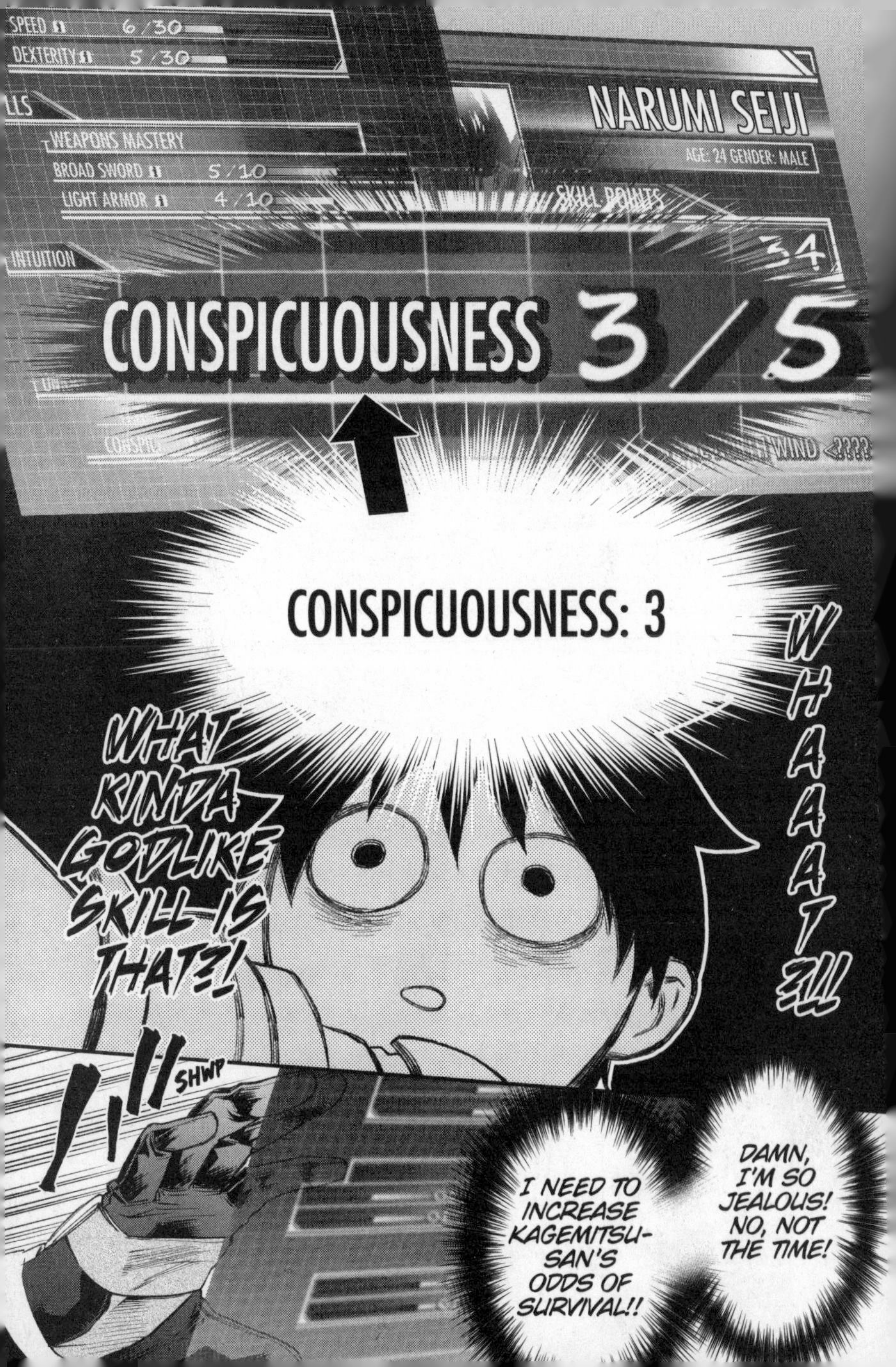
SPEED 6/30
DEXTERITY 5/30
NARUMI SEIJI
AGE: 24 GENDER: MALE
WEAPONS MASTERY
BROAD SWORD 5/10
LIGHT ARMOR 4/10
SKILL POINTS
34
INTUITION
CONSPICUOUSNESS 3/5
CONSPICUOUSNESS: 3
WHAAAAT?!!
WHAT KINDA GODLIKE SKILL IS THAT?!
DAMN, I'M SO JEALOUS! NO, NOT THE TIME!
I NEED TO INCREASE KAGEMITSU-SAN'S ODDS OF SURVIVAL!!
SHWP

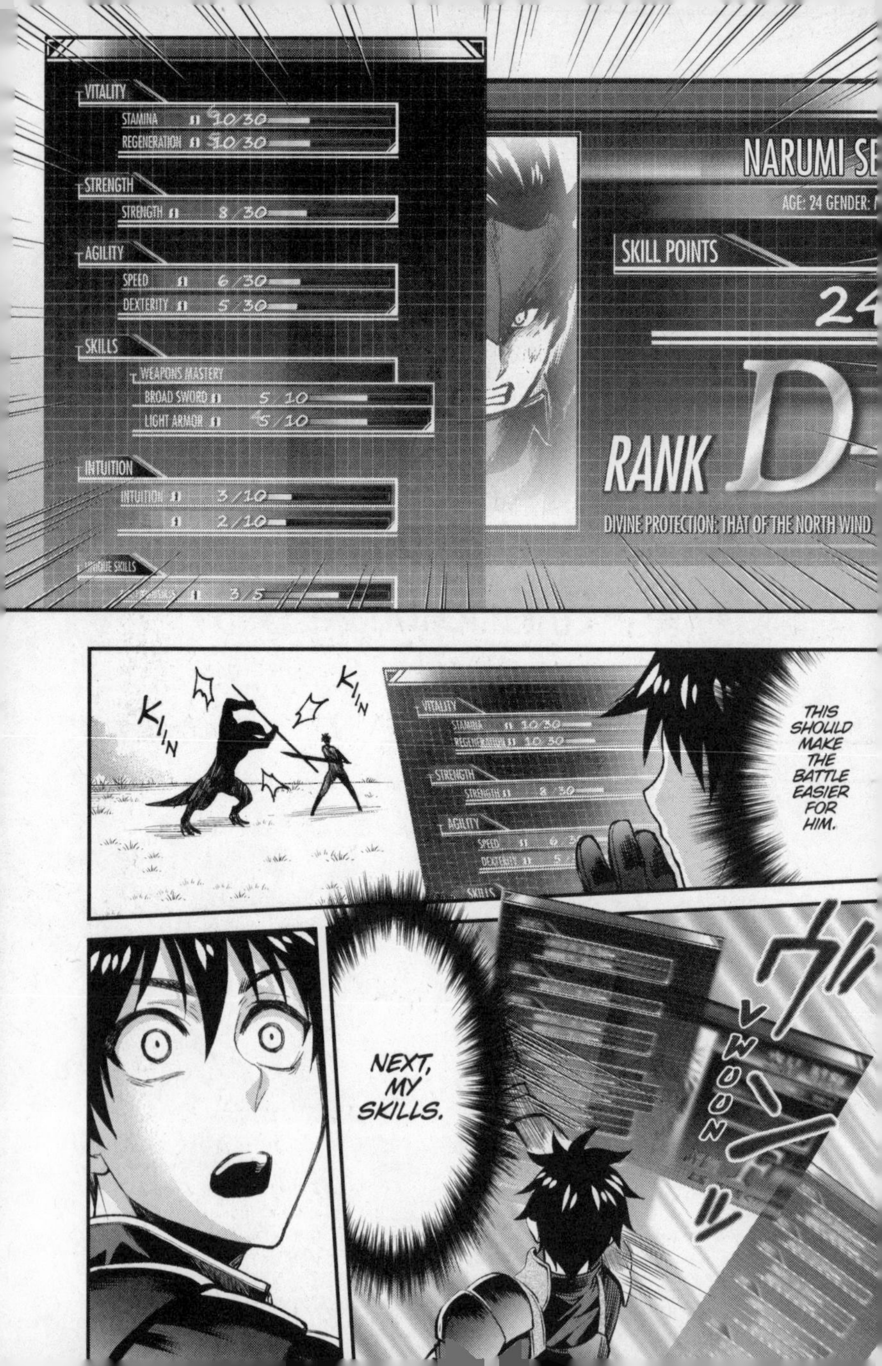
VITALITY
STAMINA 10/30
REGENERATION 10/30
STRENGTH
STRENGTH 8/30
AGILITY
SPEED 6/30
DEXTERITY 5/30
SKILLS
WEAPONS MASTERY
BROAD SWORD 5/10
LIGHT ARMOR 5/10
INTUITION
INTUITION 3/10
2/10
3/5
NARUMI SE
AGE: 24 GENDER:
SKILL POINTS
24
RANK D
DIVINE PROTECTION: THAT OF THE NORTH WIND
THIS SHOULD MAKE THE BATTLE EASIER FOR HIM.
VITALITY
STAMINA 10/30
REGENERATION 10/30
STRENGTH
STRENGTH 8/30
AGILITY
SPEED 6
DEXTERITY 5
SKILLS
KIIN
KIIN
VWOON
NEXT, MY SKILLS.

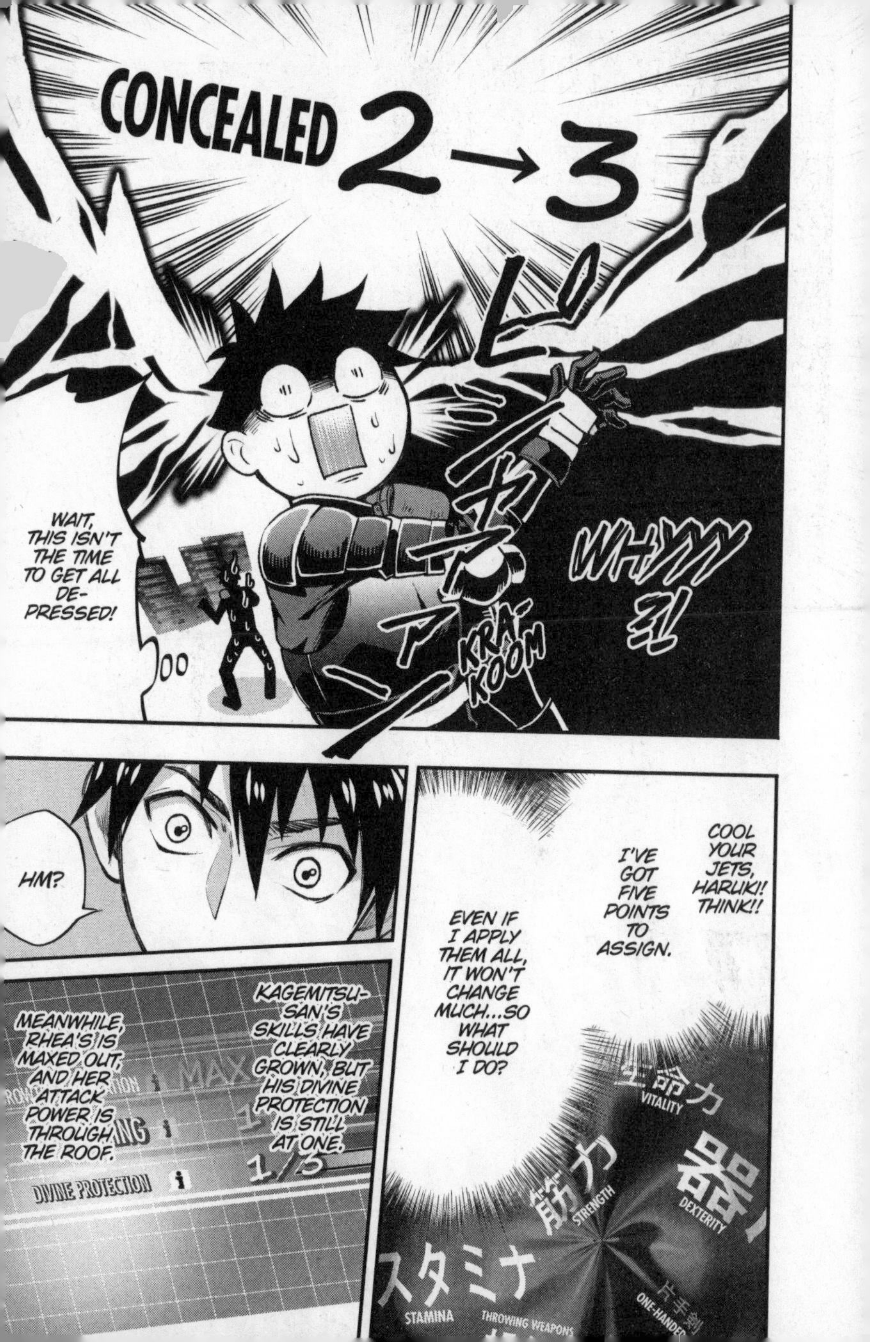
CONCEALED 2→3
WHYYY ?!
KRA-KOOM
WAIT, THIS ISN'T THE TIME TO GET ALL DE-PRESSED!
COOL YOUR JETS, HARUKI!! THINK!!
I'VE GOT FIVE POINTS TO ASSIGN.
EVEN IF I APPLY THEM ALL, IT WON'T CHANGE MUCH...SO WHAT SHOULD I DO?
生命力
VITALITY
筋力
STRENGTH
器
DEXTERITY
スタミナ
STAMINA
THROWING WEAPONS
片手剣
ONE-HANDED
HM?
KAGEMITSU-SAN'S SKILLS HAVE CLEARLY GROWN, BUT HIS DIVINE PROTECTION IS STILL AT ONE.
MEANWHILE, RHEA'S IS MAXED OUT, AND HER ATTACK POWER IS THROUGH THE ROOF.
MAX
1/5
DIVINE PROTECTION

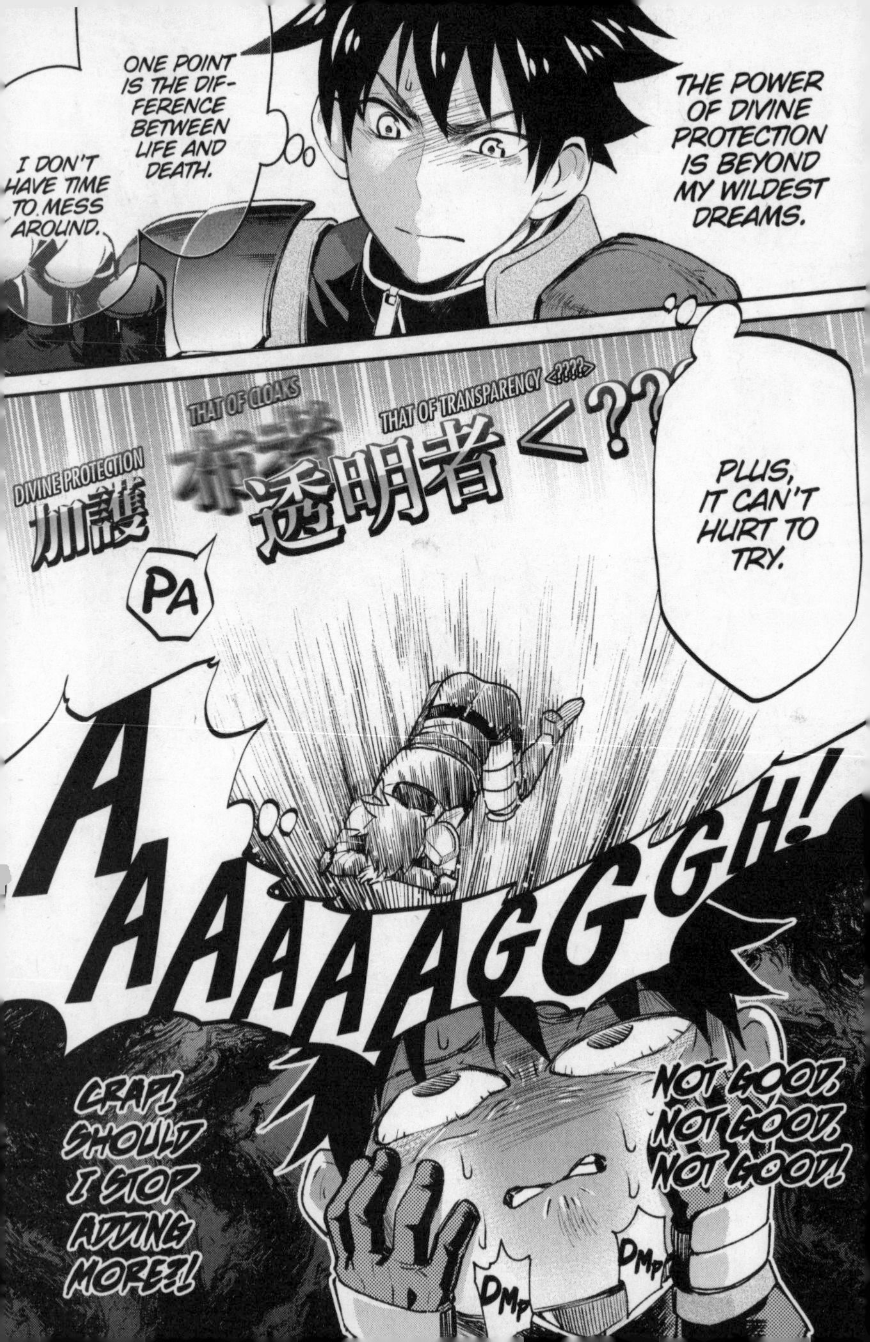
THE POWER OF DIVINE PROTECTION IS BEYOND MY WILDEST DREAMS.
ONE POINT IS THE DIF-FERENCE BETWEEN LIFE AND DEATH.
I DON'T HAVE TIME TO MESS AROUND.
PLUS, IT CAN'T HURT TO TRY.
DIVINE PROTECTION
加護
THAT OF CLOAKS
THAT OF TRANSPARENCY <????>
透明者
PA
AAAAAAGGGH!
NOT GOOD. NOT GOOD. NOT GOOD!
CRAP! SHOULD I STOP ADDING MORE?!
DMP
DMP

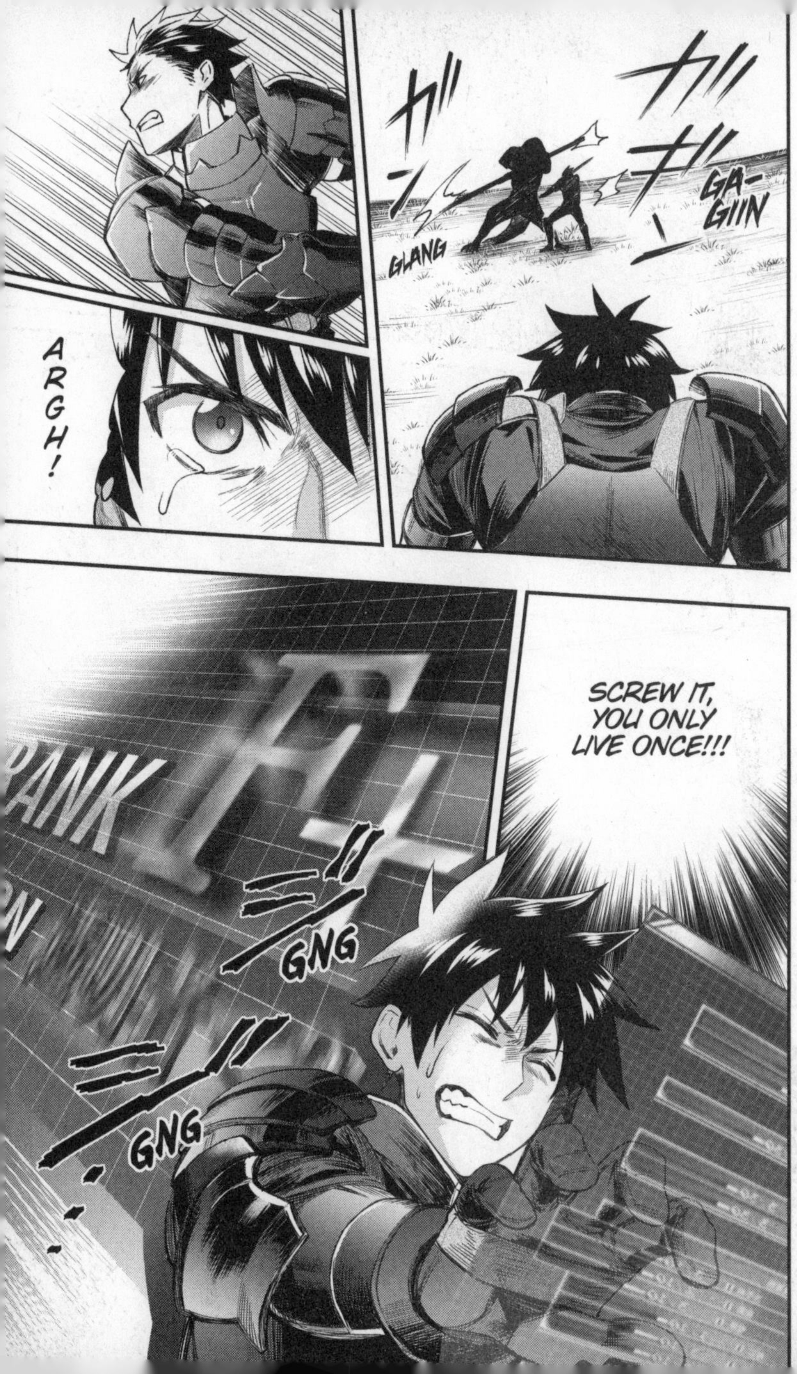
GA-GIIN
GLANG
ARGH!
SCREW IT, YOU ONLY LIVE ONCE!!!
RANK
GNG
GNG

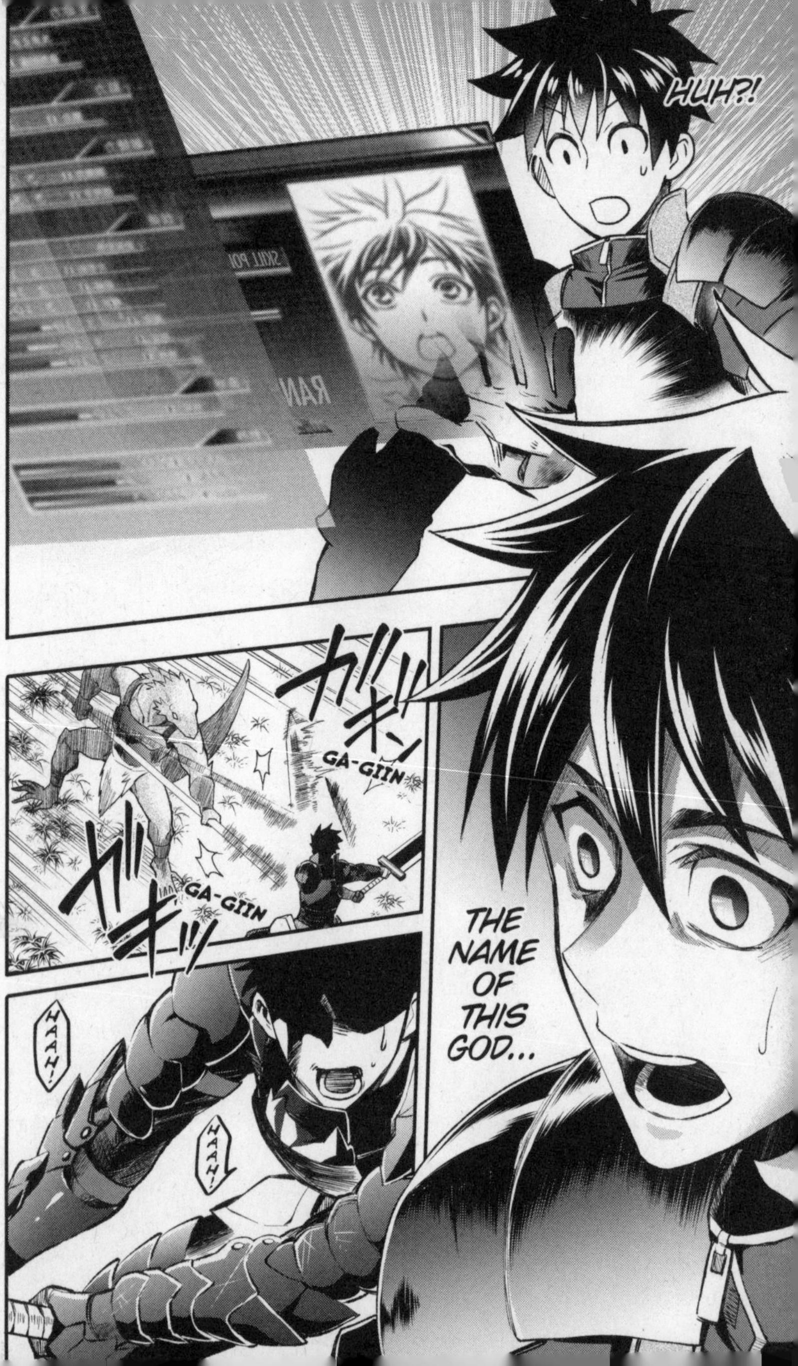
HUH?!
THE NAME OF THIS GOD...
GA-GIIN
GA-GIIN
HAAH!
HAAH!

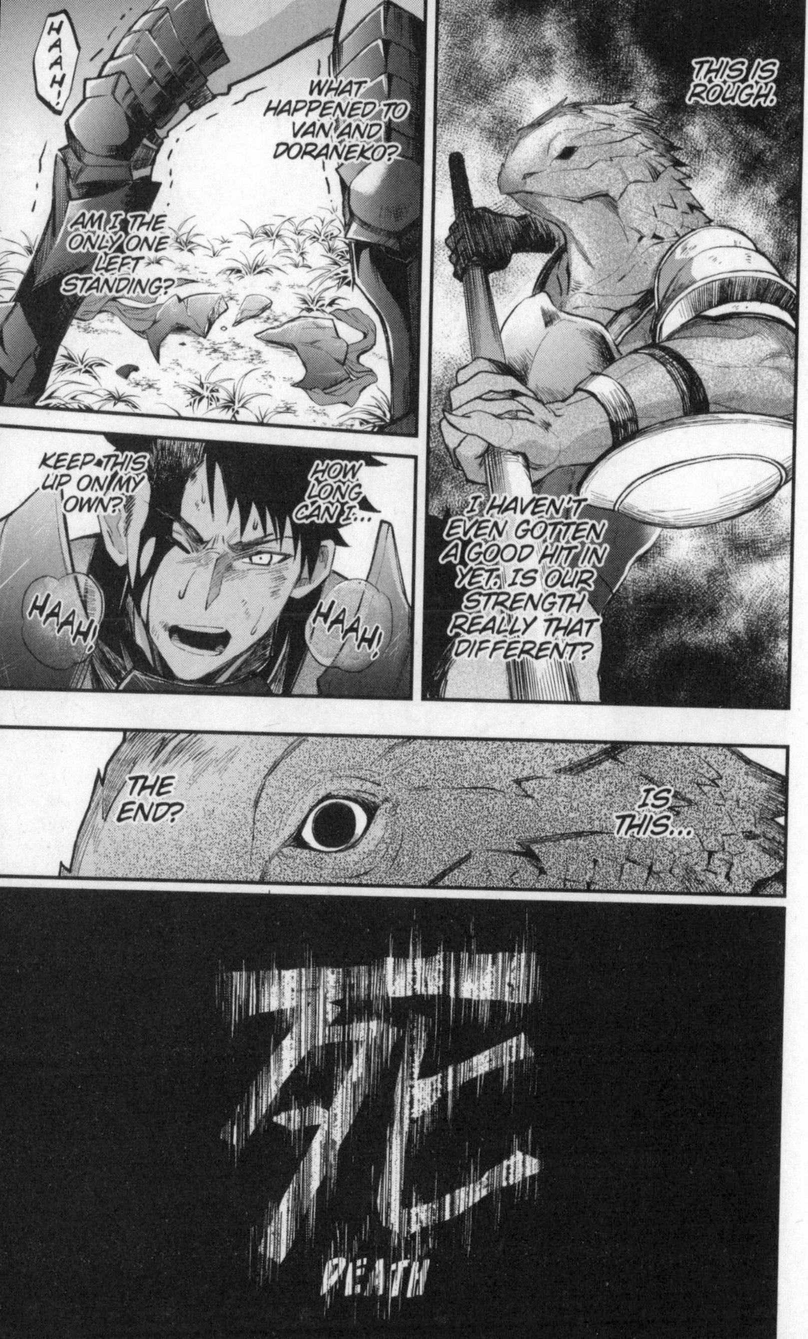
THIS IS ROUGH.
I HAVEN'T EVEN GOTTEN A GOOD HIT IN YET. IS OUR STRENGTH REALLY THAT DIFFERENT?
HAAAH!
WHAT HAPPENED TO VAN AND DORANEKO?
AM I THE ONLY ONE LEFT STANDING?
HOW LONG CAN I...
KEEP THIS UP ON MY OWN?
HAAAH!
HAAAH!
IS THIS...
THE END?
死
DEATH

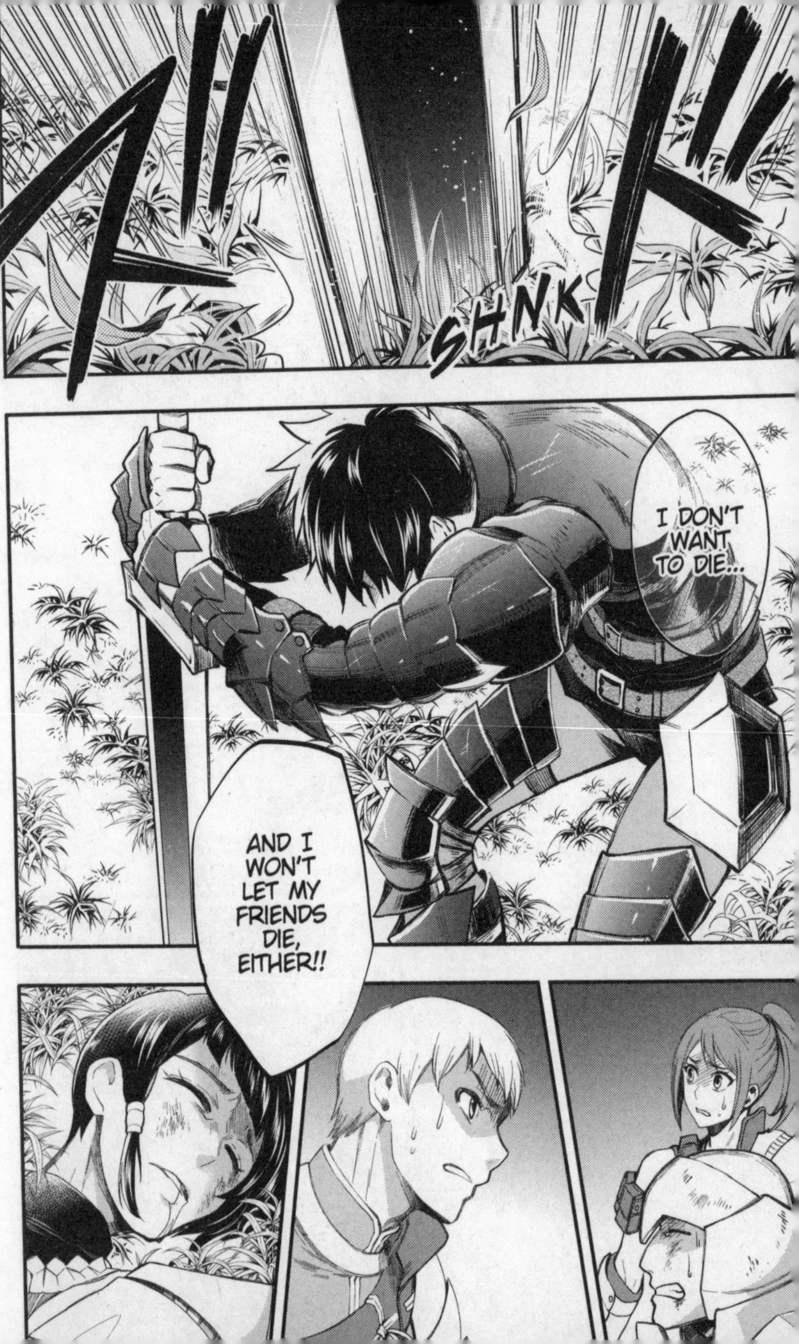
SHNK
I DON'T WANT TO DIE...
AND I WON'T LET MY FRIENDS DIE, EITHER!!

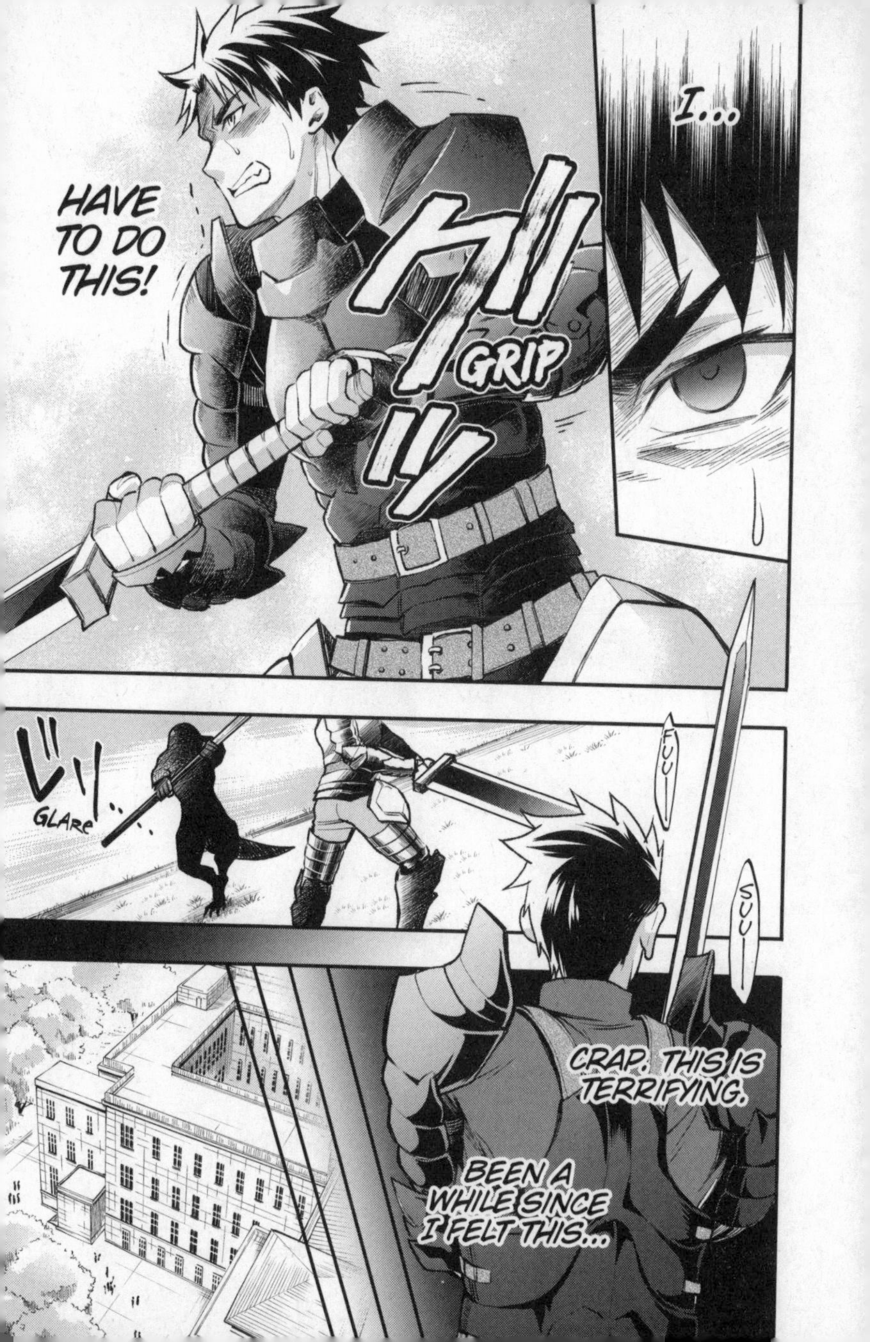
I...
HAVE TO DO THIS!
GRIP
GLARE
FUU
SUU
CRAP. THIS IS TERRIFYING.
BEEN A WHILE SINCE I FELT THIS...

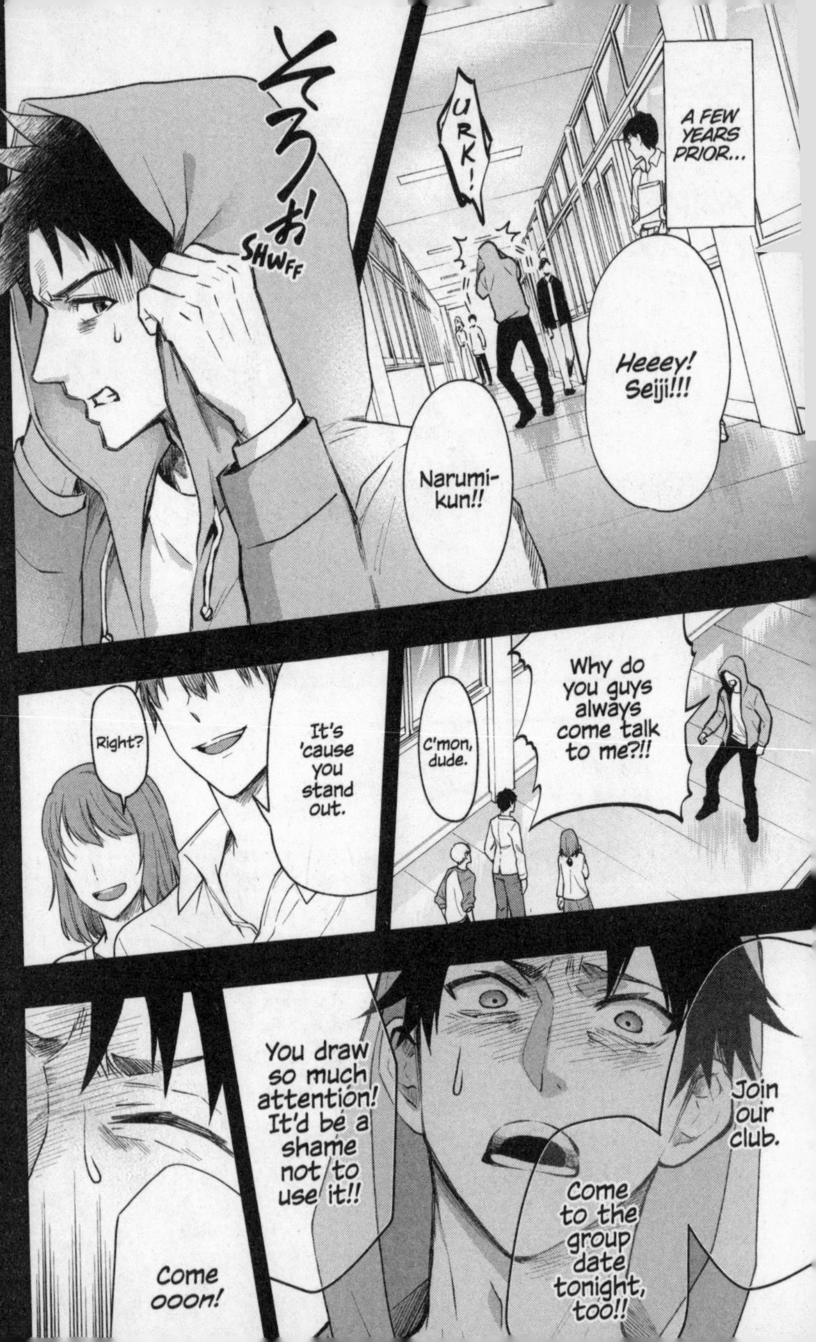
A FEW YEARS PRIOR...
Heeey! Seiji!!!
Narumi-kun!!
URK!
そろうお!
SHWFF
Why do you guys always come talk to me?!!
C'mon, dude.
It's 'cause you stand out.
Right?
Join our club.
Come to the group date tonight, too!!
You draw so much attention! It'd be a shame not to use it!!
Come ooon!

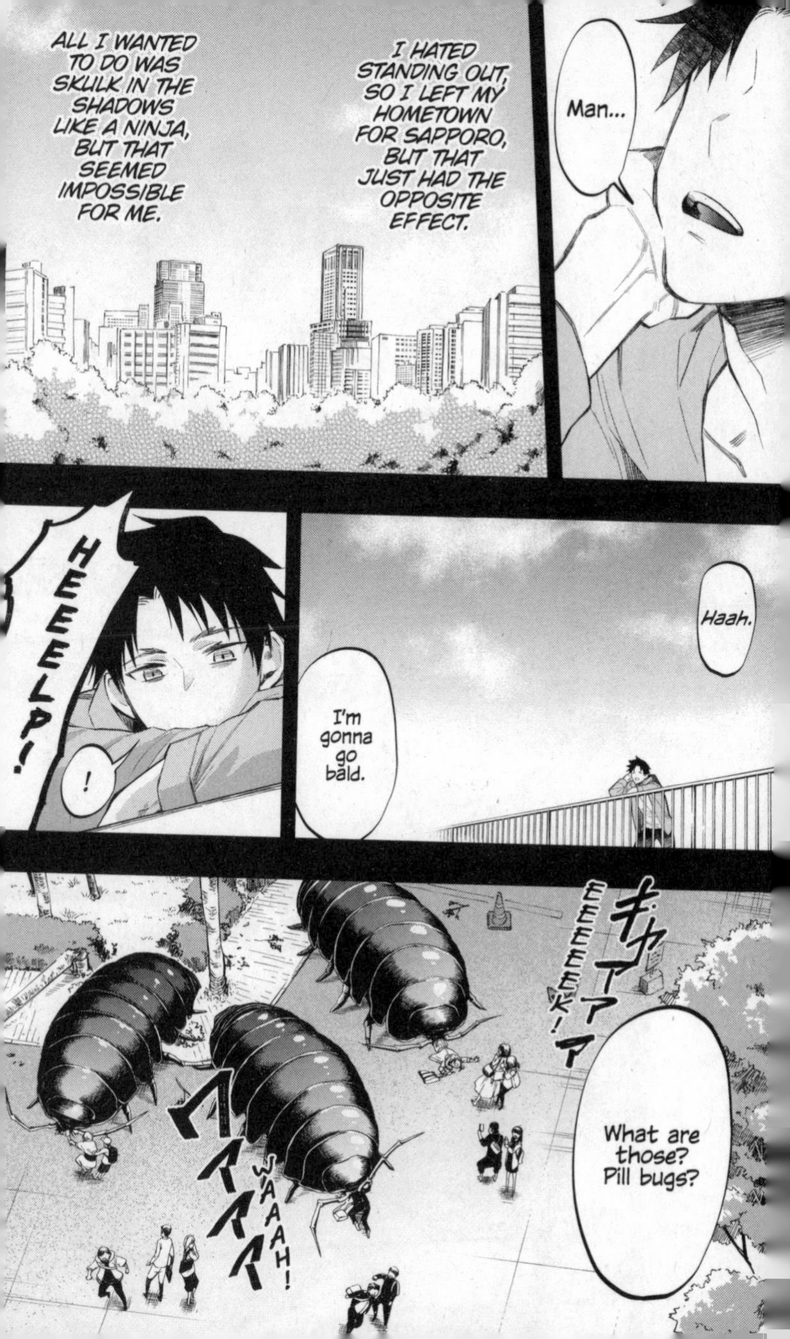
Man...
I HATED STANDING OUT, SO I LEFT MY HOMETOWN FOR SAPPORO, BUT THAT JUST HAD THE OPPOSITE EFFECT.
ALL I WANTED TO DO WAS SKULK IN THE SHADOWS LIKE A NINJA, BUT THAT SEEMED IMPOSSIBLE FOR ME.
Haah.
I'm gonna go bald.
HEEEELP!
!
EEEEEEEK!
What are those? Pill bugs?
WAAAAH!

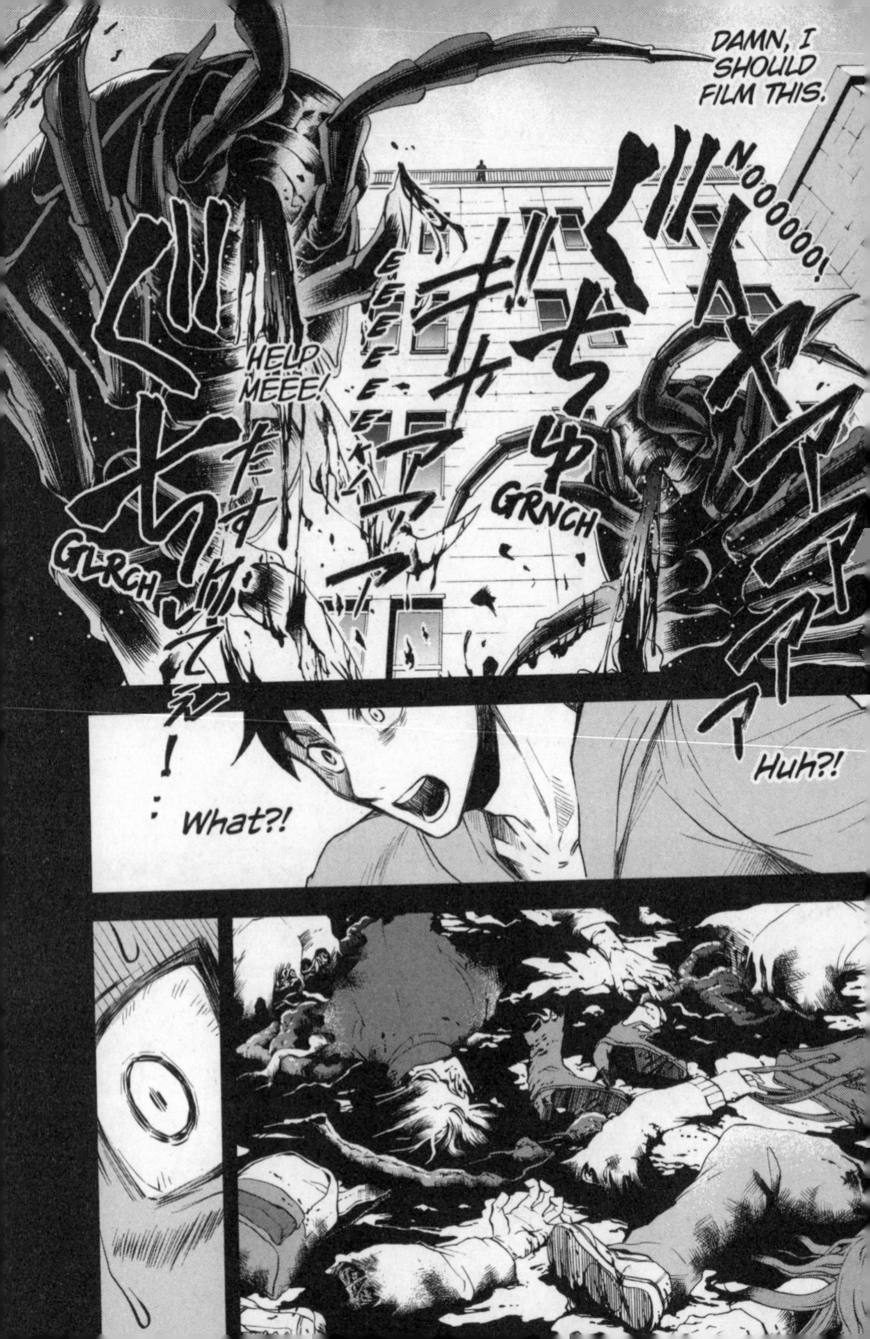
DAMN, I SHOULD FILM THIS.
NOOOOOOO!
GRNCH
HELP MEEE!
GLRCH
Huh?!
What?!

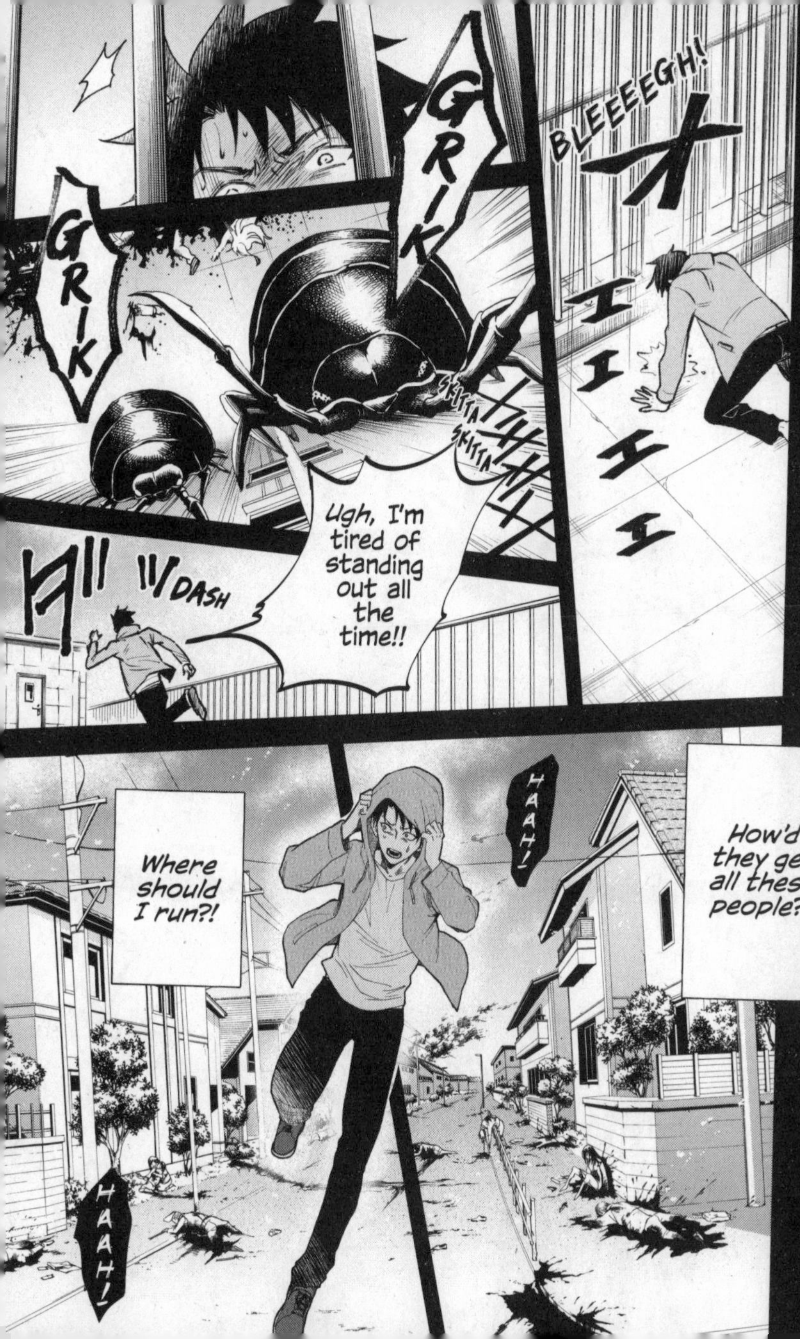
BLEEEEGH!
GRIK
GRIK
SKITTA
SKITTA
Ugh, I'm tired of standing out all the time!!
DASH
How'd they get all these people?!
HAAH!
Where should I run?!
HAAH!

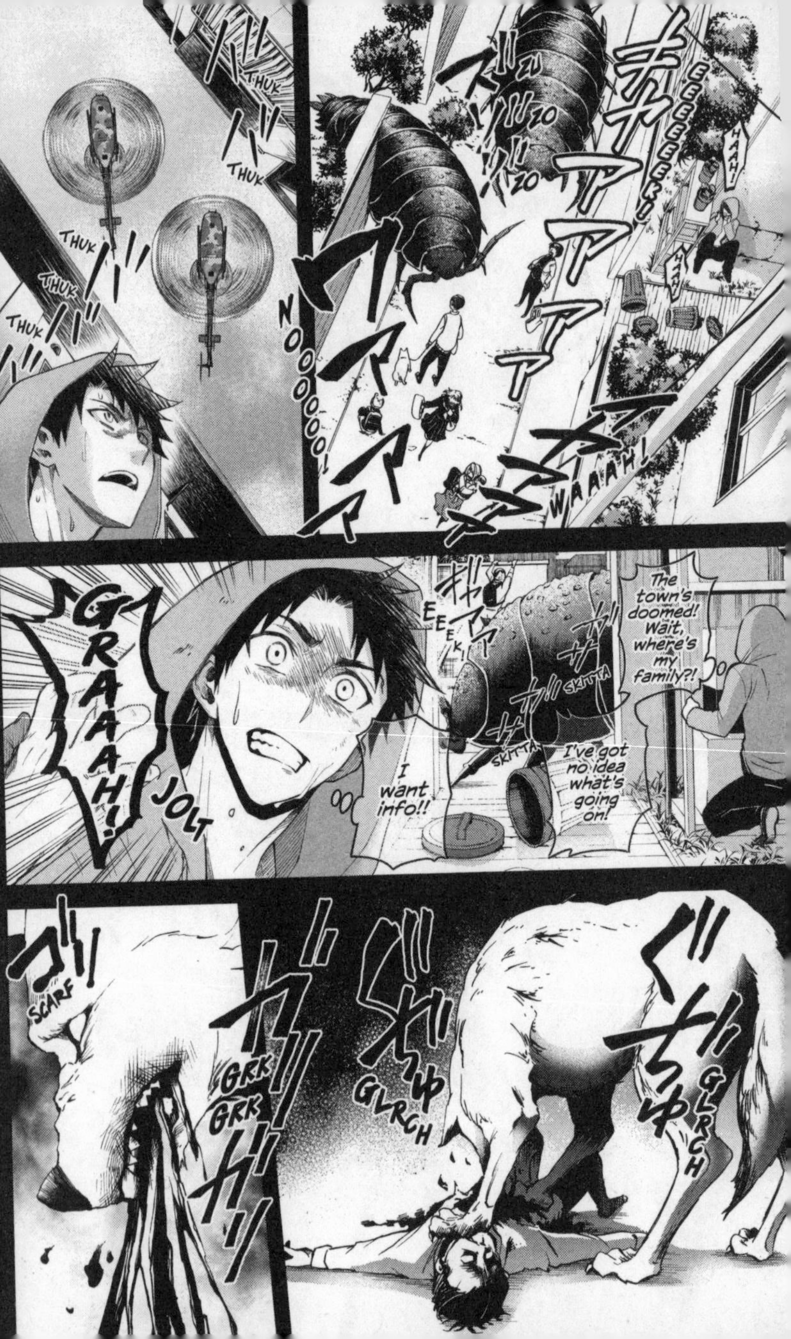
EEEEEEEK!
HAAH!
HAAH
ZU ZU
ZO ZO
NOOOOOOO!
WAAAAH!
THUK
THUK
THUK
THUK
THUK
The town's doomed! Wait, where's my family?!
I've got no idea what's going on!
SKITTA
SKITTA
EEEK!
I want info!!
JOLT
GRAAAAH!
GLRCH
GLRCH
GRK GRK
SCARF

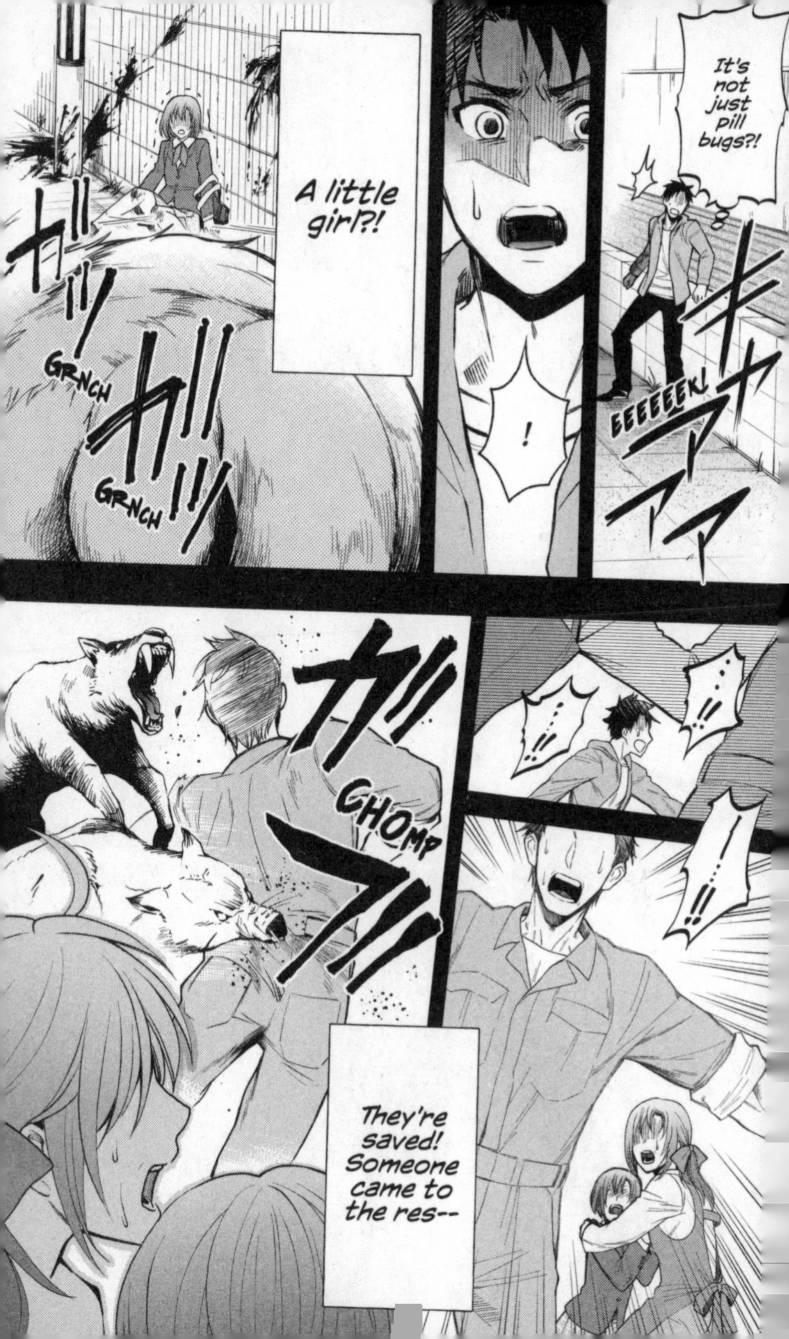
It's not just pill bugs?!
EEEEEEK!
!
A little girl?!
GRNCH
GRNCH
...!!
!!
...!!
They're saved! Someone came to the res--
CHOMP

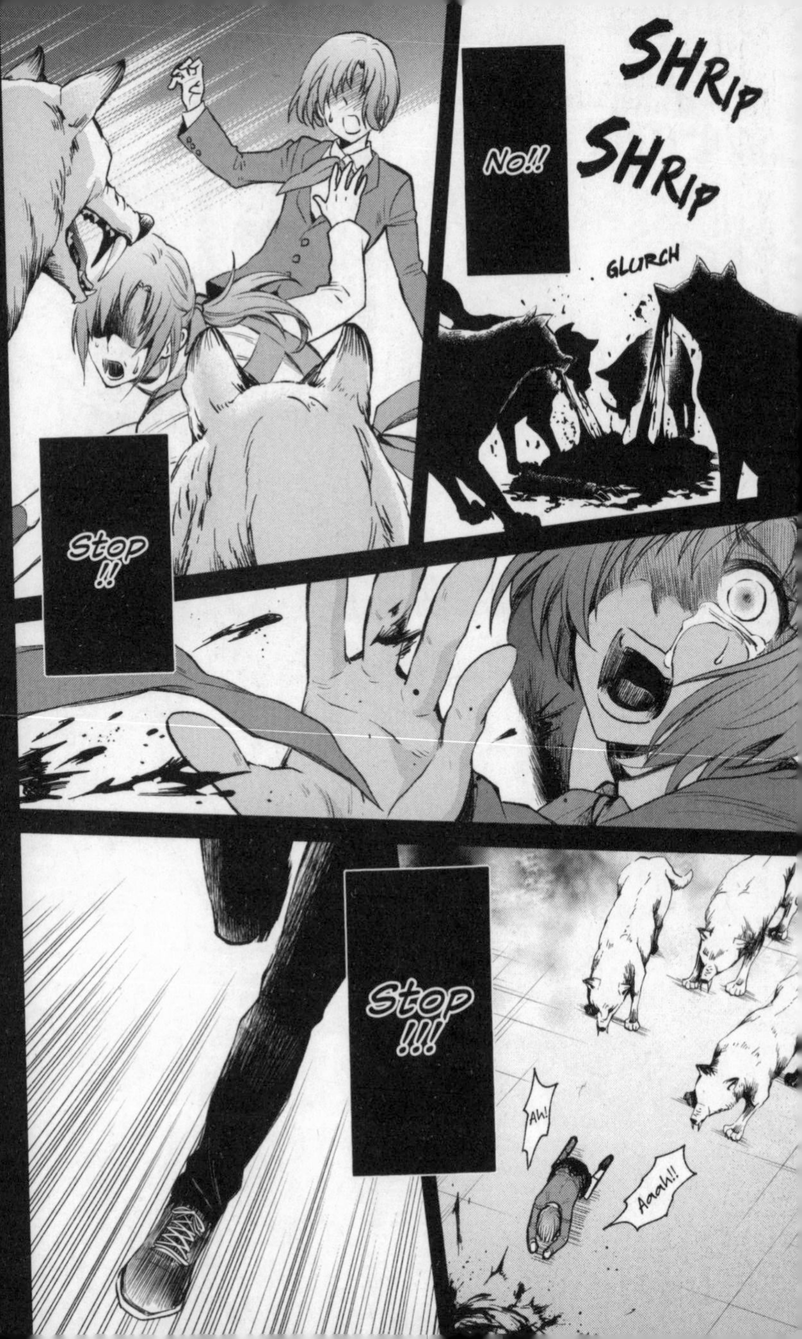
SHRIP
SHRIP
No!!
GLURCH
Stop !!
Stop !!!
Ah!
Aaaah!!

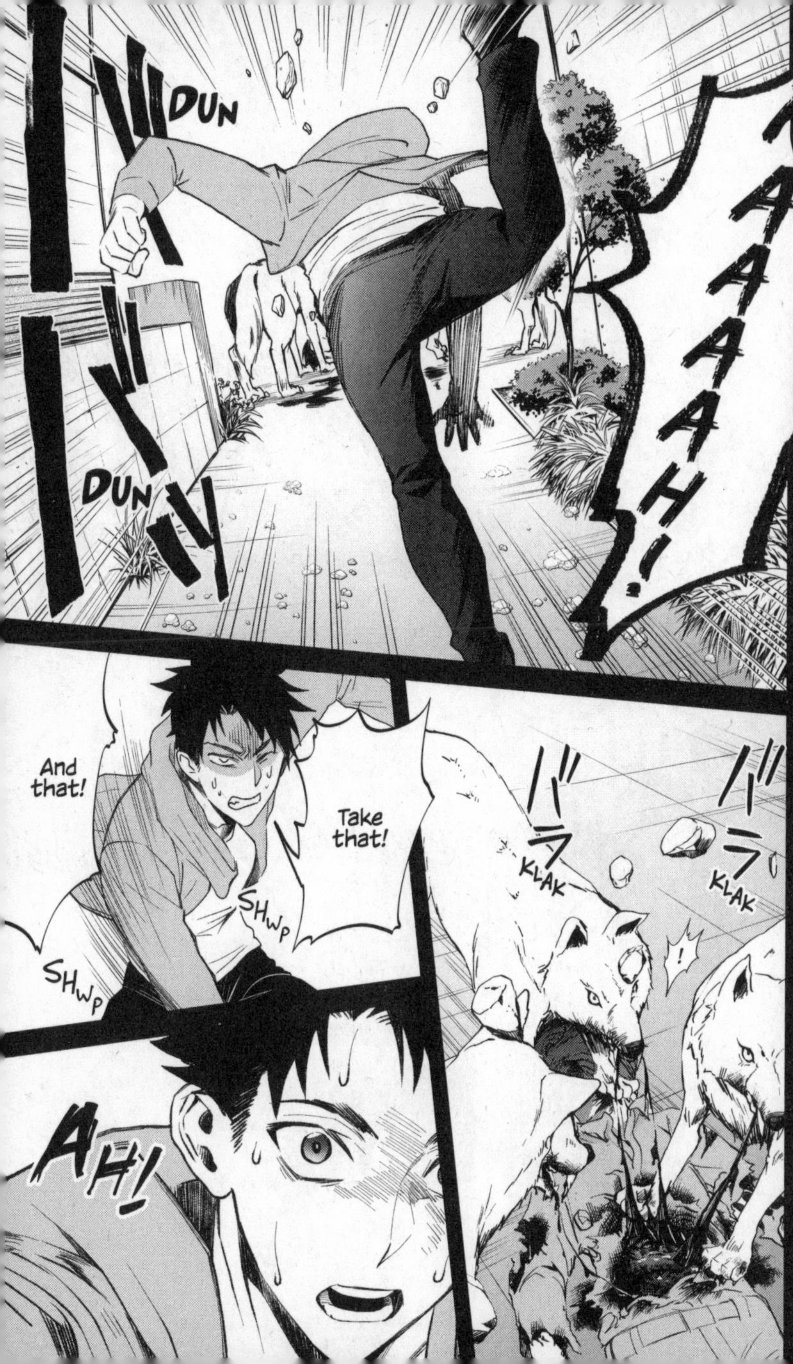
RAAAAH!
DUN
DUN
バラ
KLAK
バラ
KLAK
!
Take that!
And that!
SHWP
SHWP
AH!

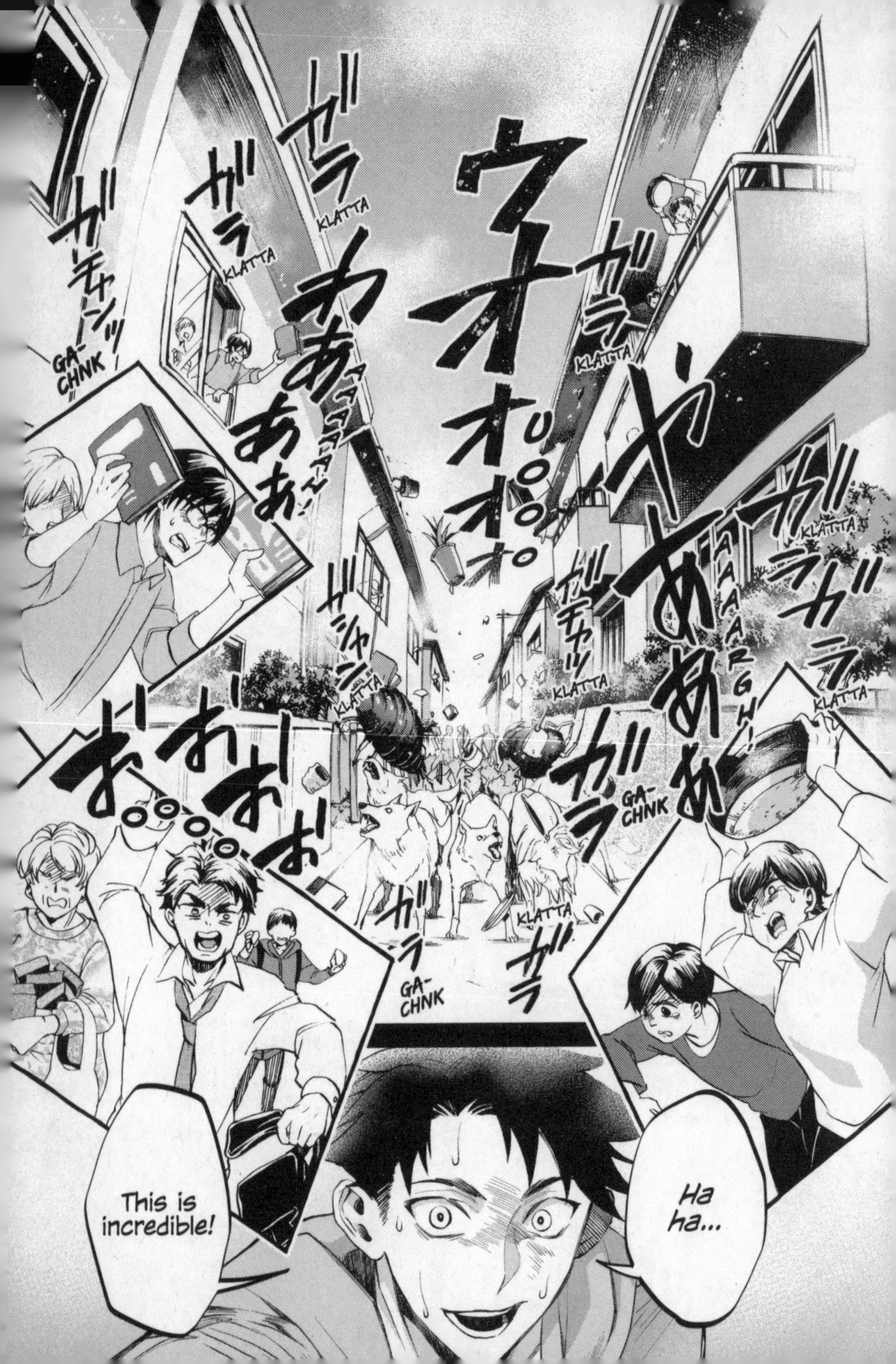
KLATTA
AAAARGH!
KLATTA
KLATTA
KLATTA
GA-CHNK
UOOO
KLATTA
KLATTA
AAAAAAAH!
GA-CHNK
KLATTA
KLATTA
GA-CHNK
Ha ha...
This is incredible!

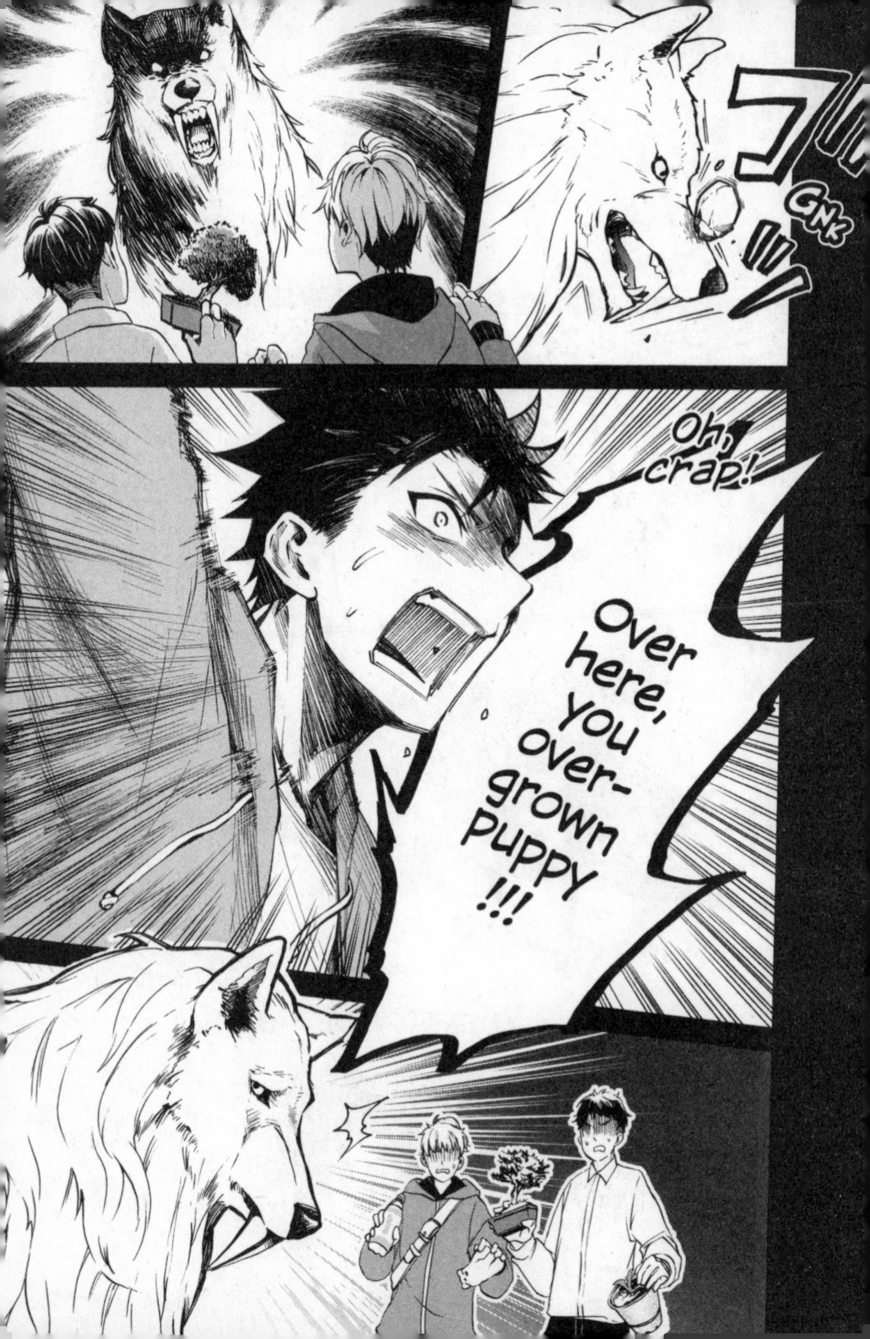
Gnk
Oh, crap!
Over here, you over-grown puppy!!!

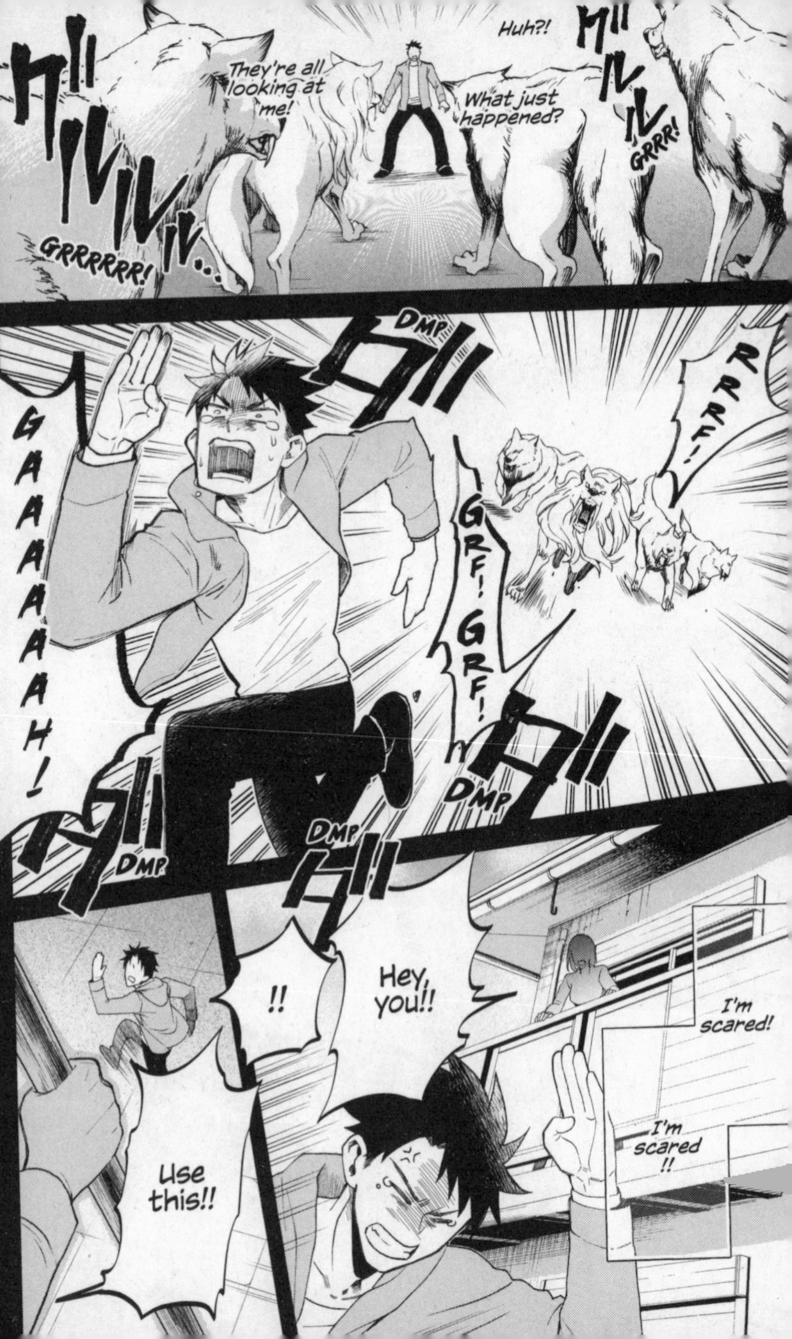
Huh?!
GRRR!
What just happened?
They're all looking at me!
GRRRRRR!
RRRF!
DMP
GRF! GRF!
DMP
GAAAAAAAAAH!
DMP
DMP
I'm scared!
I'm scared!!
Hey, you!!
!!
Use this!!

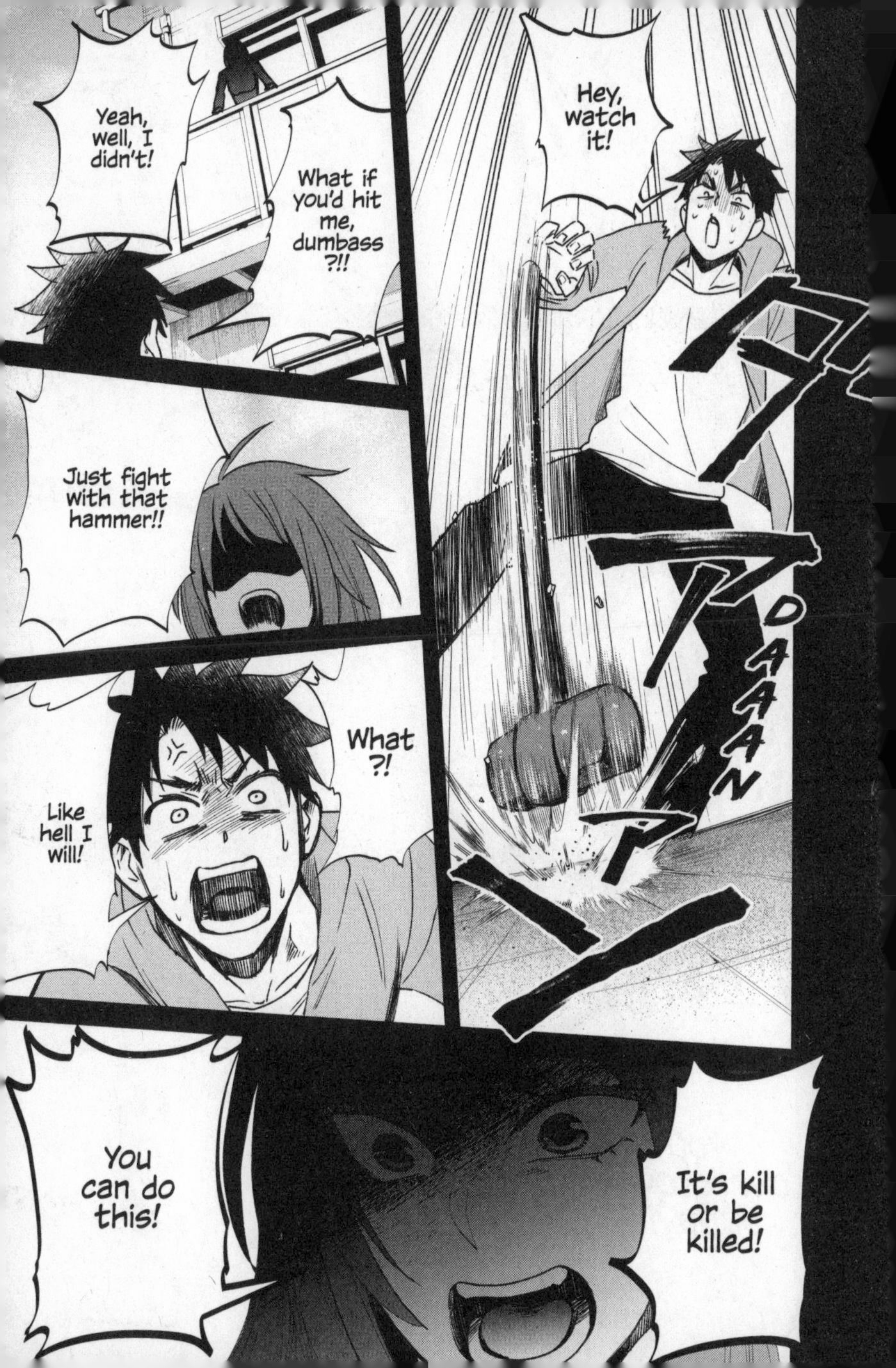
Hey, watch it!
DOAAAAN
What if you'd hit me, dumbass ?!!
Yeah, well, I didn't!
Just fight with that hammer!!
What ?!
Like hell I will!
It's kill or be killed!
You can do this!

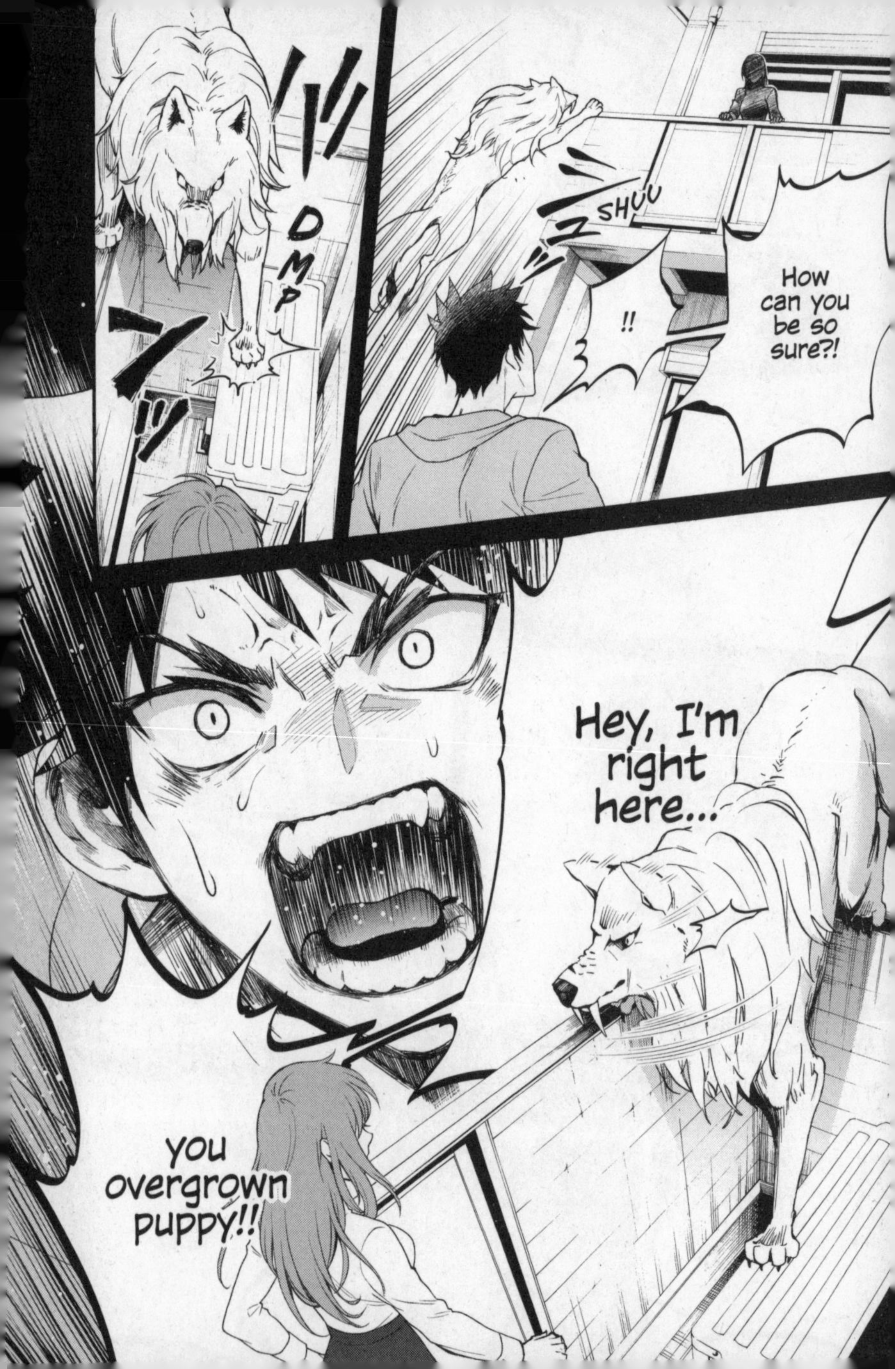
SHUU
How can you be so sure?!
!!
DMP
Hey, I'm right here...
you overgrown puppy!!

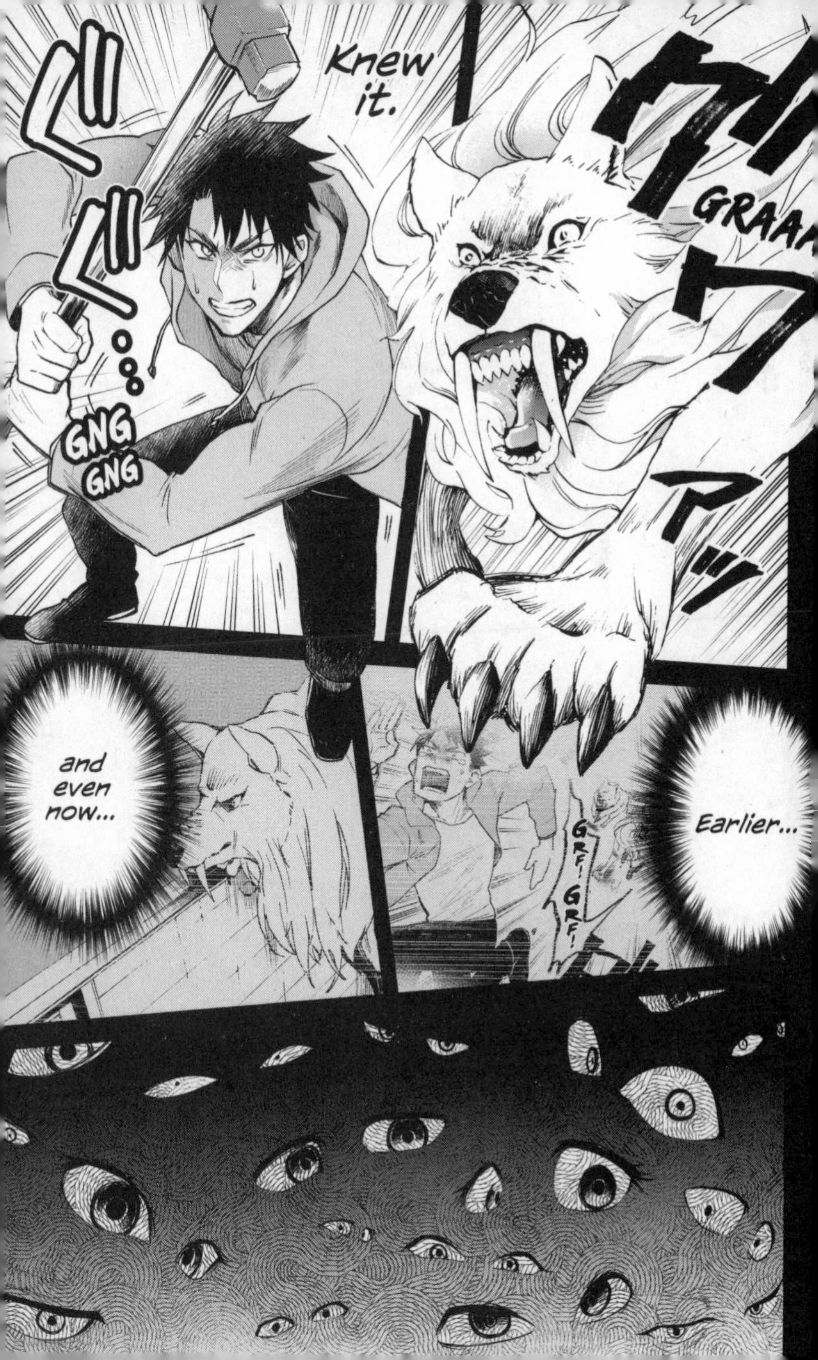
GRAAA
Knew it.
GNG GNG
Earlier...
GRF! GRF!
and even now...

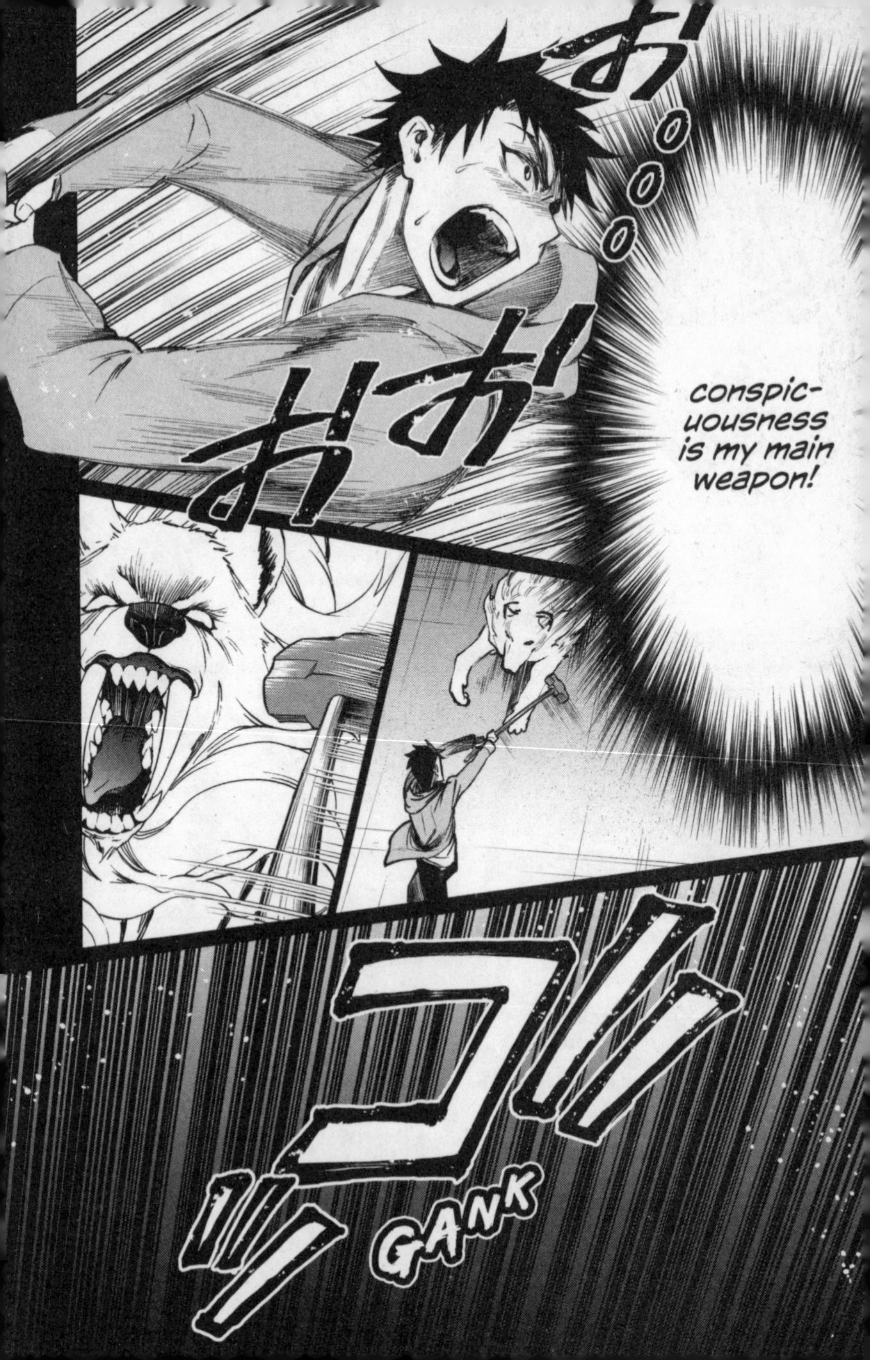
conspic-
uousness
is my main
weapon!
GANK

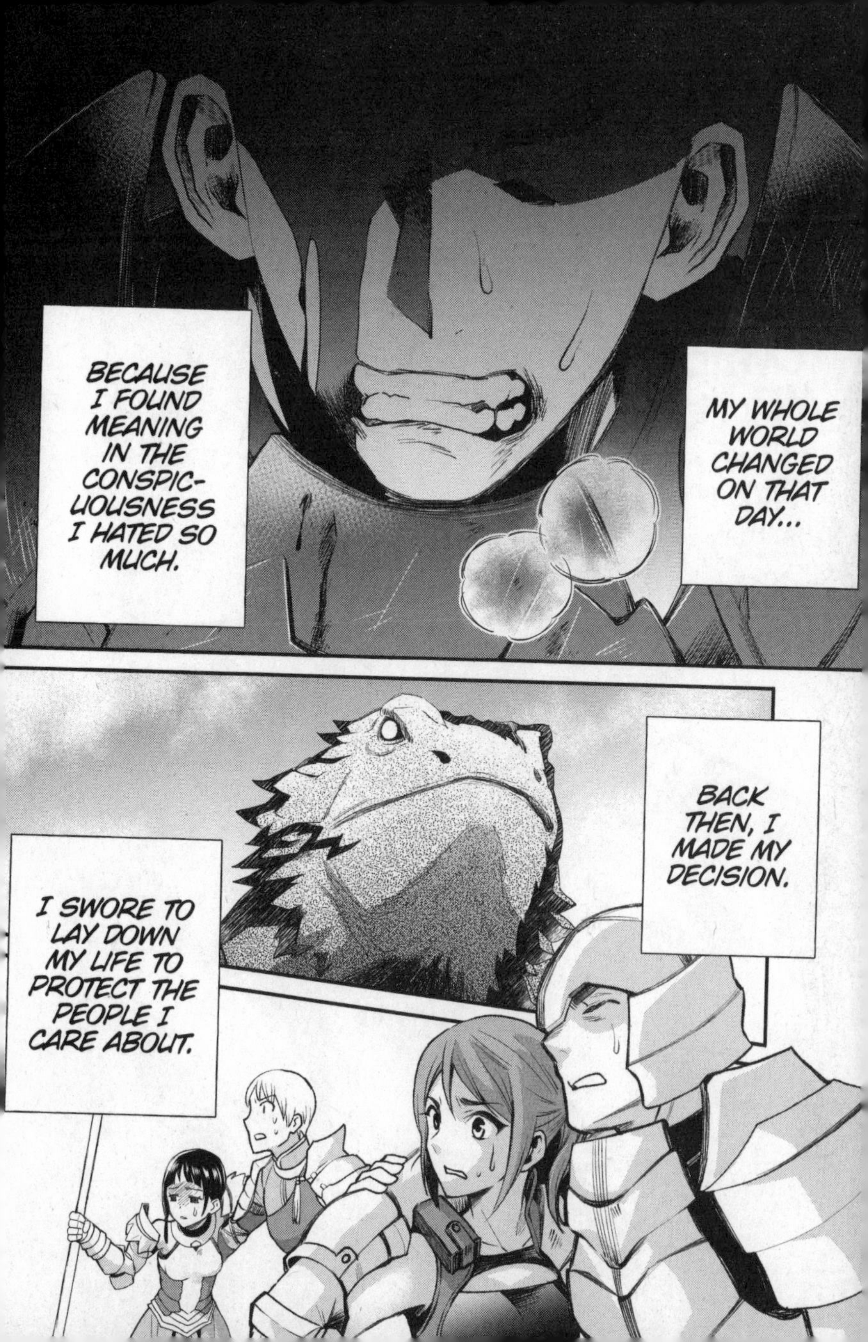
MY WHOLE WORLD CHANGED ON THAT DAY...
BECAUSE I FOUND MEANING IN THE CONSPIC-UOUSNESS I HATED SO MUCH.
BACK THEN, I MADE MY DECISION.
I SWORE TO LAY DOWN MY LIFE TO PROTECT THE PEOPLE I CARE ABOUT.

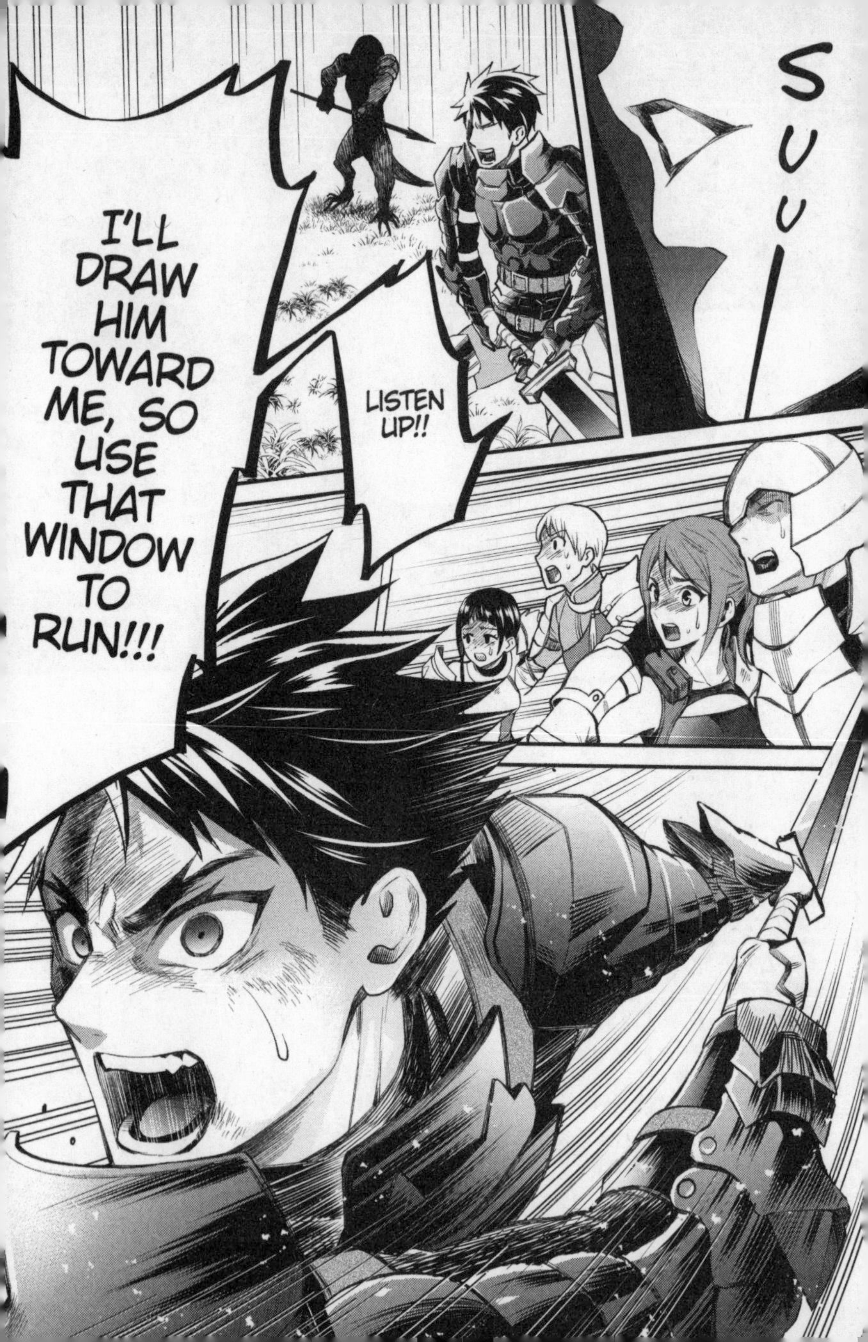
SUU
LISTEN UP!!
I'LL DRAW HIM TOWARD ME, SO USE THAT WINDOW TO RUN!!!

CALL TO ADVENTURE!

DEFEATING DUNGEONS

WITH A SKILL BOARD

5

CALL TO ADVENTURE!

DEFEATING DUNGEONS

WITH A SKILL BOARD

5

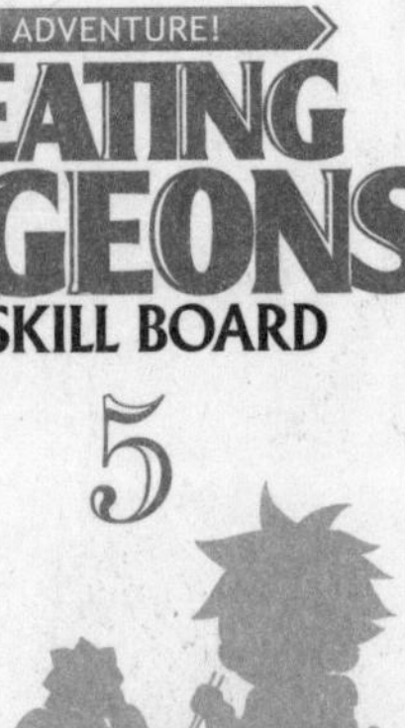

Chapter 23

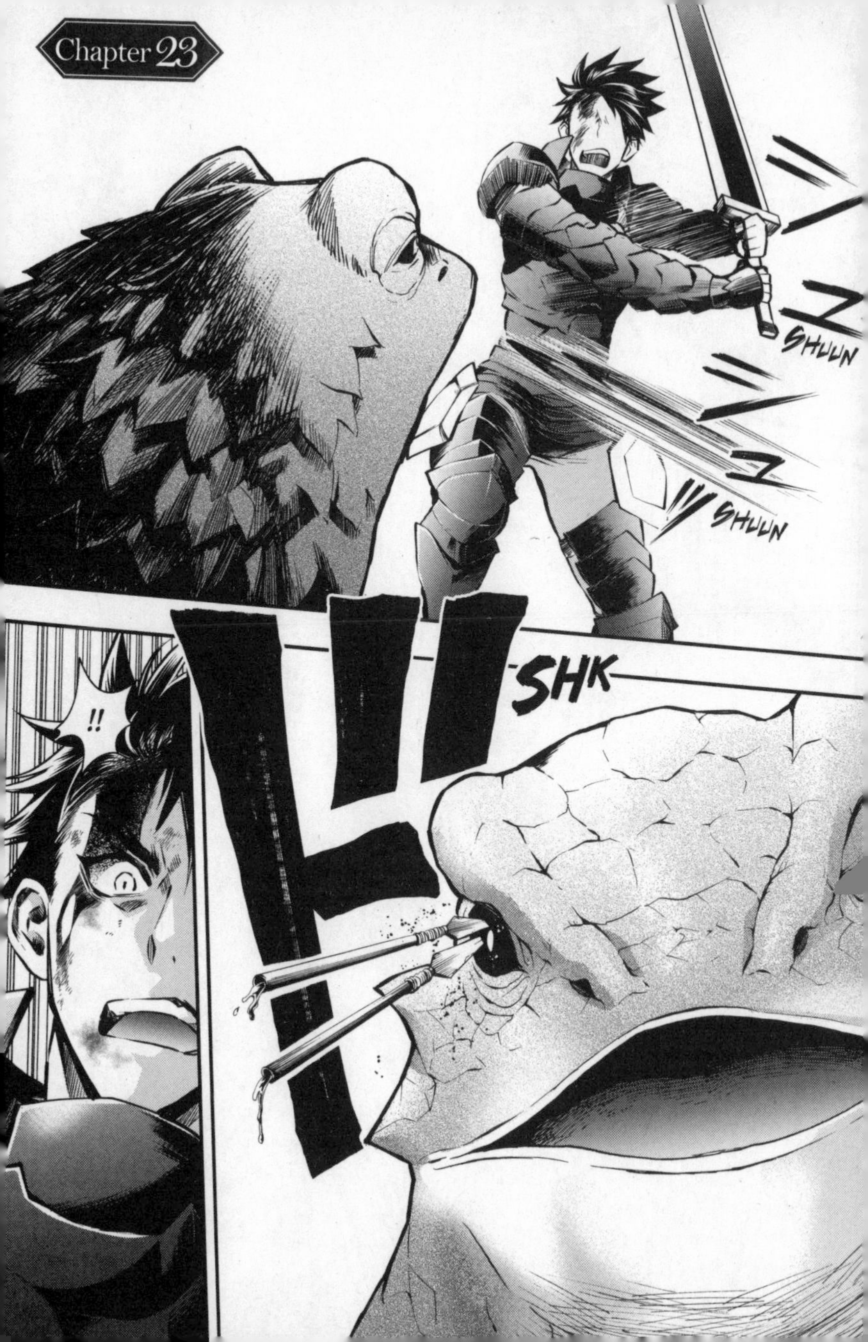
SHUUN
SHUUN
SHK
!!

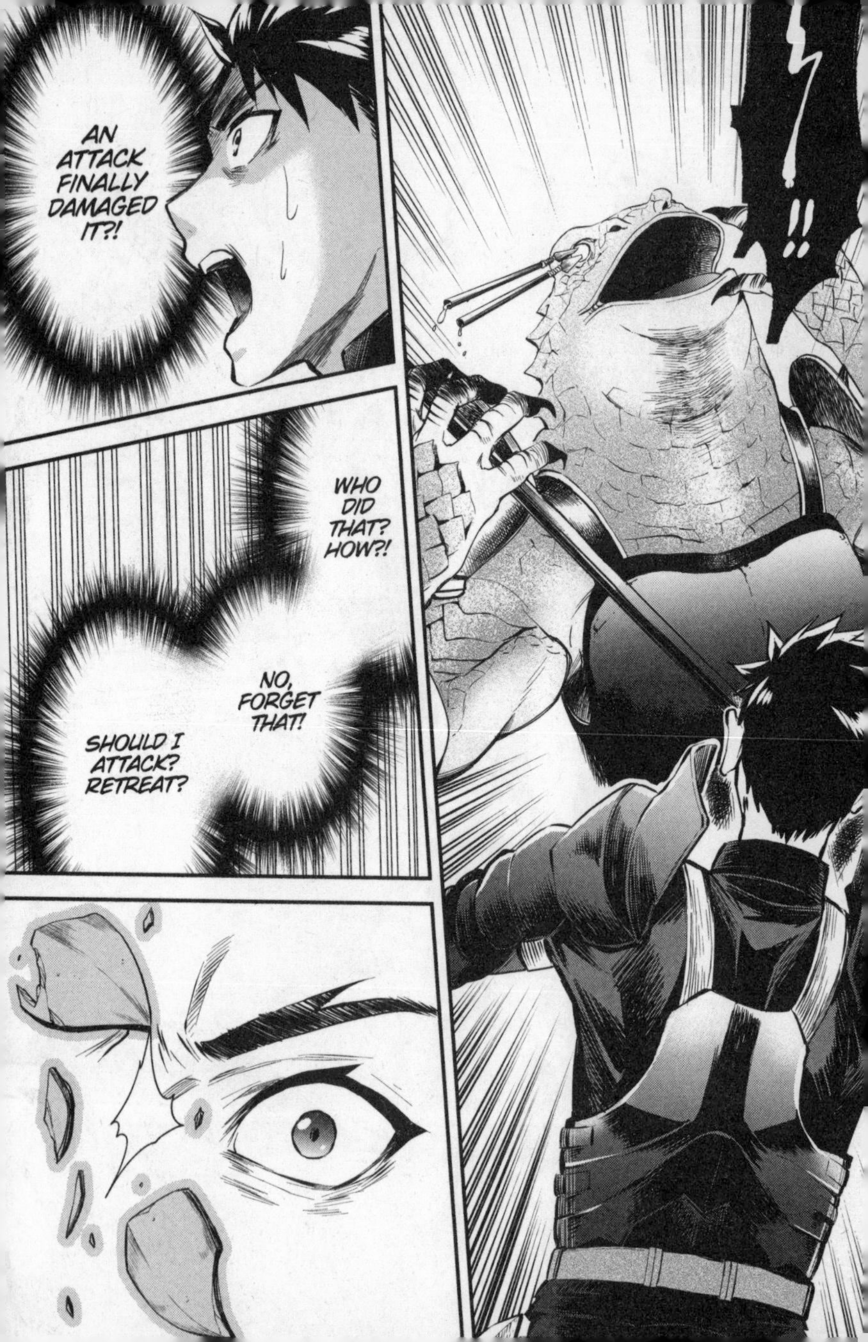
!!
AN ATTACK FINALLY DAMAGED IT?!
WHO DID THAT? HOW?!
NO, FORGET THAT!
SHOULD I ATTACK? RETREAT?

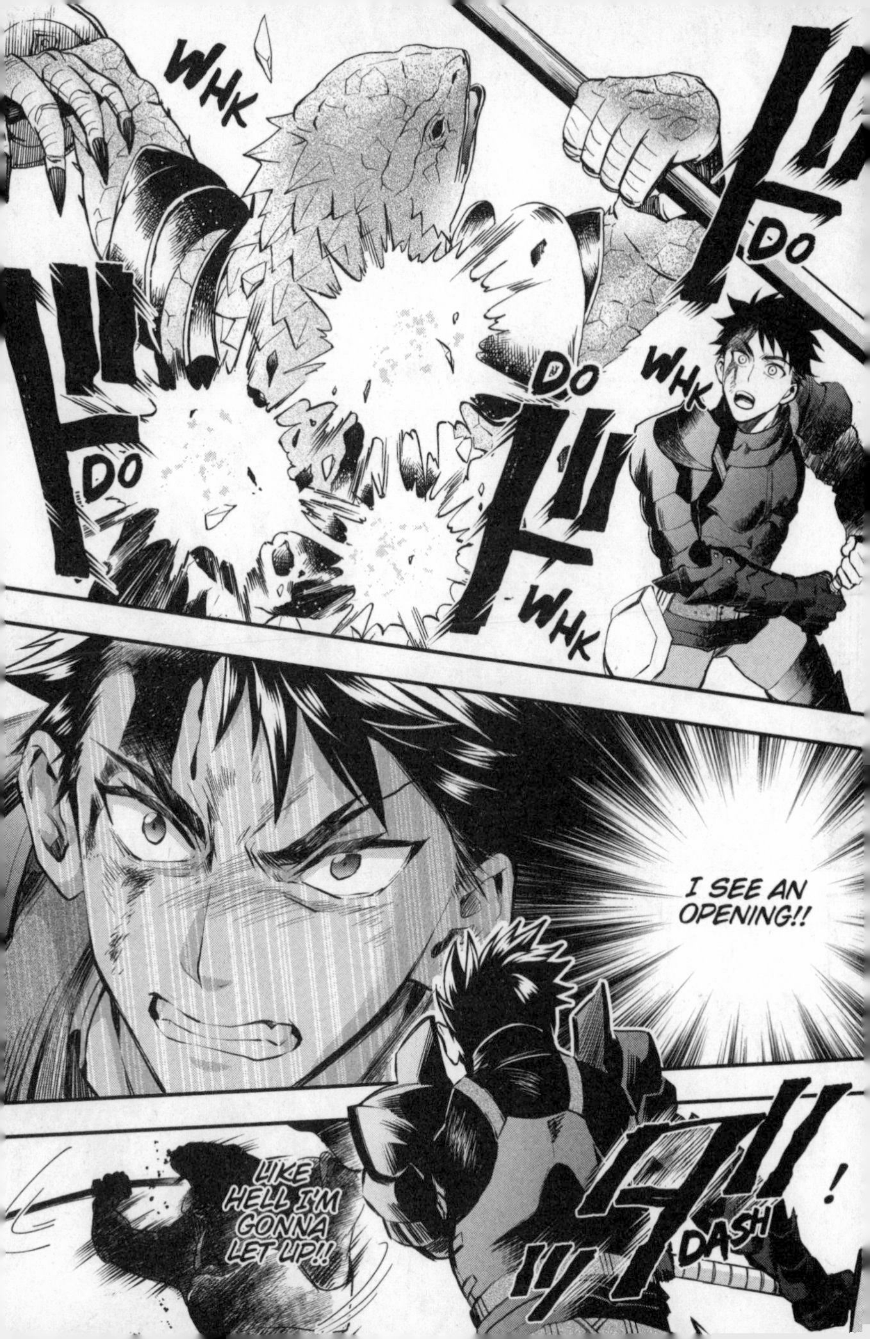
DO
WHK
DO
WHK
DO
WHK
I SEE AN OPENING!!
DASH
LIKE HELL I'M GONNA LET UP!!

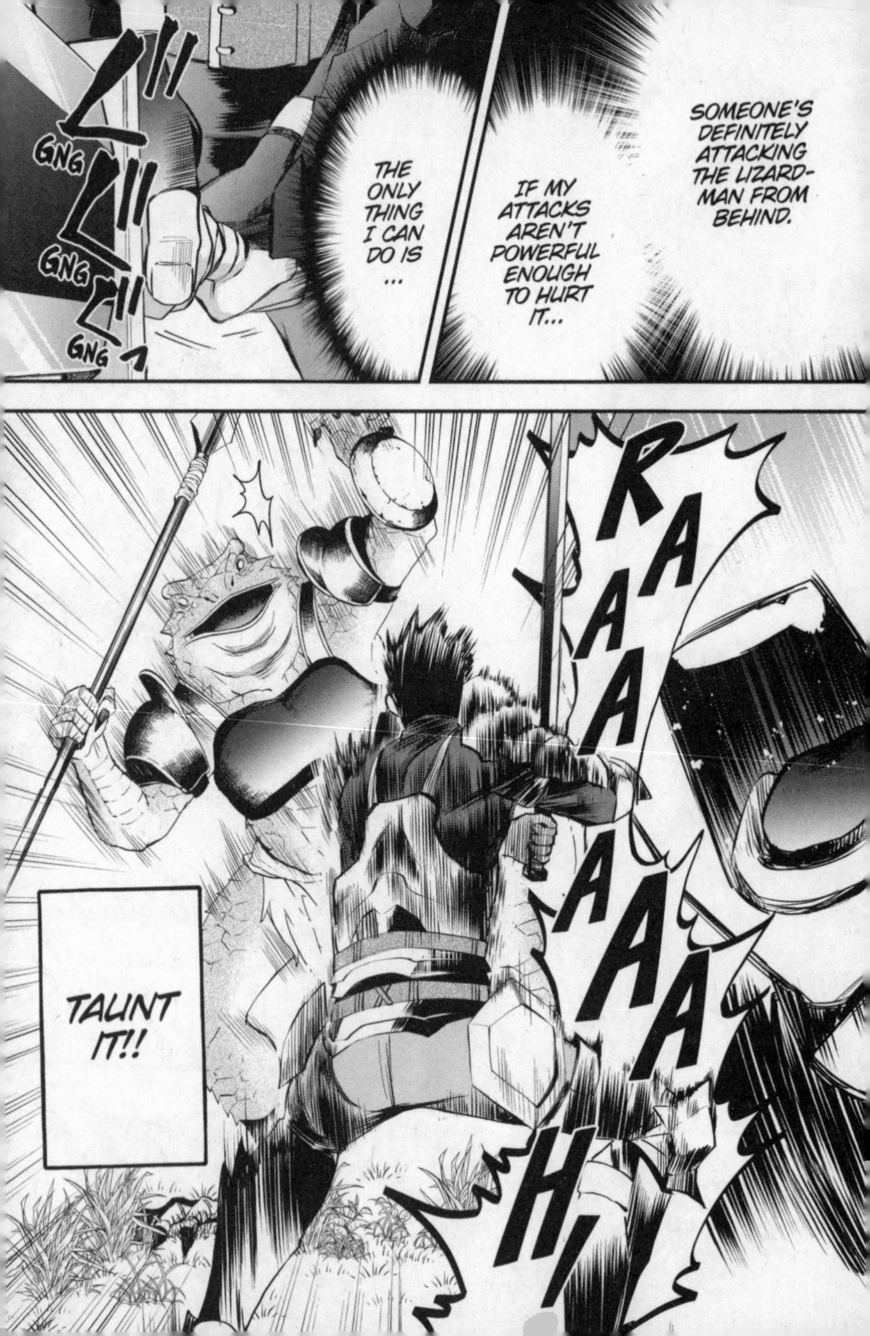
SOMEONE'S DEFINITELY ATTACKING THE LIZARD-MAN FROM BEHIND.
IF MY ATTACKS AREN'T POWERFUL ENOUGH TO HURT IT...
THE ONLY THING I CAN DO IS ...
GNG
GNG
GNG
RAAAAAAAH!
TAUNT IT!!

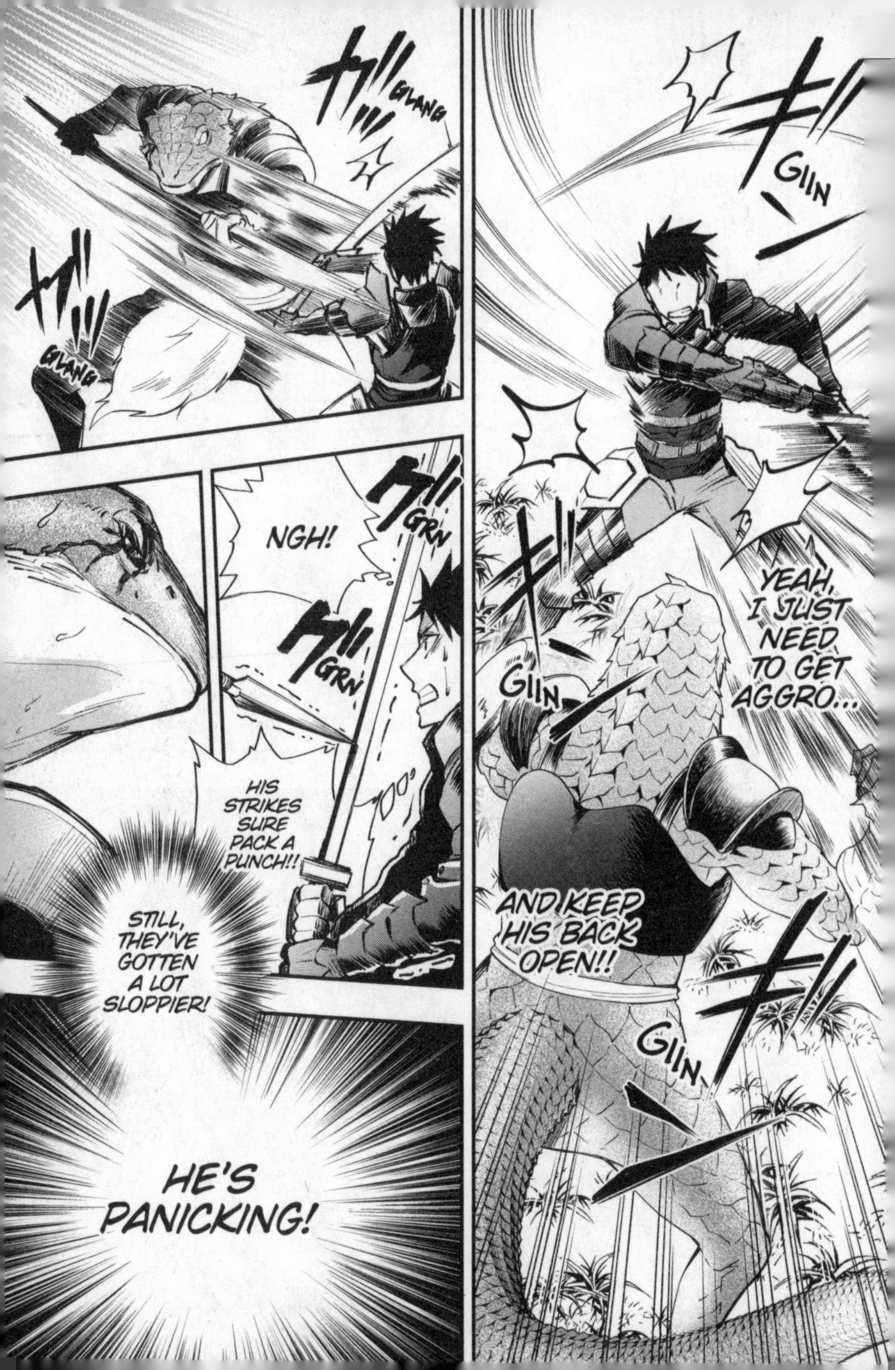
CLANG
CLANG
NGH!
GRRN
GRRN
HIS STRIKES SURE PACK A PUNCH!!
STILL, THEY'VE GOTTEN A LOT SLOPPIER!
HE'S PANICKING!
GIIN
GIIN
YEAH, I JUST NEED TO GET AGGRO...
AND KEEP HIS BACK OPEN!!
GIIN

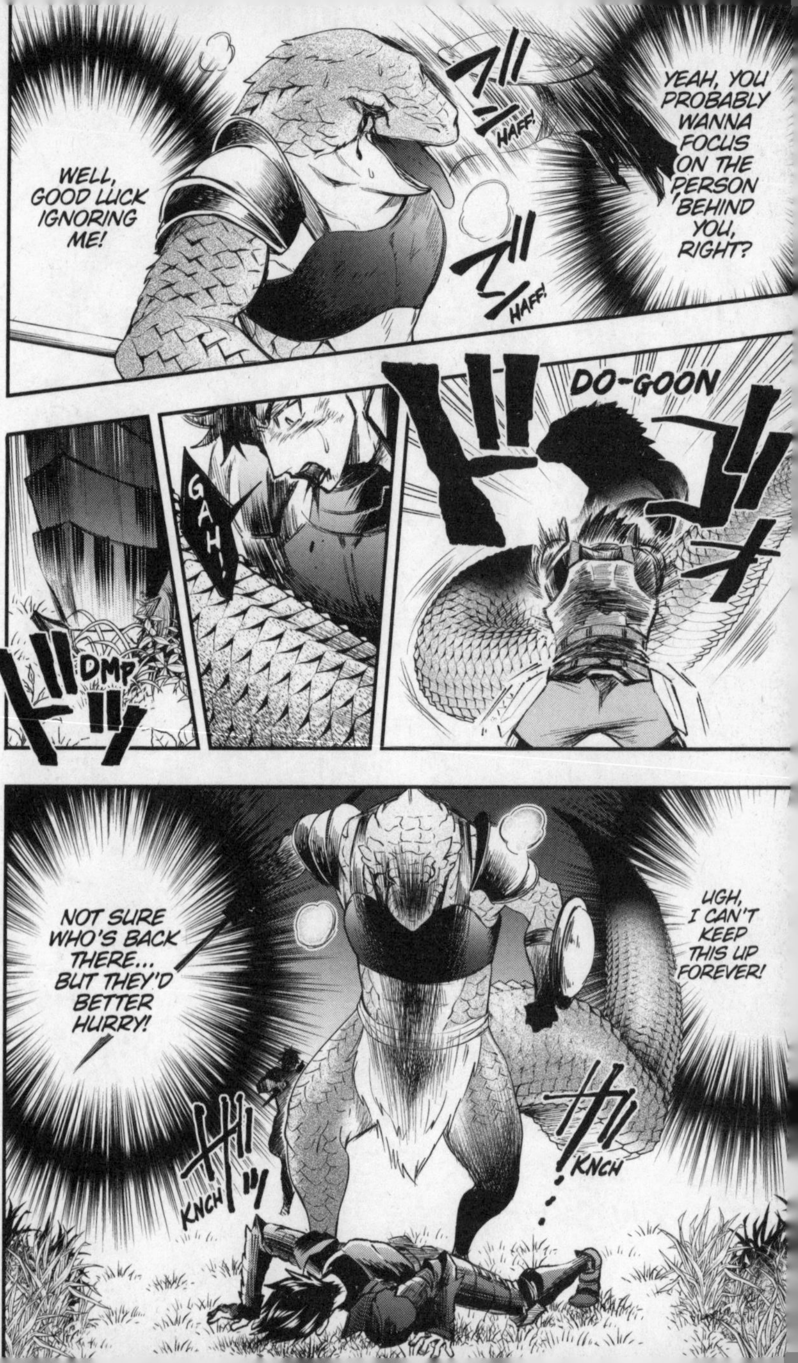
YEAH, YOU PROBABLY WANNA FOCUS ON THE PERSON BEHIND YOU, RIGHT?
HAFF!
HAFF!
WELL, GOOD LUCK IGNORING ME!
DO-GOON
GAH!
DMP
UGH, I CAN'T KEEP THIS UP FOREVER!
KNCH
NOT SURE WHO'S BACK THERE... BUT THEY'D BETTER HURRY!
KNCH

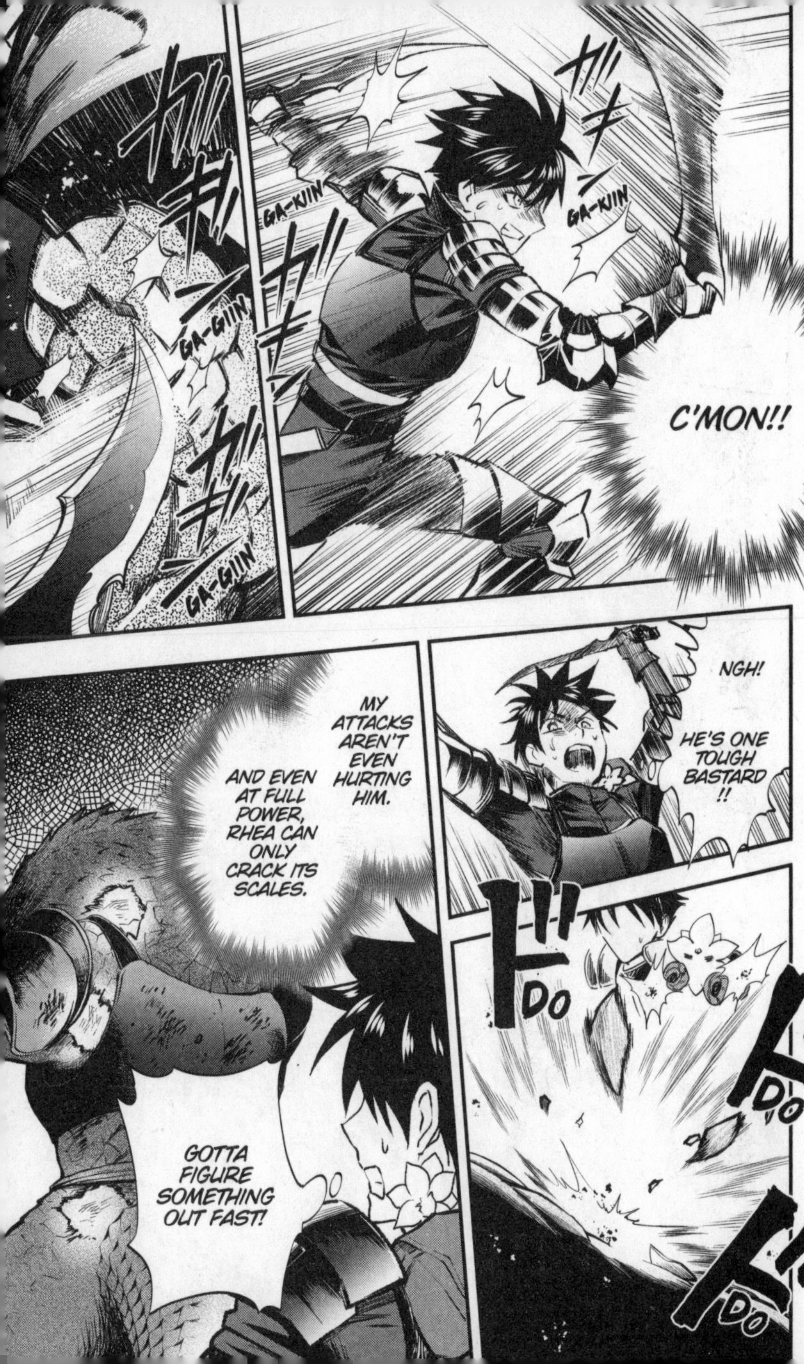

GA-KIIN
C'MON!!
GA-KIIN
GA-GIIN
GA-GIIN
NGH!
HE'S ONE TOUGH BASTARD!!
DO
DO
DO
MY ATTACKS AREN'T EVEN HURTING HIM.
AND EVEN AT FULL POWER, RHEA CAN ONLY CRACK ITS SCALES.
GOTTA FIGURE SOMETHING OUT FAST!

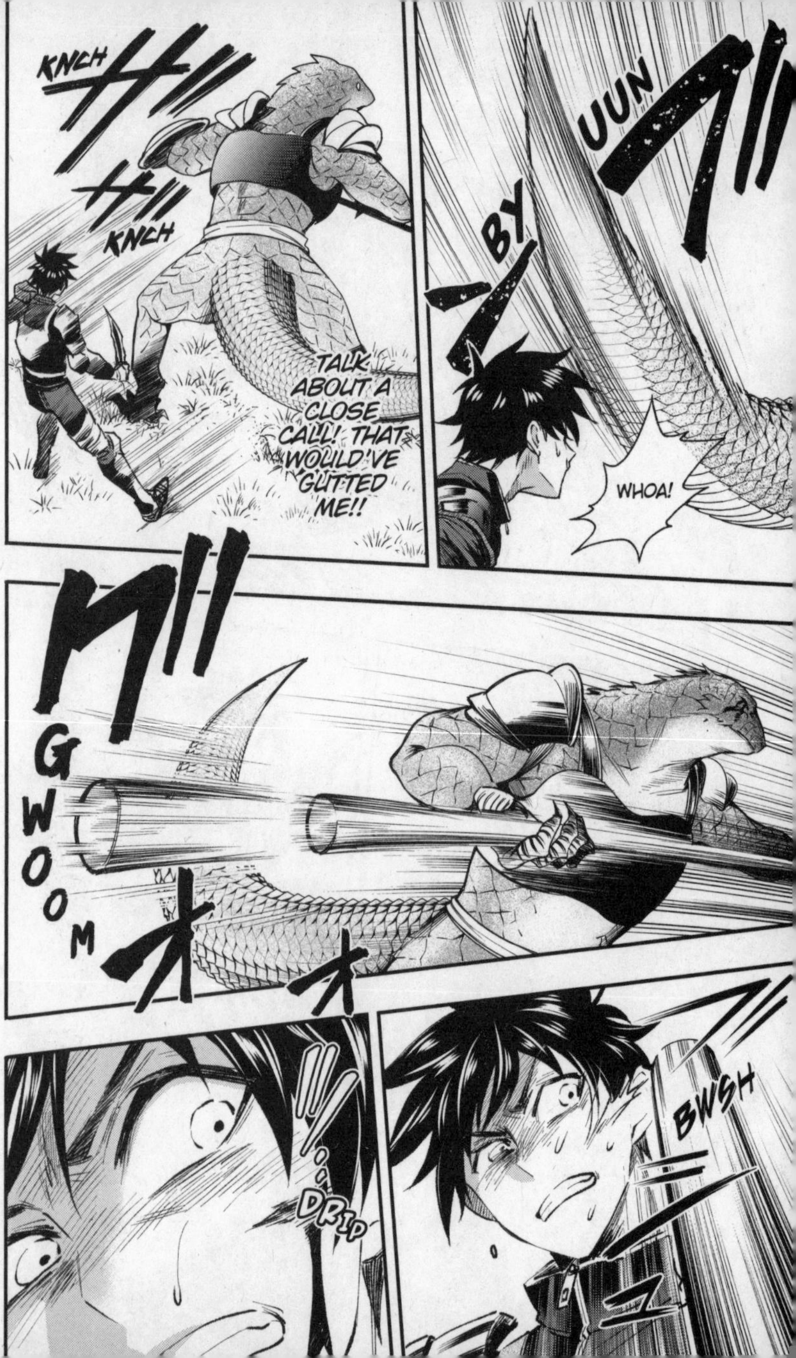
BYUUN
WHOA!
KNCH
KNCH
TALK ABOUT A CLOSE CALL! THAT WOULD'VE GUTTED ME!!
GWOOOM
BWSH
DRIP

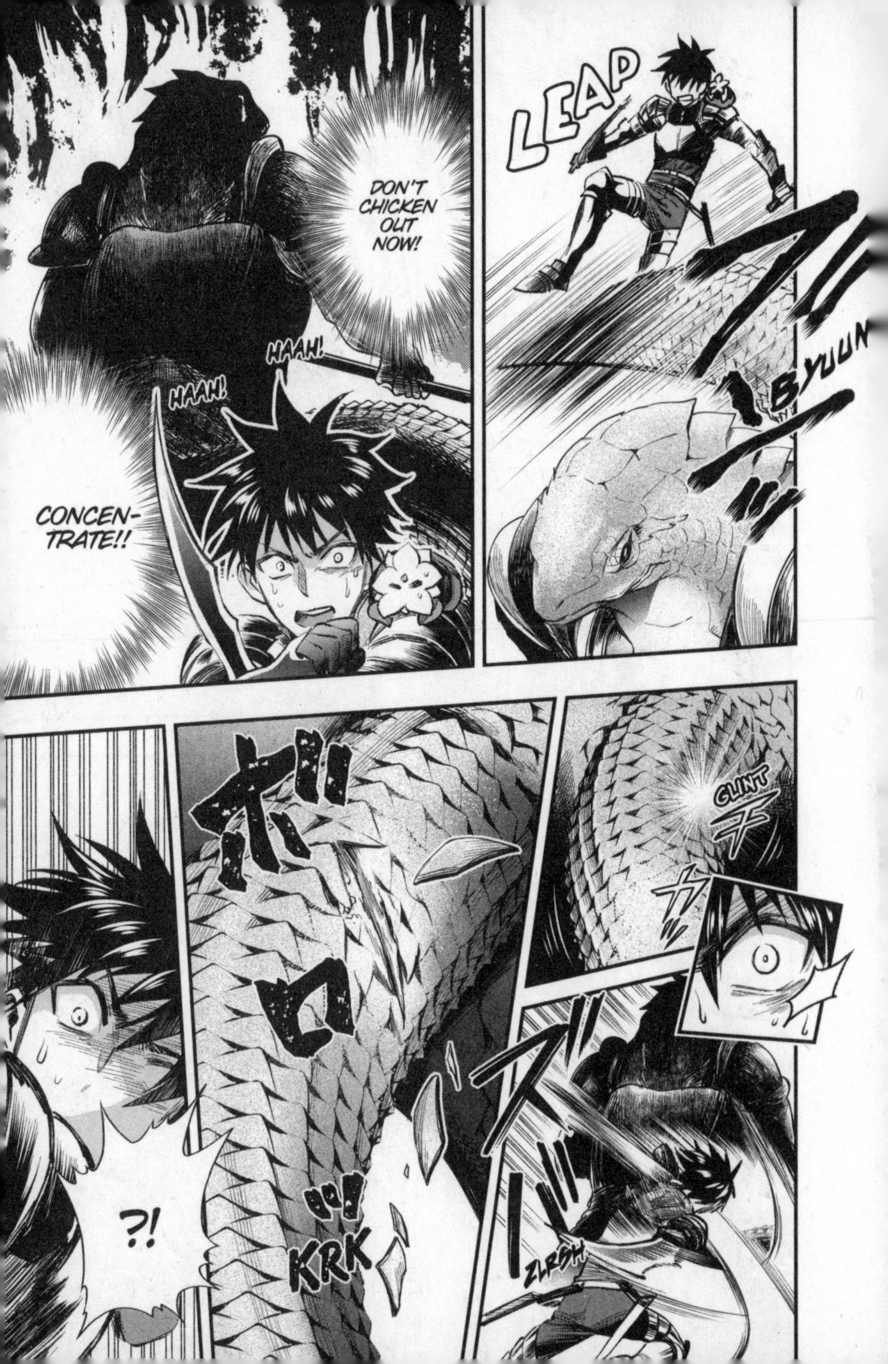
LEAP
BYUUN
DON'T CHICKEN OUT NOW!
HAAH!
HAAH!
CONCENTRATE!!
GLINT
ZLRSH
KRK
?!

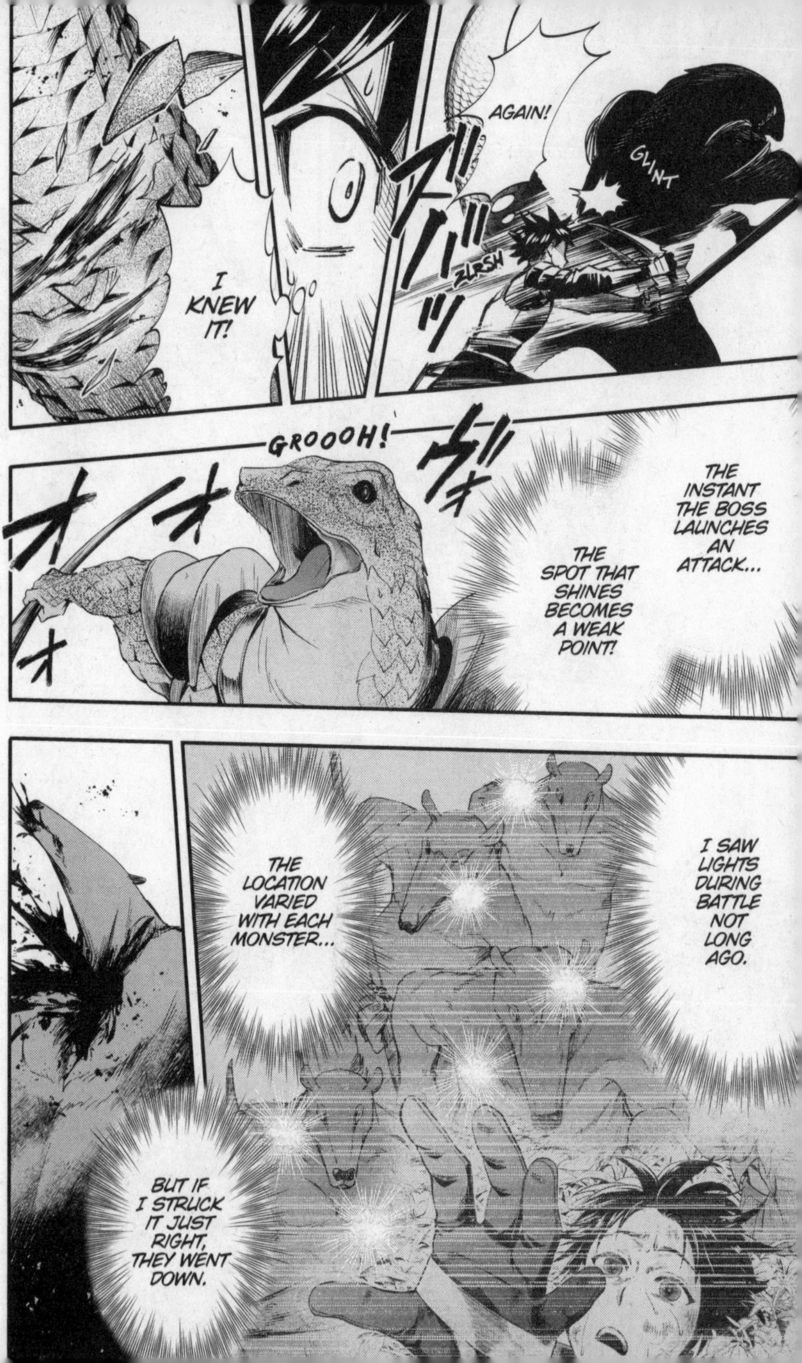
AGAIN!
GLINT
ZLRSH
I KNEW IT!
GROOOH!
THE INSTANT THE BOSS LAUNCHES AN ATTACK...
THE SPOT THAT SHINES BECOMES A WEAK POINT!
I SAW LIGHTS DURING BATTLE NOT LONG AGO.
THE LOCATION VARIED WITH EACH MONSTER...
BUT IF I STRUCK IT JUST RIGHT, THEY WENT DOWN.

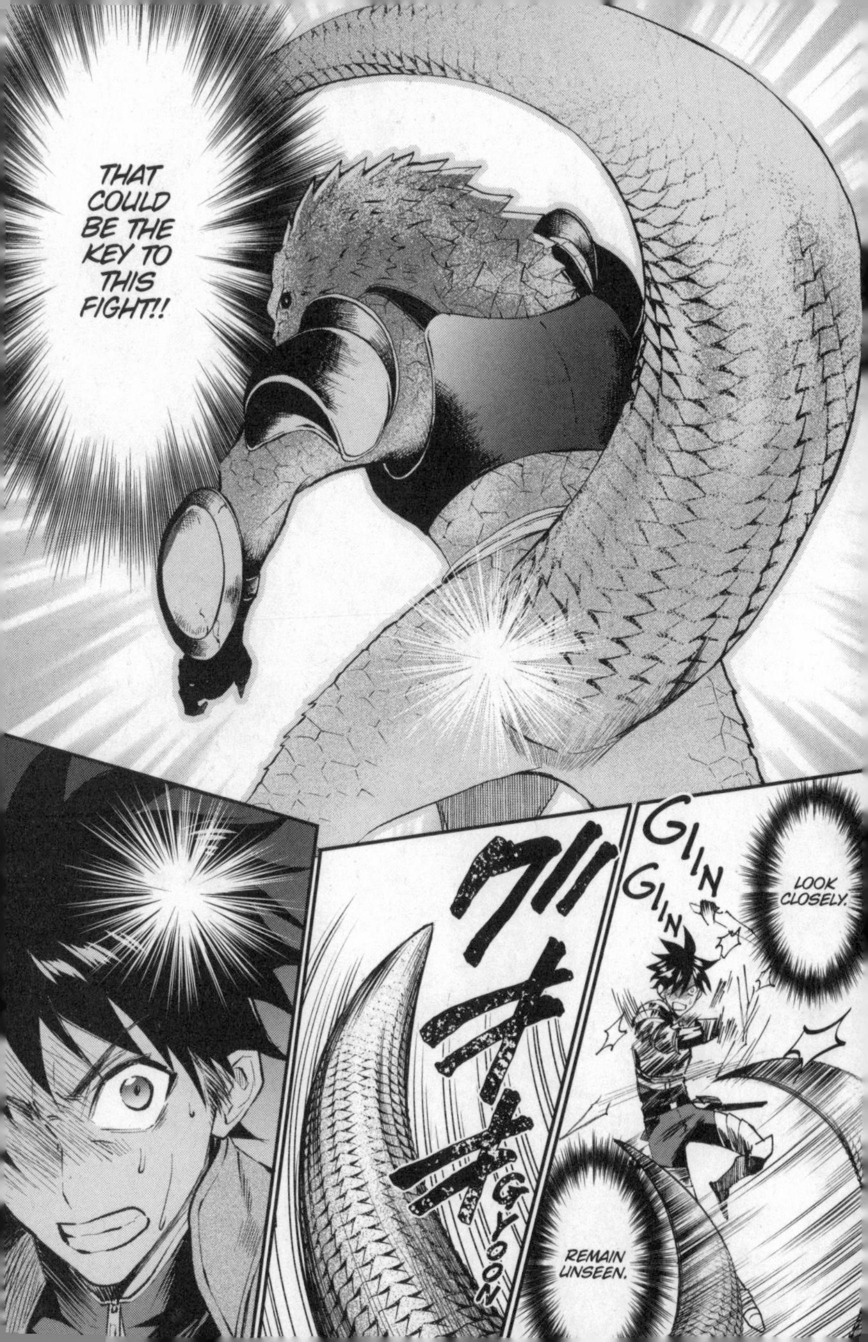
THAT COULD BE THE KEY TO THIS FIGHT!!
LOOK CLOSELY.
GIIN
GIIN
REMAIN UNSEEN.
GYOOON

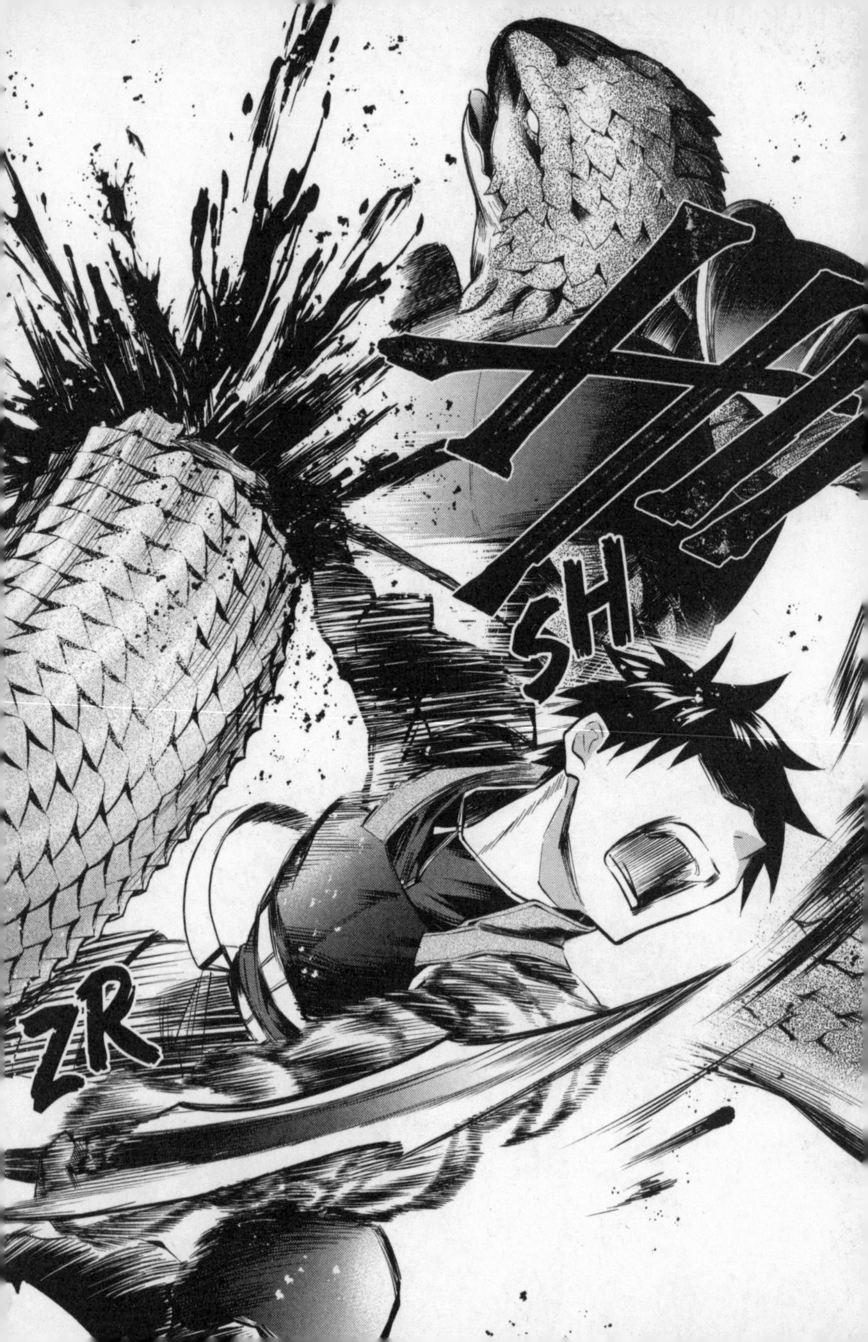
SH
ZR

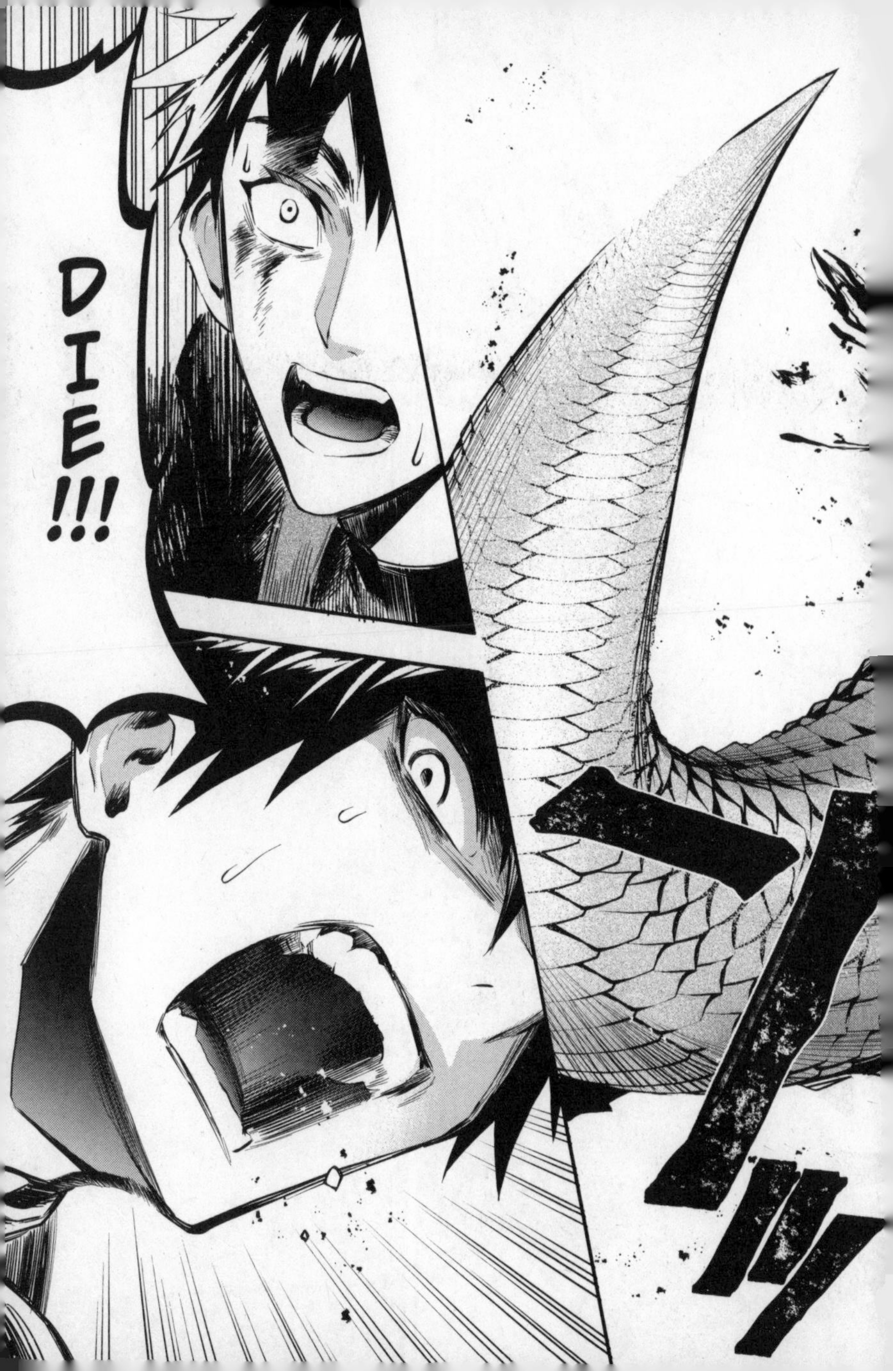
DIE!!!

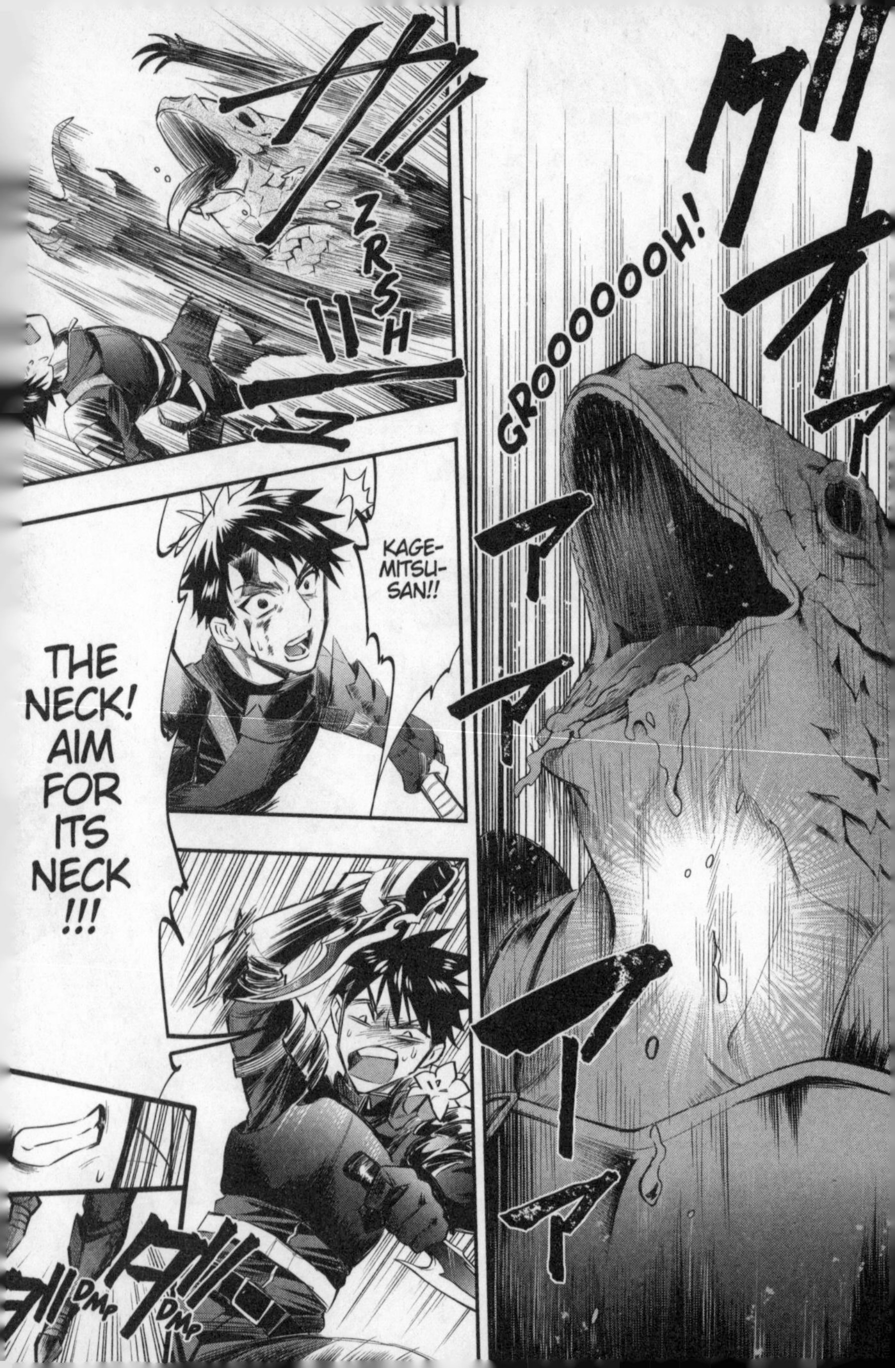

GROOOOOOH!
ZRSH
KAGE-MITSU-SAN!!
THE NECK! AIM FOR ITS NECK!!!
DMP
DMP

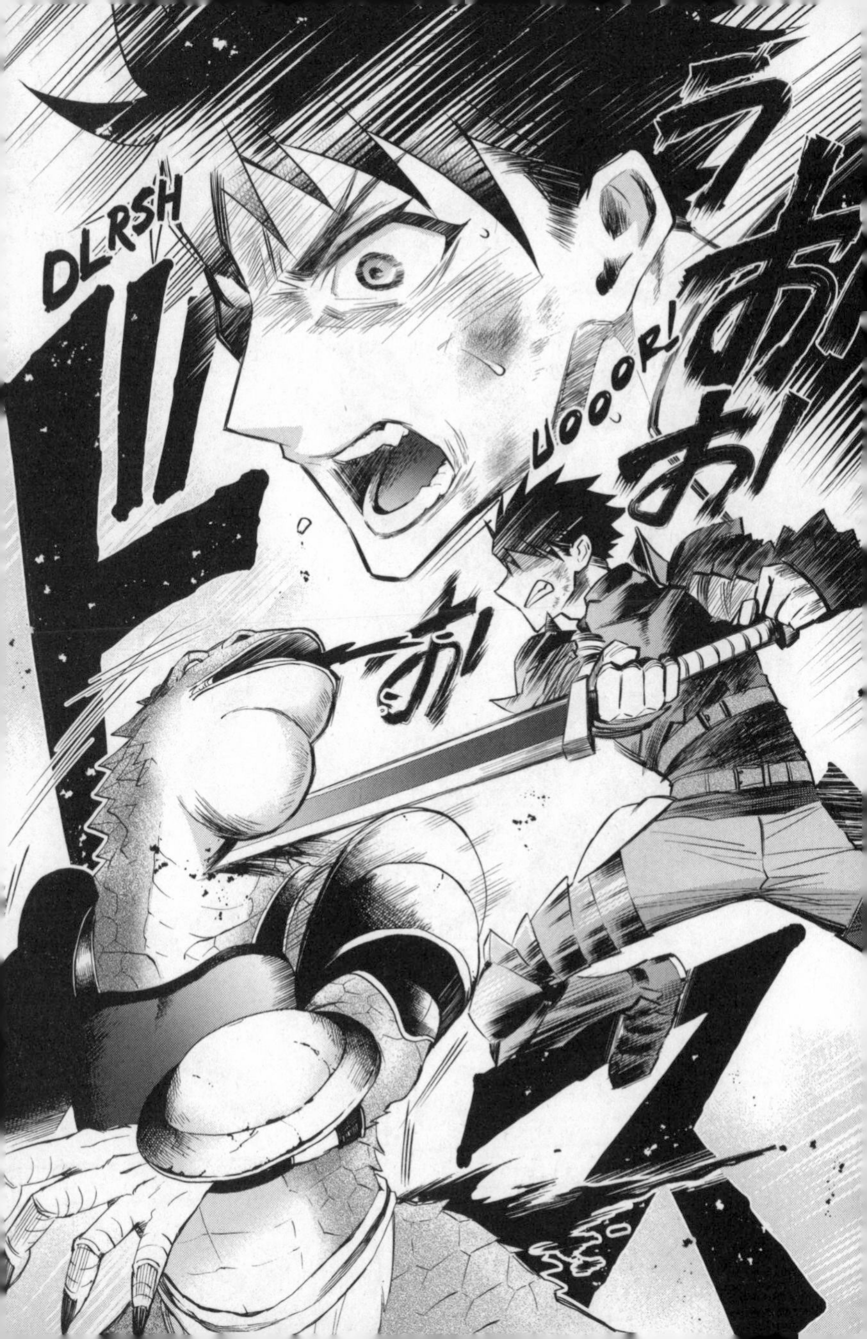
うおおお
UOOOOR!
DLRSH

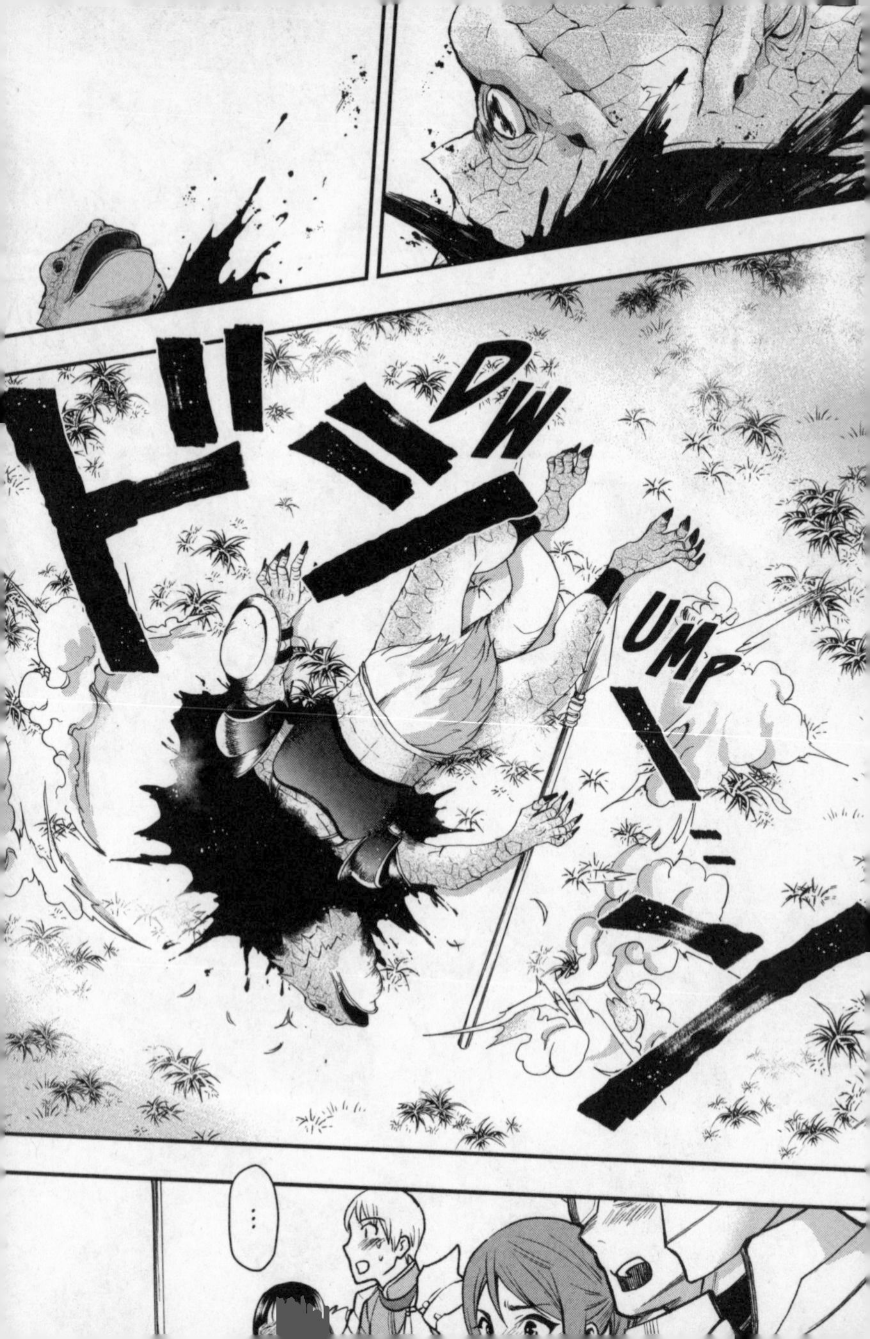
DWUMP
...

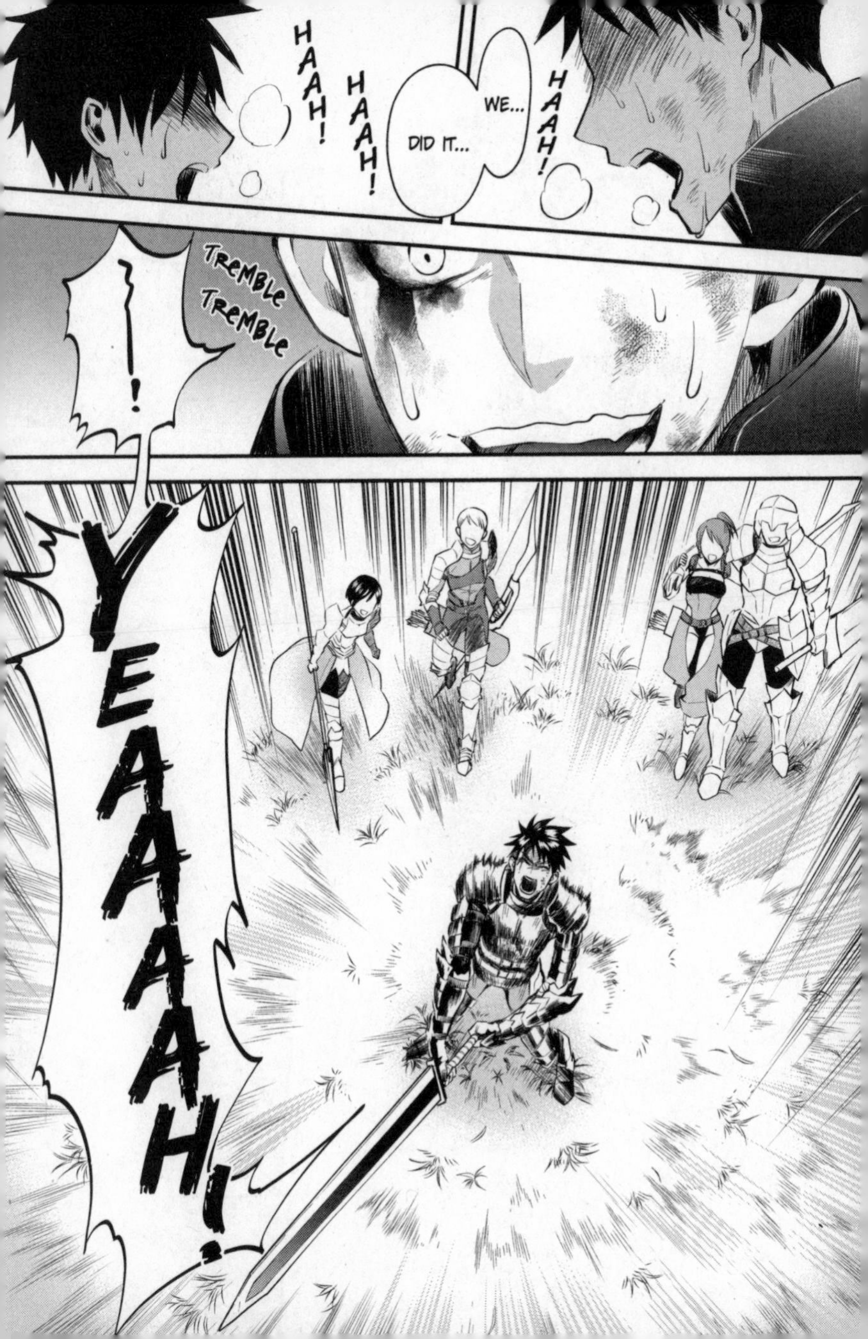
HAAAH!
WE... DID IT...
HAAAH!
HAAAH!
TREMBLE TREMBLE
—!
YEAAAAH!

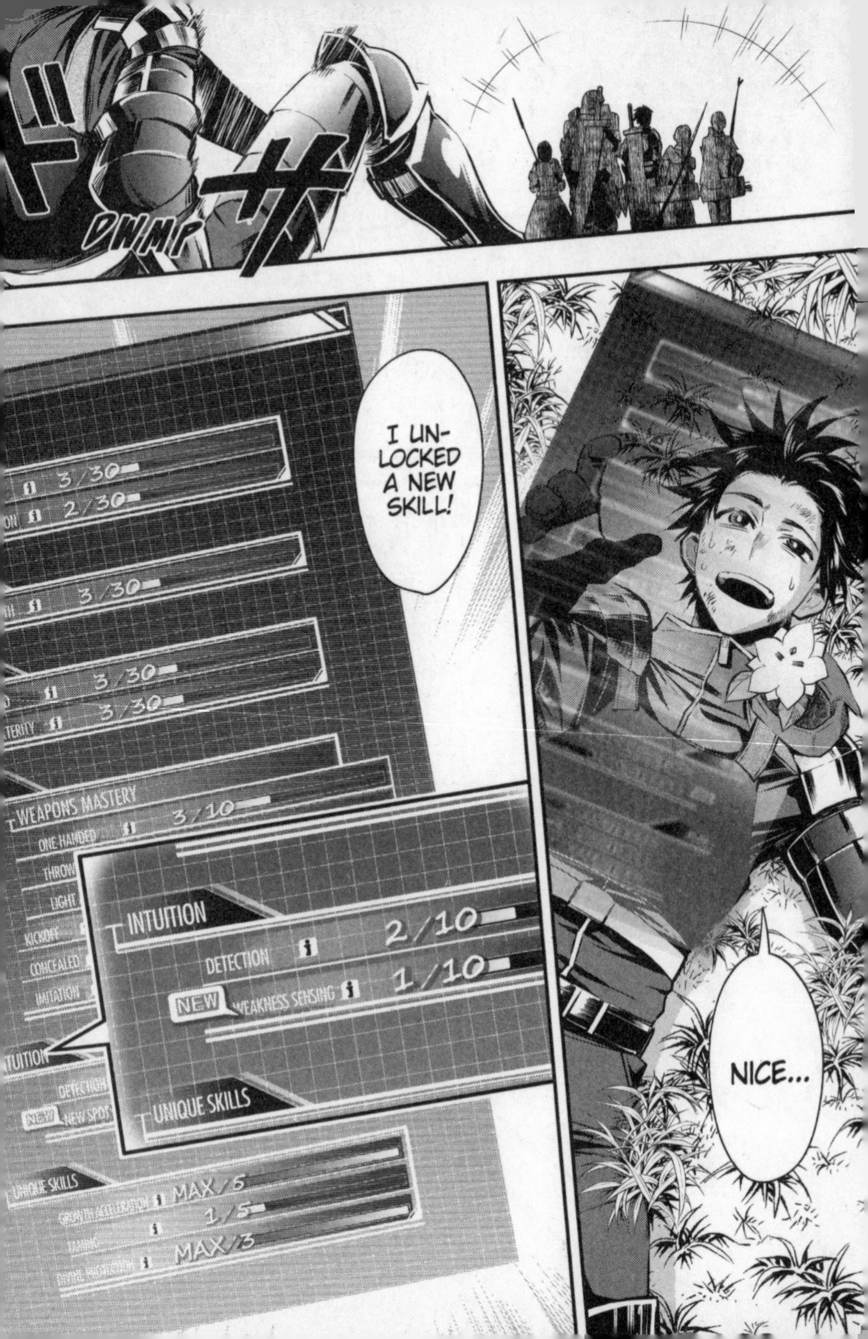
DWMP
NICE...
I UN-LOCKED A NEW SKILL!
3/30
2/30
3/30
3/30
3/30
WEAPONS MASTERY 3/10
ONE-HANDED
THROW
LIGHT
KICKOFF
CONCEALED
IMITATION
INTUITION 2/10
DETECTION
NEW WEAKNESS SENSING 1/10
UNIQUE SKILLS
UNIQUE SKILLS
GROWTH ACCELERATION MAX/5
TAMING 1/5
DIVINE PROTECTION MAX/3

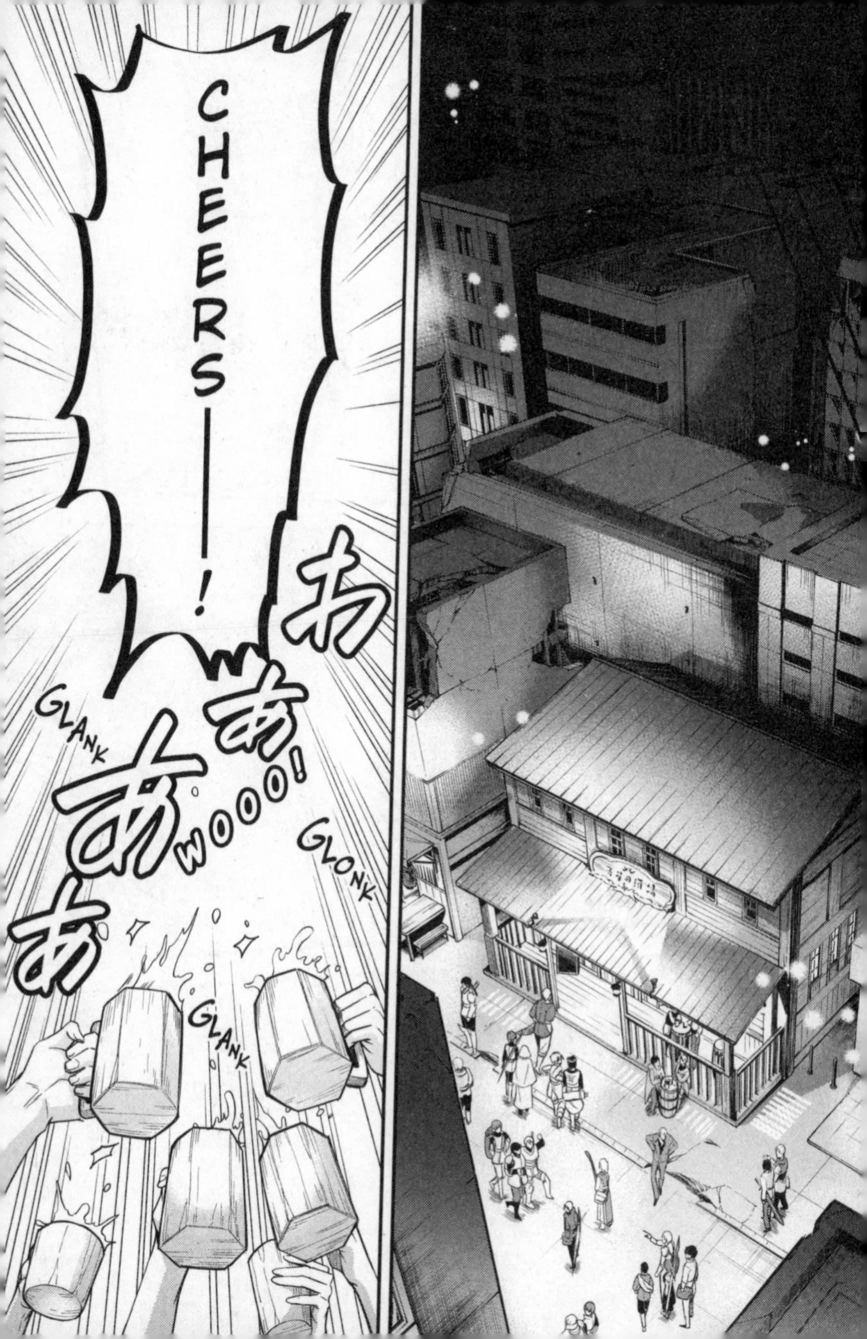
CHEERS——!
わあああ
WOOOO!
GLONK
GLANK
GLANK

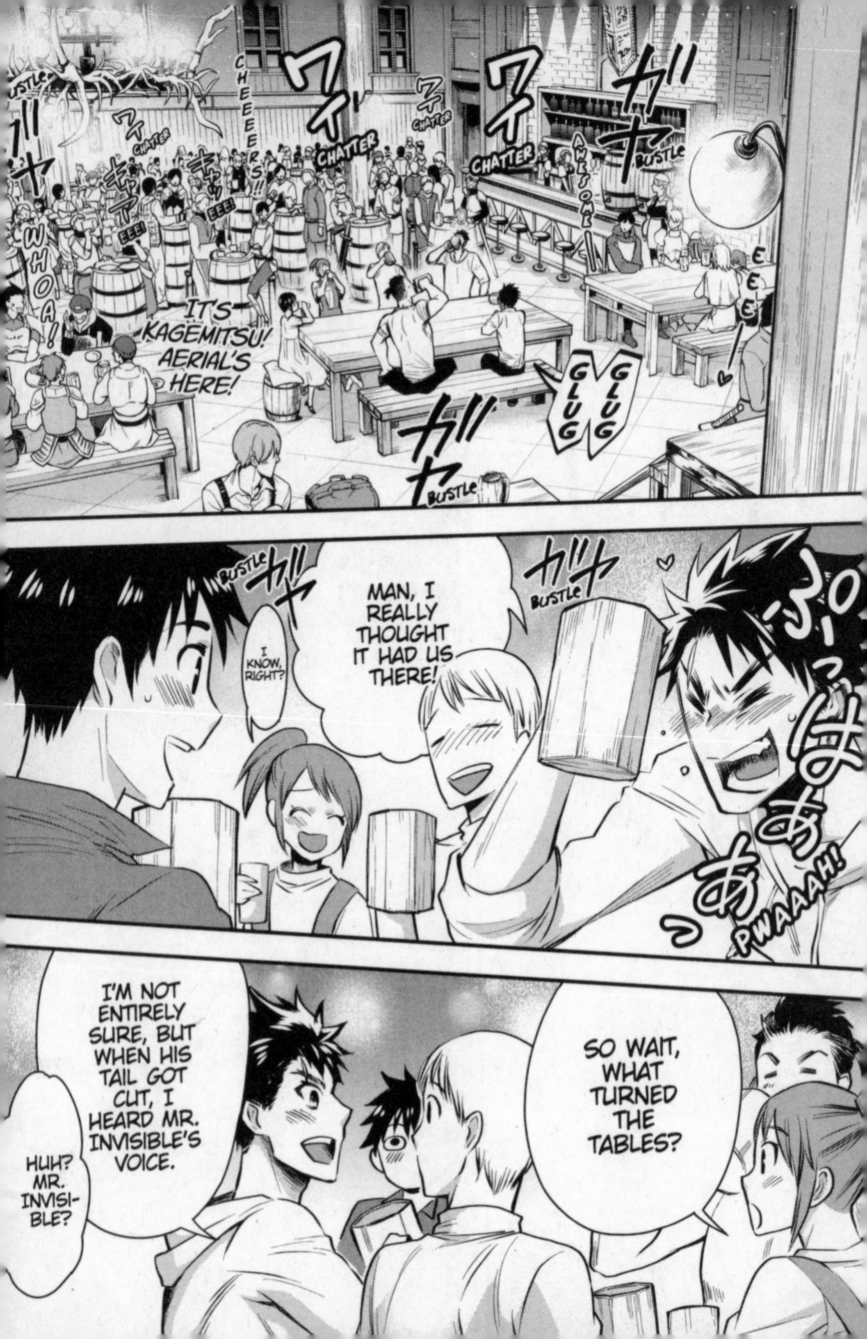
ガヤ
BUSTLE
ワイ
CHATTER
AWESOME!!
EEEE!
ワイ
CHATTER
CHEEEEERS!!
ワイ
CHATTER
キャア
EEE!
キャッ
EEE!
ガヤ
BUSTLE
WHOA!
GLUG GLUG
IT'S KAGEMITSU! AERIAL'S HERE!
ガヤ
BUSTLE
ぷはああっ
PWAAAH!
ガヤ
BUSTLE
MAN, I REALLY THOUGHT IT HAD US THERE!
ガヤ
BUSTLE
I KNOW, RIGHT?
SO WAIT, WHAT TURNED THE TABLES?
I'M NOT ENTIRELY SURE, BUT WHEN HIS TAIL GOT CUT, I HEARD MR. INVISIBLE'S VOICE.
HUH? MR. INVISIBLE?

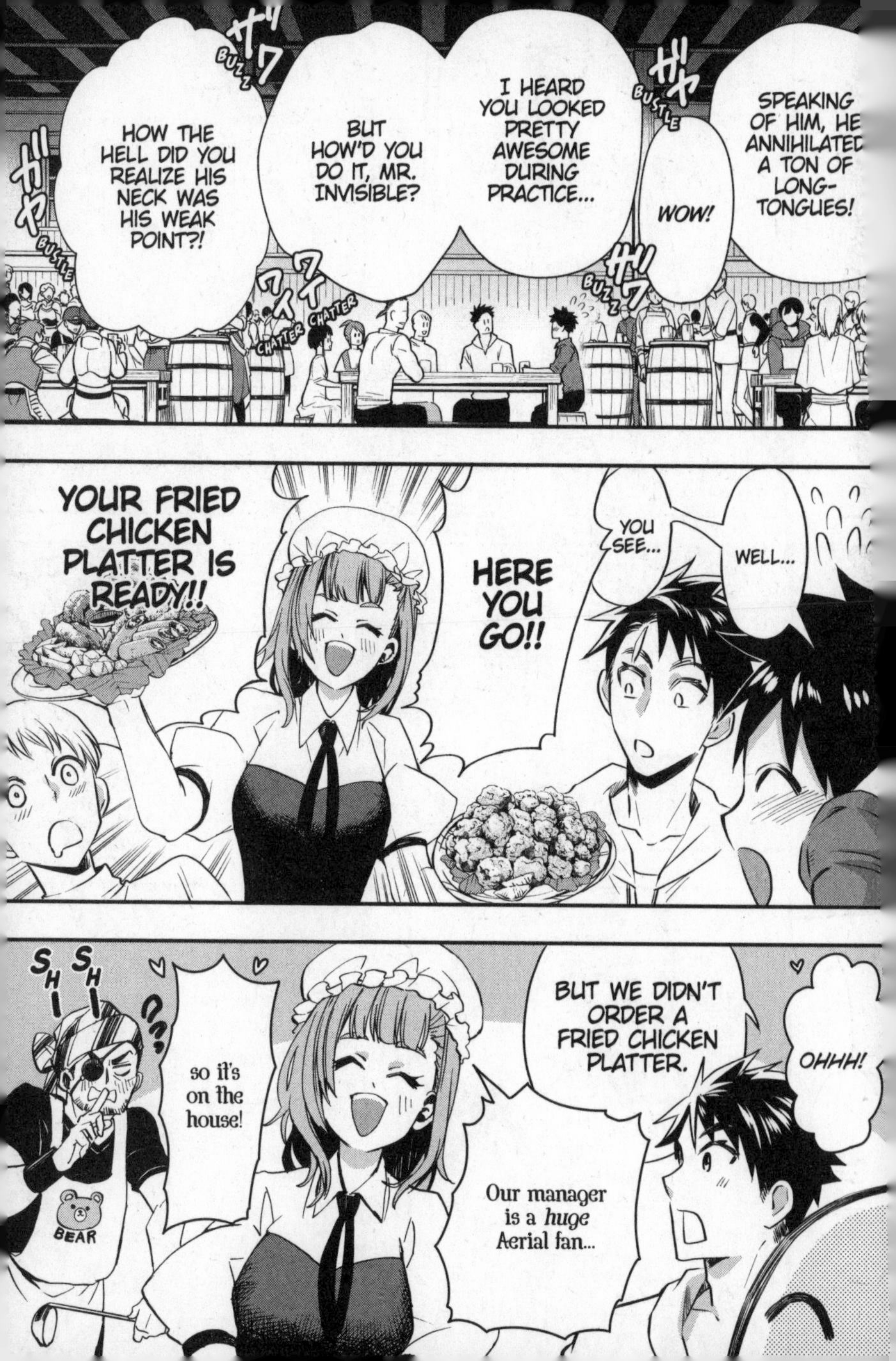
SPEAKING OF HIM, HE ANNIHILATED A TON OF LONG-TONGUES!
BUSTLE
WOW!
BUZZ
I HEARD YOU LOOKED PRETTY AWESOME DURING PRACTICE...
BUT HOW'D YOU DO IT, MR. INVISIBLE?
CHATTER CHATTER
BUZZ
HOW THE HELL DID YOU REALIZE HIS NECK WAS HIS WEAK POINT?!
BUSTLE
WELL...
YOU SEE...
HERE YOU GO!!
YOUR FRIED CHICKEN PLATTER IS READY!!
OHHH!
BUT WE DIDN'T ORDER A FRIED CHICKEN PLATTER.
Our manager is a *huge* Aerial fan...
so it's on the house!
??
SHI SHI

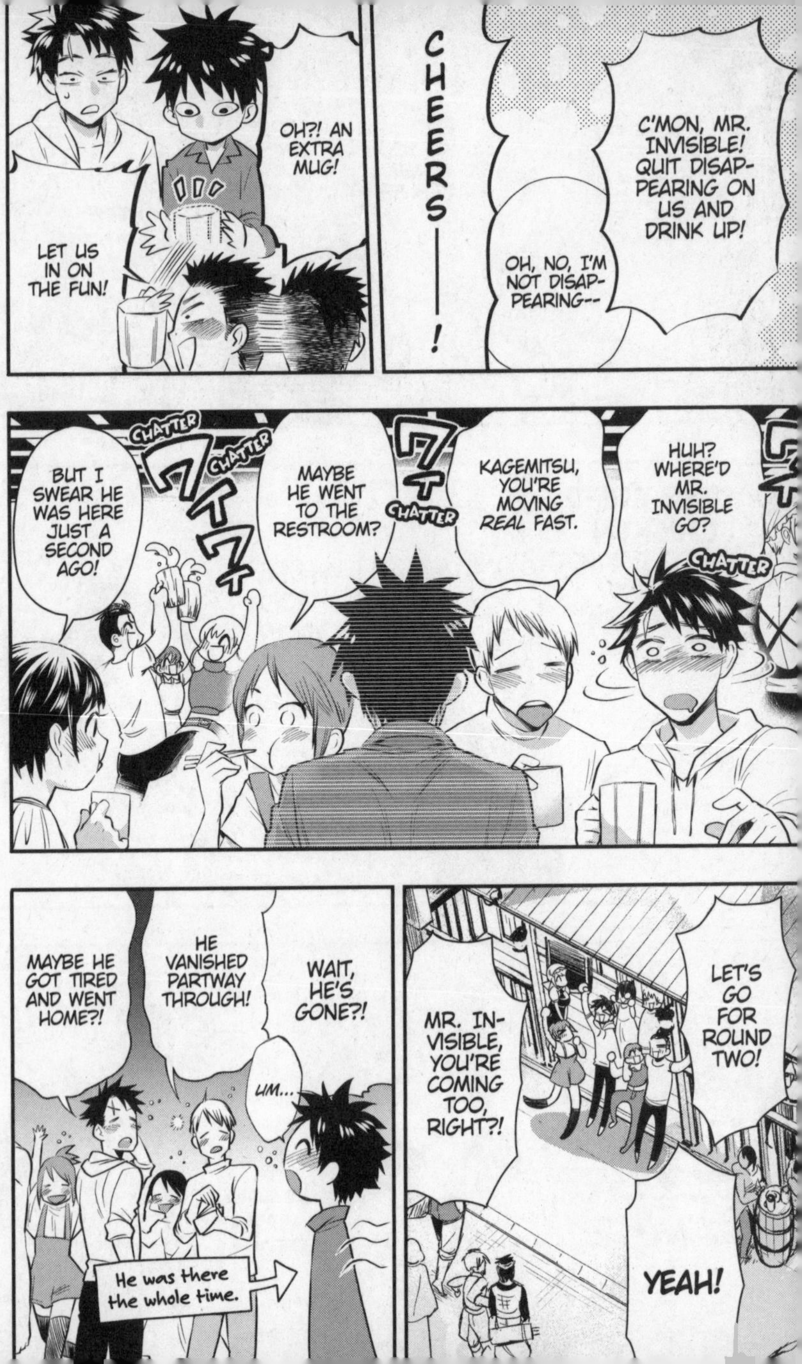
C'MON, MR. INVISIBLE! QUIT DISAPPEARING ON US AND DRINK UP!
OH, NO, I'M NOT DISAPPEARING--
CHEERS—!
OH?! AN EXTRA MUG!
LET US IN ON THE FUN!
HUH? WHERE'D MR. INVISIBLE GO?
KAGEMITSU, YOU'RE MOVING REAL FAST.
MAYBE HE WENT TO THE RESTROOM?
BUT I SWEAR HE WAS HERE JUST A SECOND AGO!
LET'S GO FOR ROUND TWO!
MR. INVISIBLE, YOU'RE COMING TOO, RIGHT?!
YEAH!
WAIT, HE'S GONE?!
HE VANISHED PARTWAY THROUGH!
MAYBE HE GOT TIRED AND WENT HOME?!
UM...
He was there the whole time.

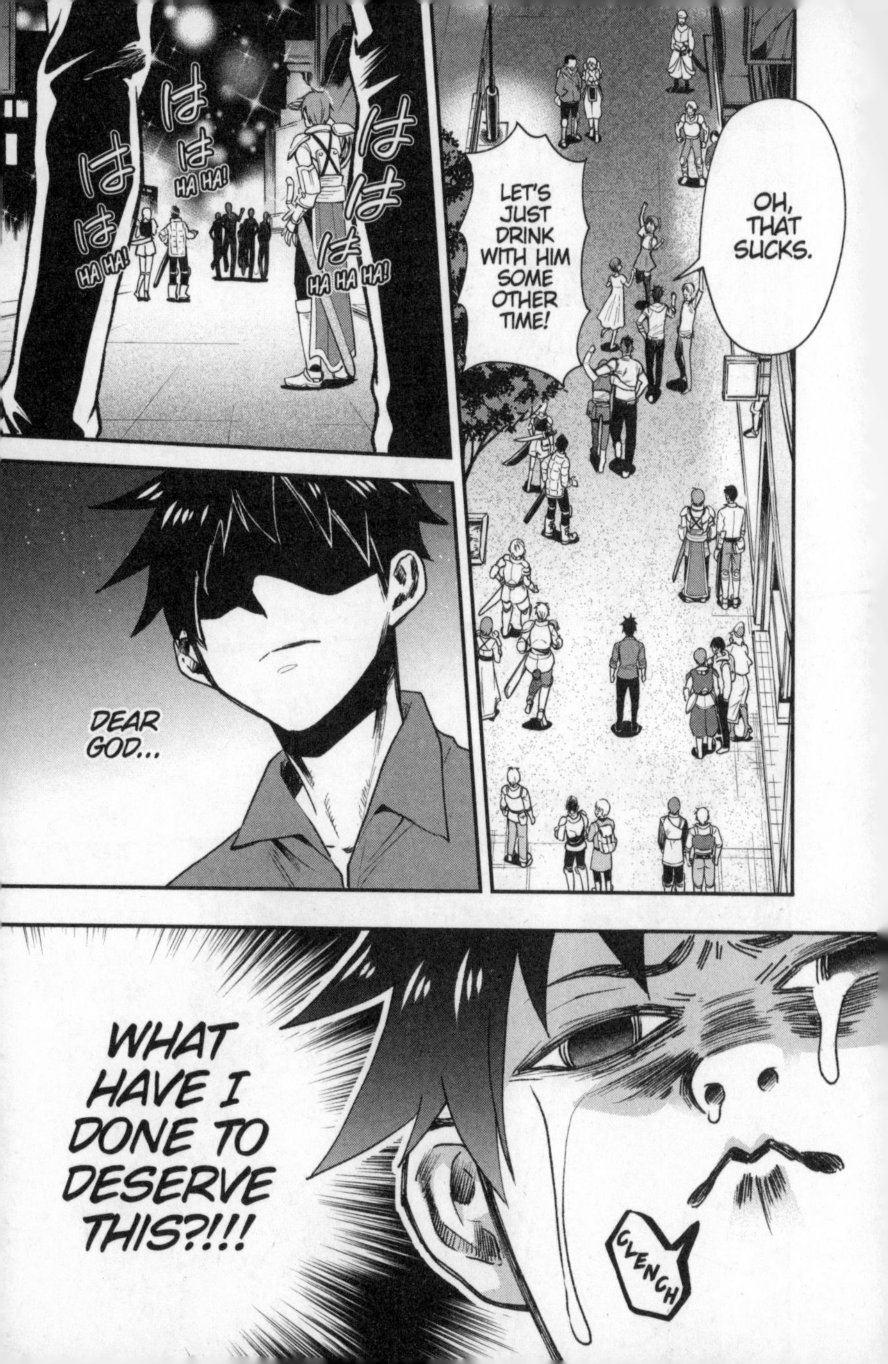
OH, THAT SUCKS.
LET'S JUST DRINK WITH HIM SOME OTHER TIME!
ははは
HA HA HA!
はは
HA HA!
はは
HA HA!
DEAR GOD...
WHAT HAVE I DONE TO DESERVE THIS?!!!
CLENCH

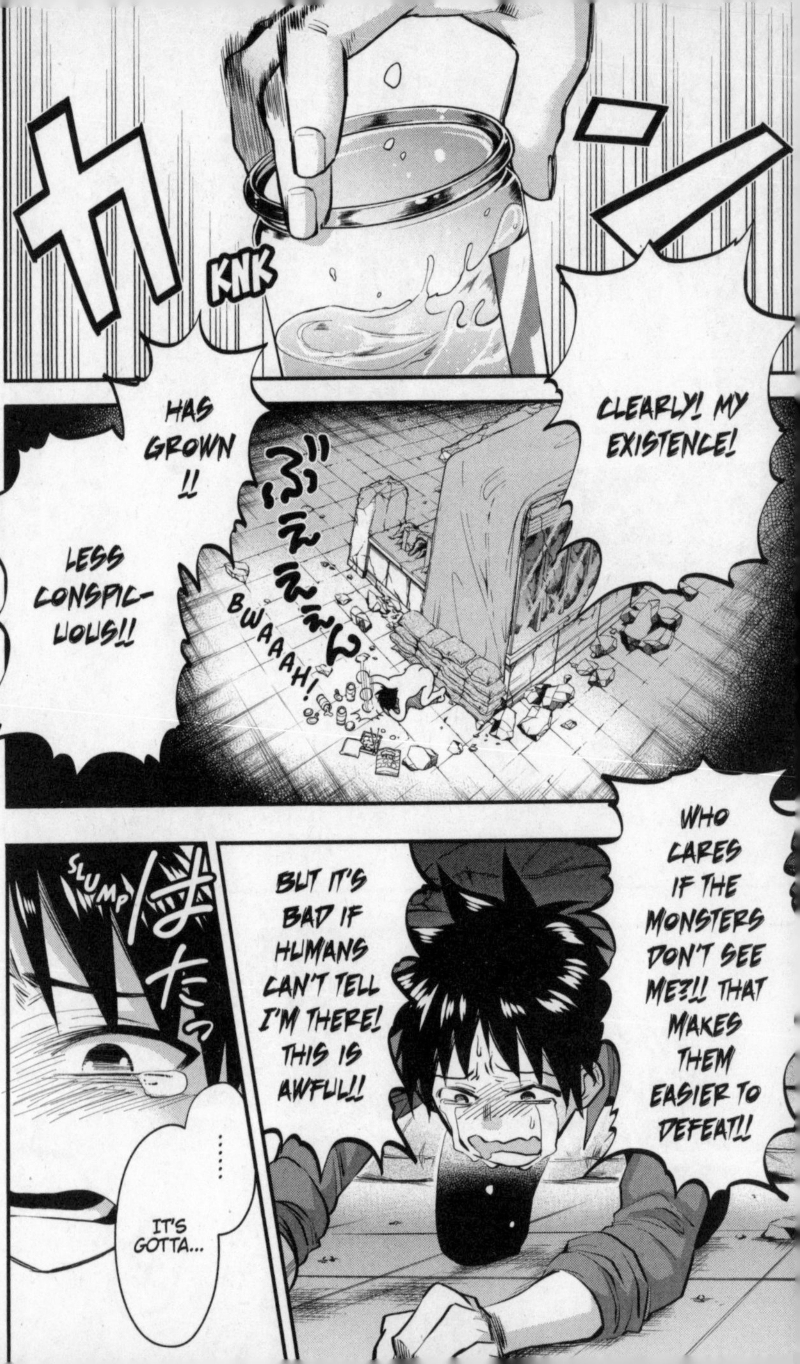
KNK
CLEARLY! MY EXISTENCE!
HAS GROWN !!
LESS CONSPIC-UOUS!!
BWAAAAH!
WHO CARES IF THE MONSTERS DON'T SEE ME?!! THAT MAKES THEM EASIER TO DEFEAT!!
BUT IT'S BAD IF HUMANS CAN'T TELL I'M THERE! THIS IS AWFUL!!
SLUMP
......
IT'S GOTTA...

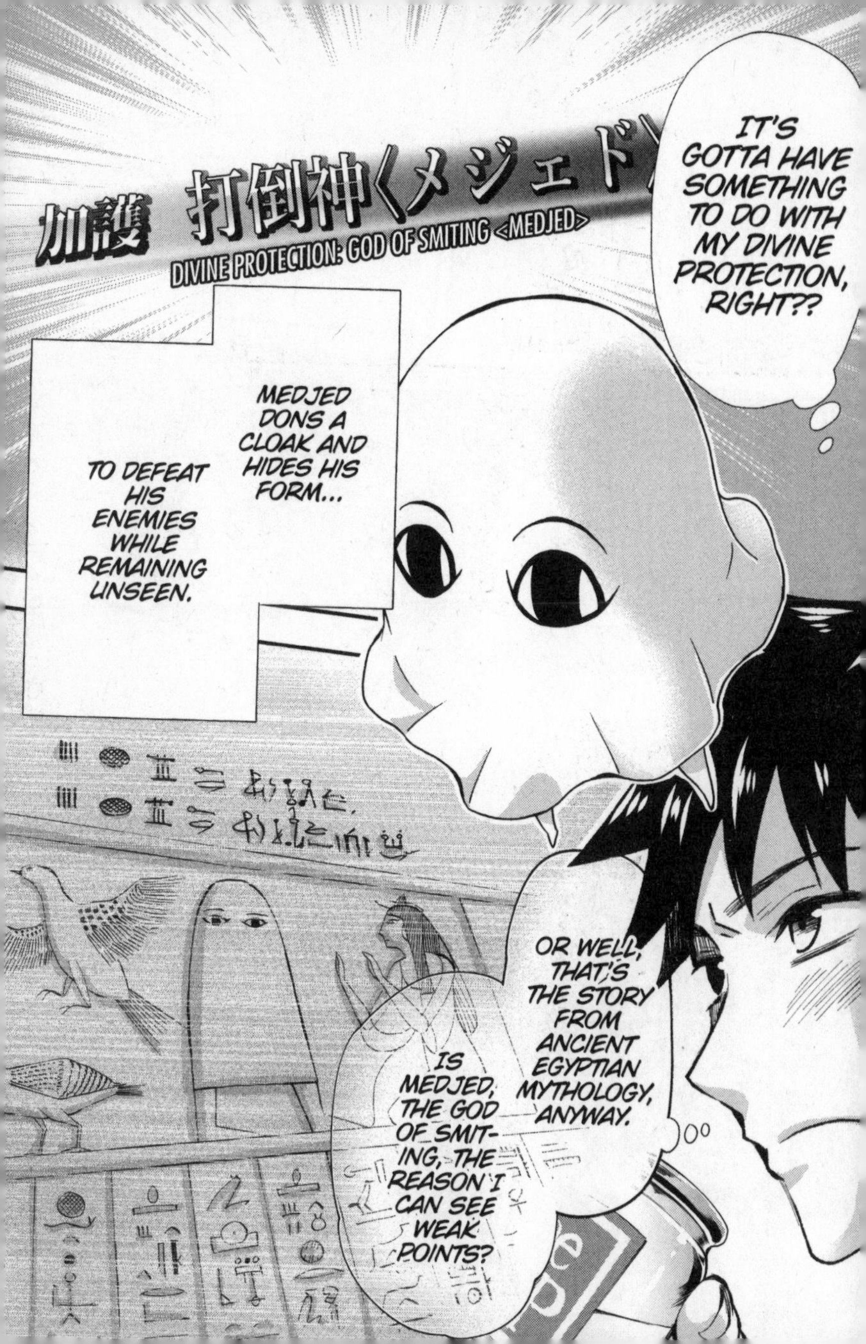

IT'S GOTTA HAVE SOMETHING TO DO WITH MY DIVINE PROTECTION, RIGHT??
加護　打倒神〈メジェド
DIVINE PROTECTION: GOD OF SMITING <MEDJED>
MEDJED DONS A CLOAK AND HIDES HIS FORM...
TO DEFEAT HIS ENEMIES WHILE REMAINING UNSEEN.
OR WELL, THAT'S THE STORY FROM ANCIENT EGYPTIAN MYTHOLOGY, ANYWAY.
IS MEDJED, THE GOD OF SMIT-ING, THE REASON I CAN SEE WEAK POINTS?

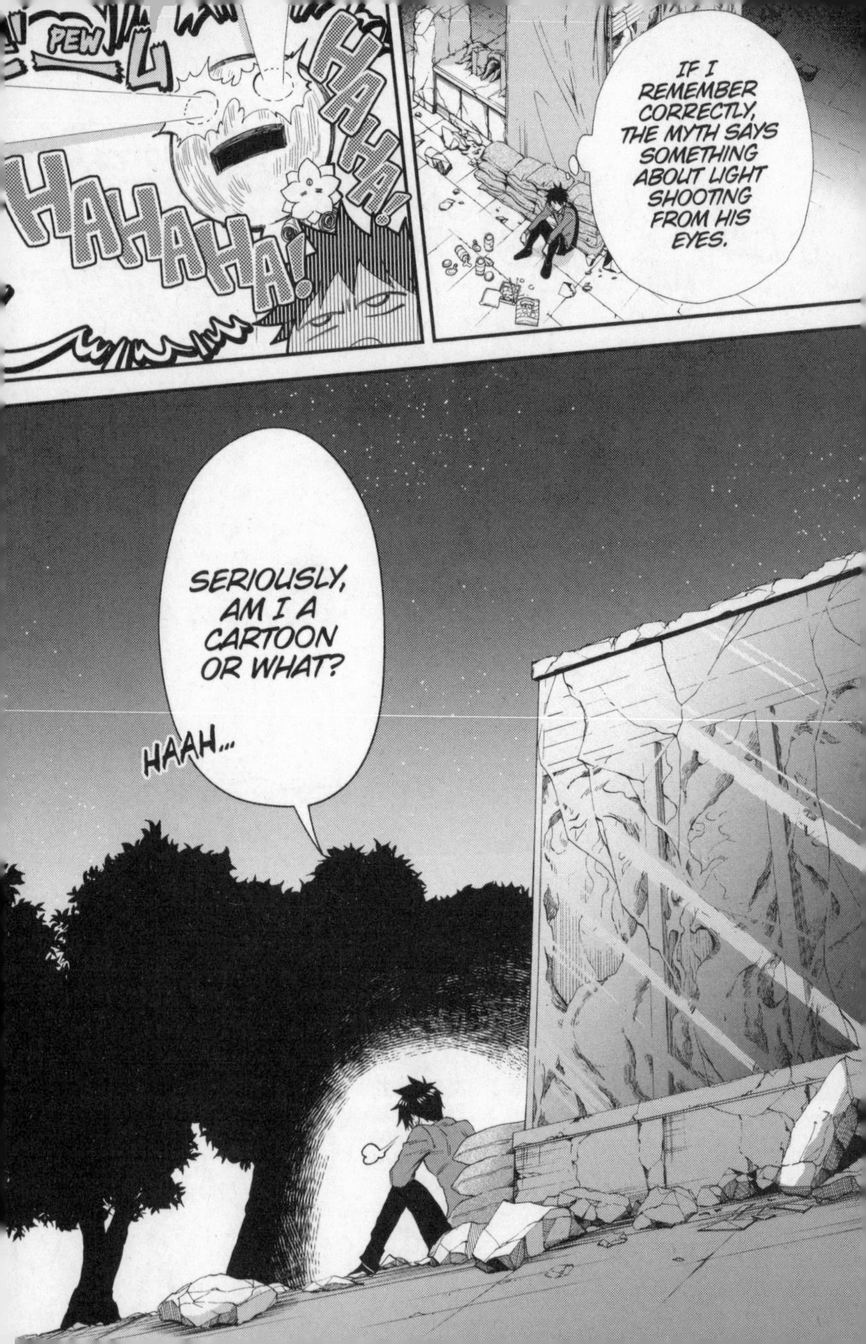
IF I REMEMBER CORRECTLY, THE MYTH SAYS SOMETHING ABOUT LIGHT SHOOTING FROM HIS EYES.
HAHA!
PEW
HAHAHAHA!
SERIOUSLY, AM I A CARTOON OR WHAT?
HAAH...

CALL TO ADVENTURE!

DEFEATING DUNGEONS

WITH A SKILL BOARD

5

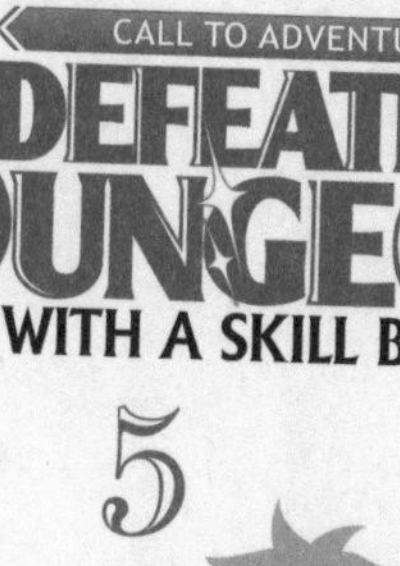

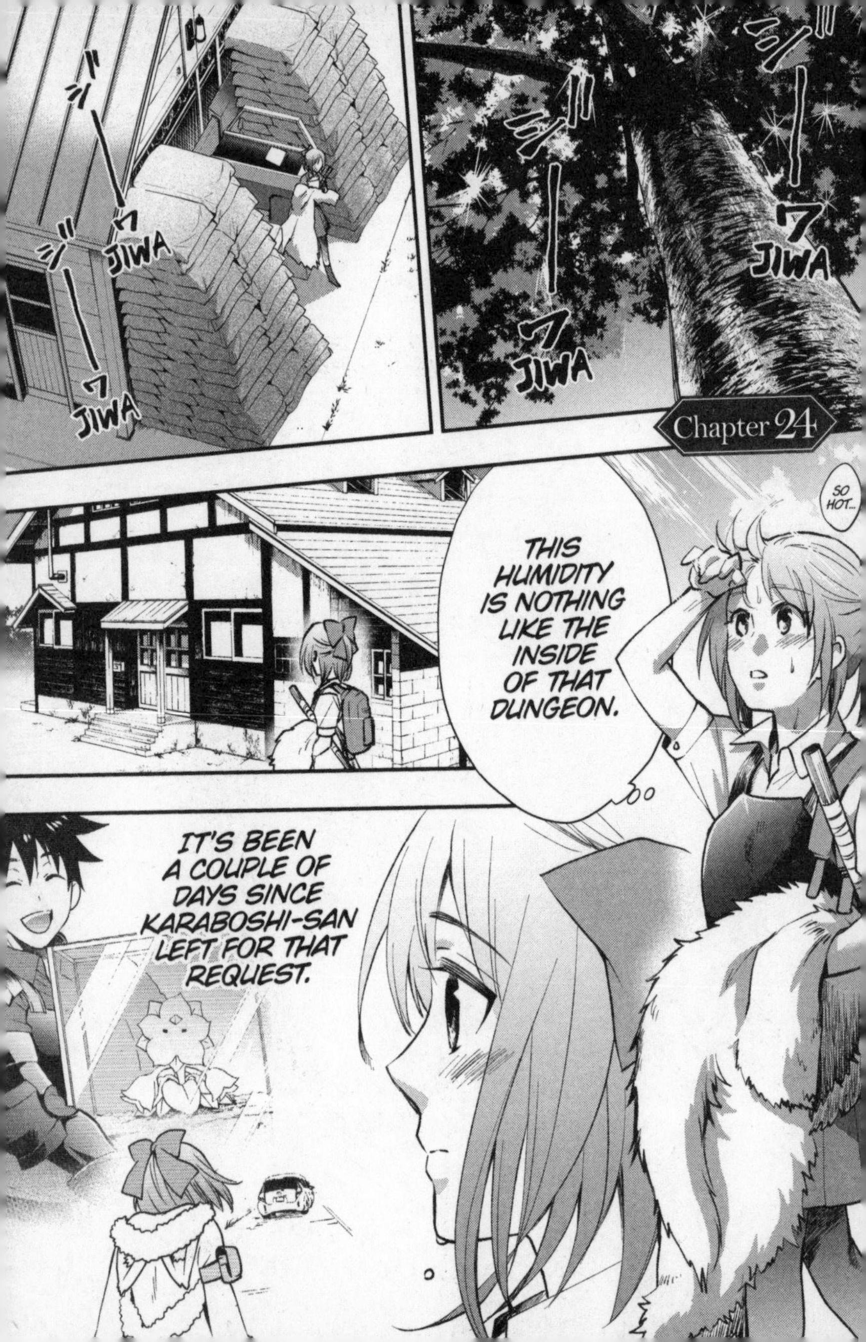
JIWA
JIWA
JIWA
JIWA
Chapter 24
SO HOT...
THIS HUMIDITY IS NOTHING LIKE THE INSIDE OF THAT DUNGEON.
IT'S BEEN A COUPLE OF DAYS SINCE KARABOSHI-SAN LEFT FOR THAT REQUEST.

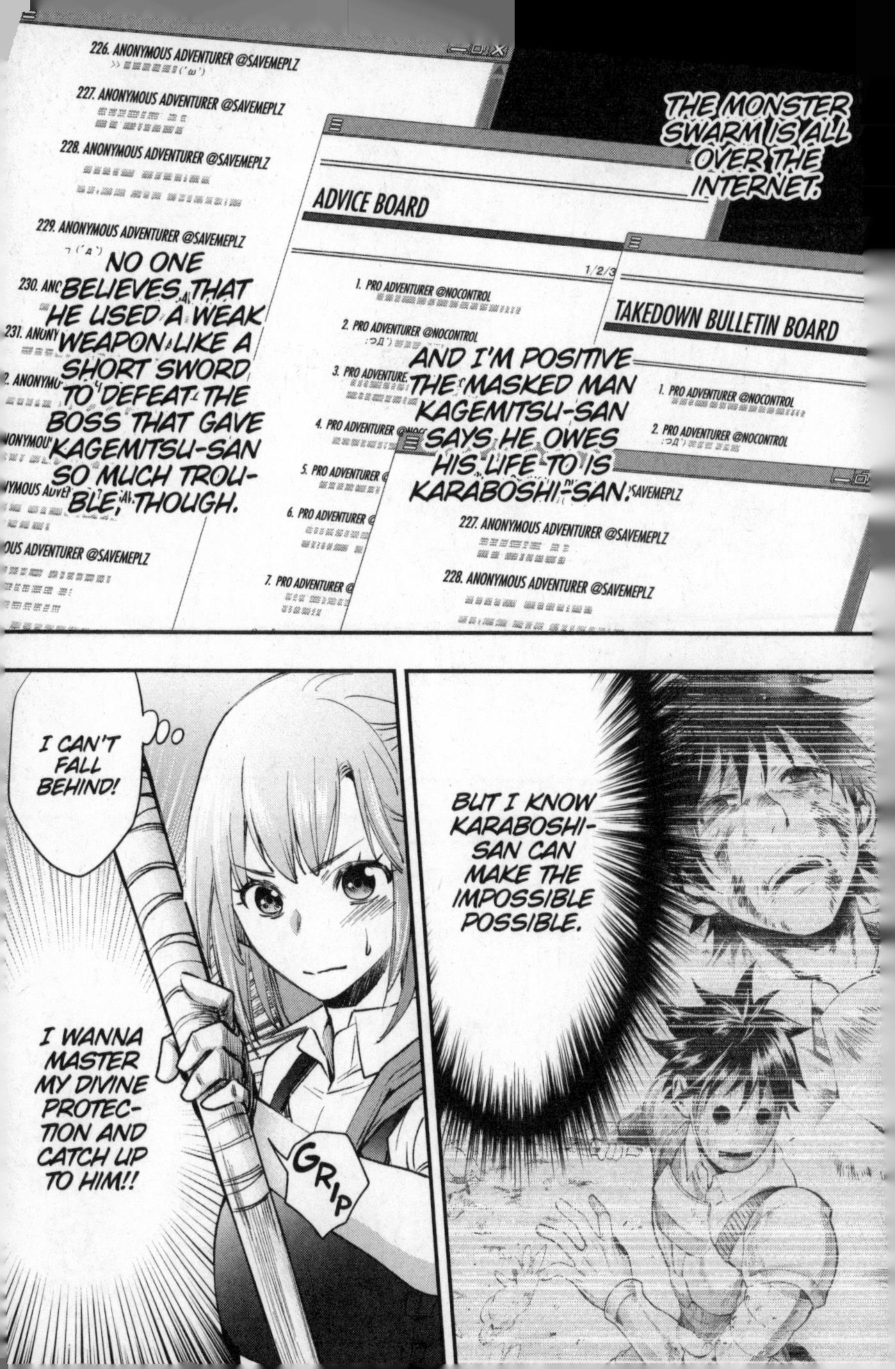
THE MONSTER SWARM IS ALL OVER THE INTERNET.
TAKEDOWN BULLETIN BOARD
1. PRO ADVENTURER @NOCONTROL
2. PRO ADVENTURER @NOCONTROL
ADVICE BOARD
1/2/3
1. PRO ADVENTURER @NOCONTROL
2. PRO ADVENTURER @NOCONTROL
227. ANONYMOUS ADVENTURER @SAVEMEPLZ
228. ANONYMOUS ADVENTURER @SAVEMEPLZ
AND I'M POSITIVE THE MASKED MAN KAGEMITSU-SAN SAYS HE OWES HIS LIFE TO IS KARABOSHI-SAN.
226. ANONYMOUS ADVENTURER @SAVEMEPLZ
227. ANONYMOUS ADVENTURER @SAVEMEPLZ
228. ANONYMOUS ADVENTURER @SAVEMEPLZ
229. ANONYMOUS ADVENTURER @SAVEMEPLZ
OUS ADVENTURER @SAVEMEPLZ
NO ONE BELIEVES THAT HE USED A WEAK WEAPON LIKE A SHORT SWORD TO DEFEAT THE BOSS THAT GAVE KAGEMITSU-SAN SO MUCH TROUBLE, THOUGH.
BUT I KNOW KARABOSHI-SAN CAN MAKE THE IMPOSSIBLE POSSIBLE.
I CAN'T FALL BEHIND!
GRIP
I WANNA MASTER MY DIVINE PROTECTION AND CATCH UP TO HIM!!

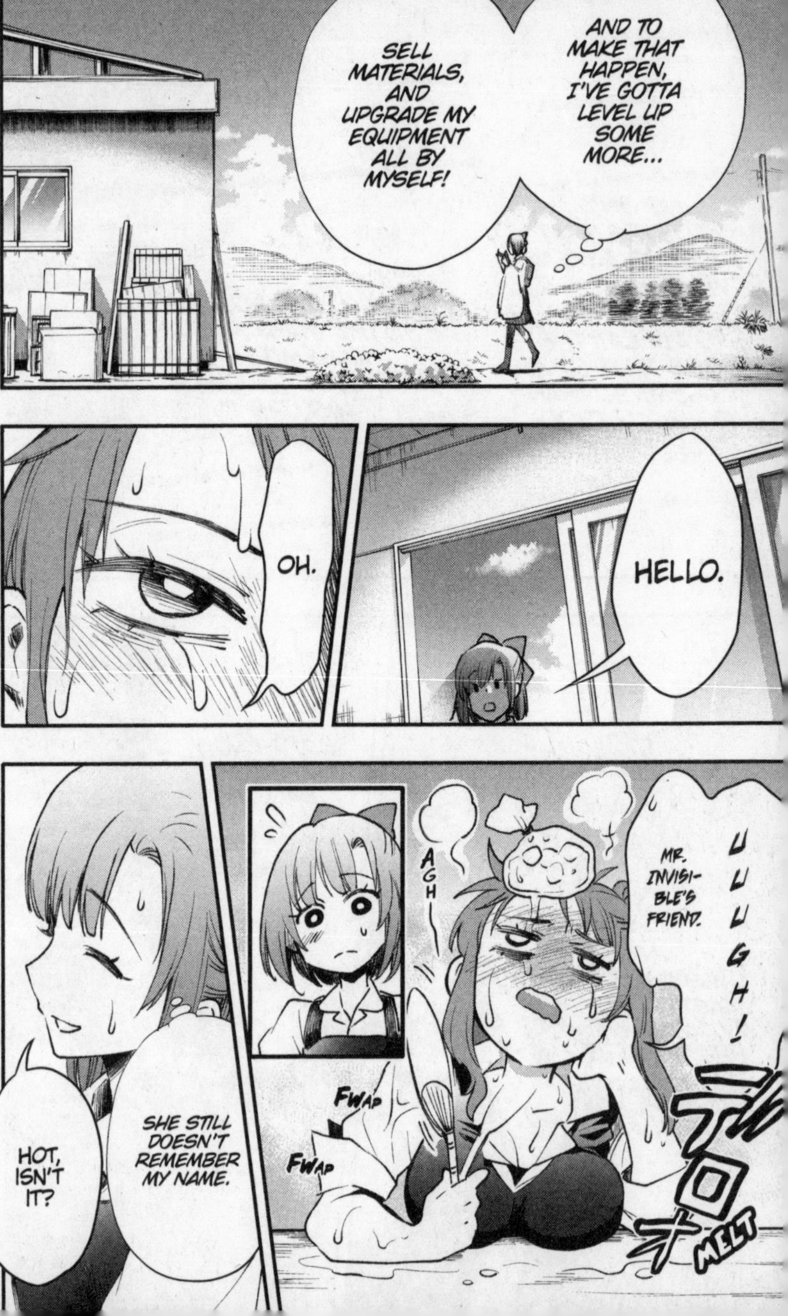
AND TO MAKE THAT HAPPEN, I'VE GOTTA LEVEL UP SOME MORE...
SELL MATERIALS, AND UPGRADE MY EQUIPMENT ALL BY MYSELF!
HELLO.
OH.
UUUGH!
MR. INVISIBLE'S FRIEND.
AGH
FWAP
FWAP
MELT
SHE STILL DOESN'T REMEMBER MY NAME.
HOT, ISN'T IT?

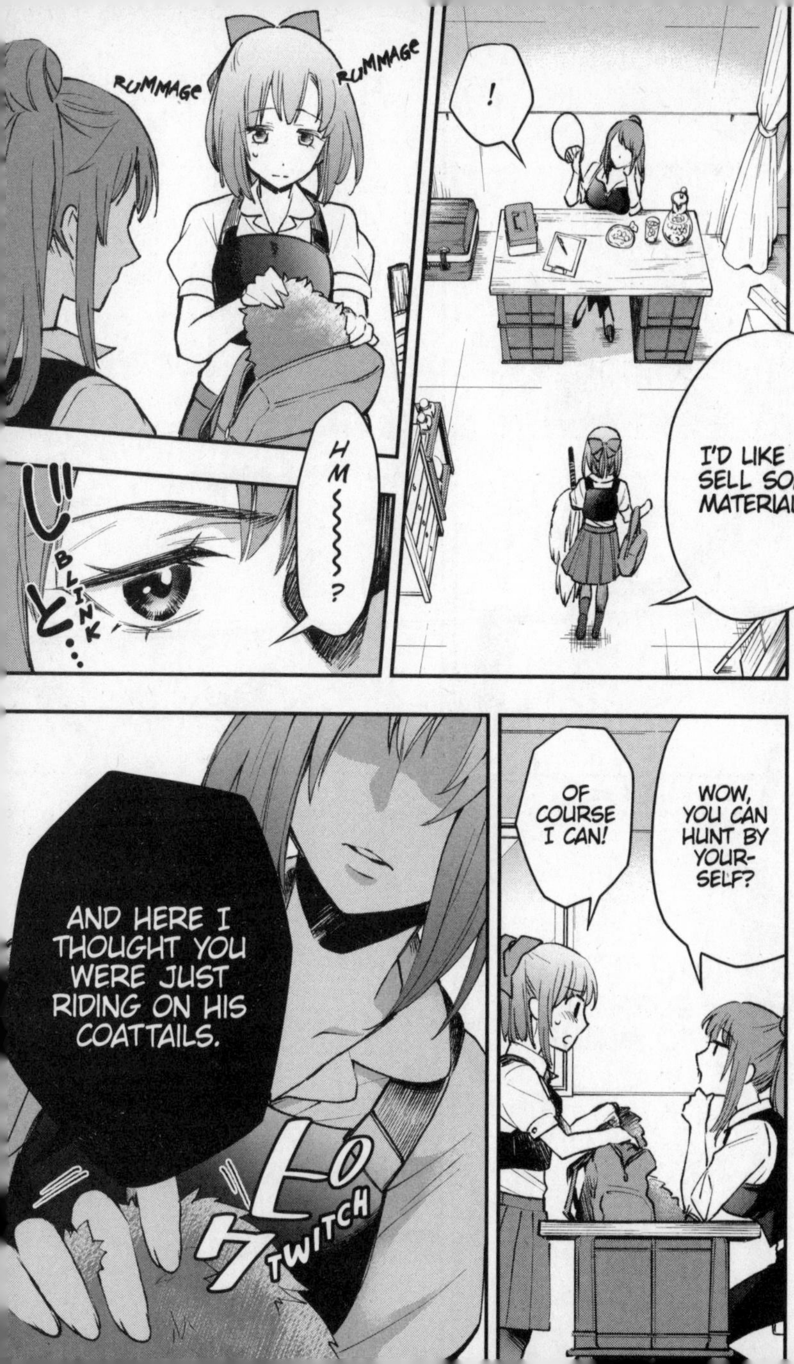
!
I'D LIKE TO SELL SOME MATERIALS.
RUMMAGE
RUMMAGE
HM~~~?
BLINK
WOW, YOU CAN HUNT BY YOURSELF?
OF COURSE I CAN!
AND HERE I THOUGHT YOU WERE JUST RIDING ON HIS COATTAILS.
TWITCH

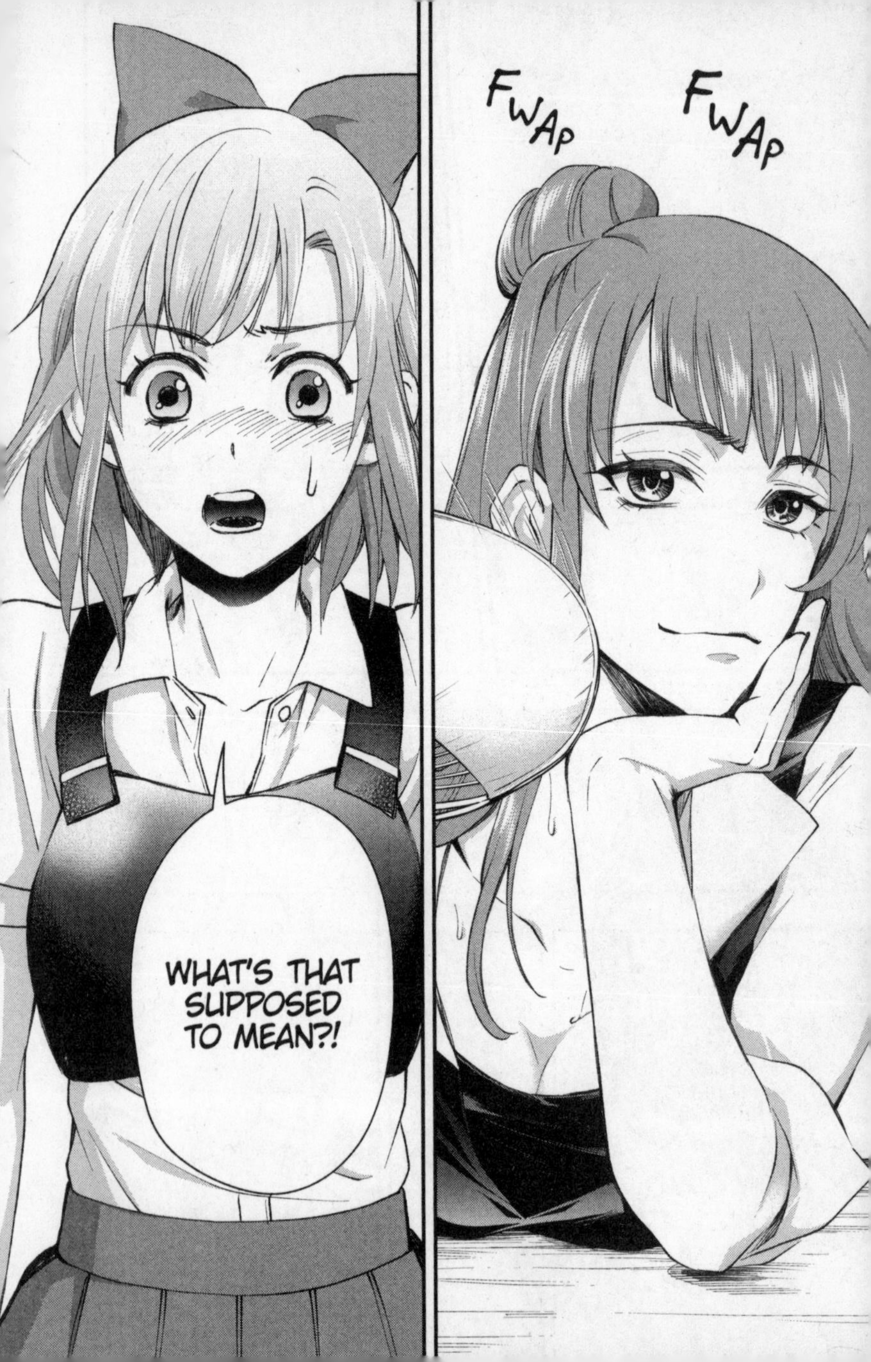
FWAP
FWAP
WHAT'S THAT SUPPOSED TO MEAN?!

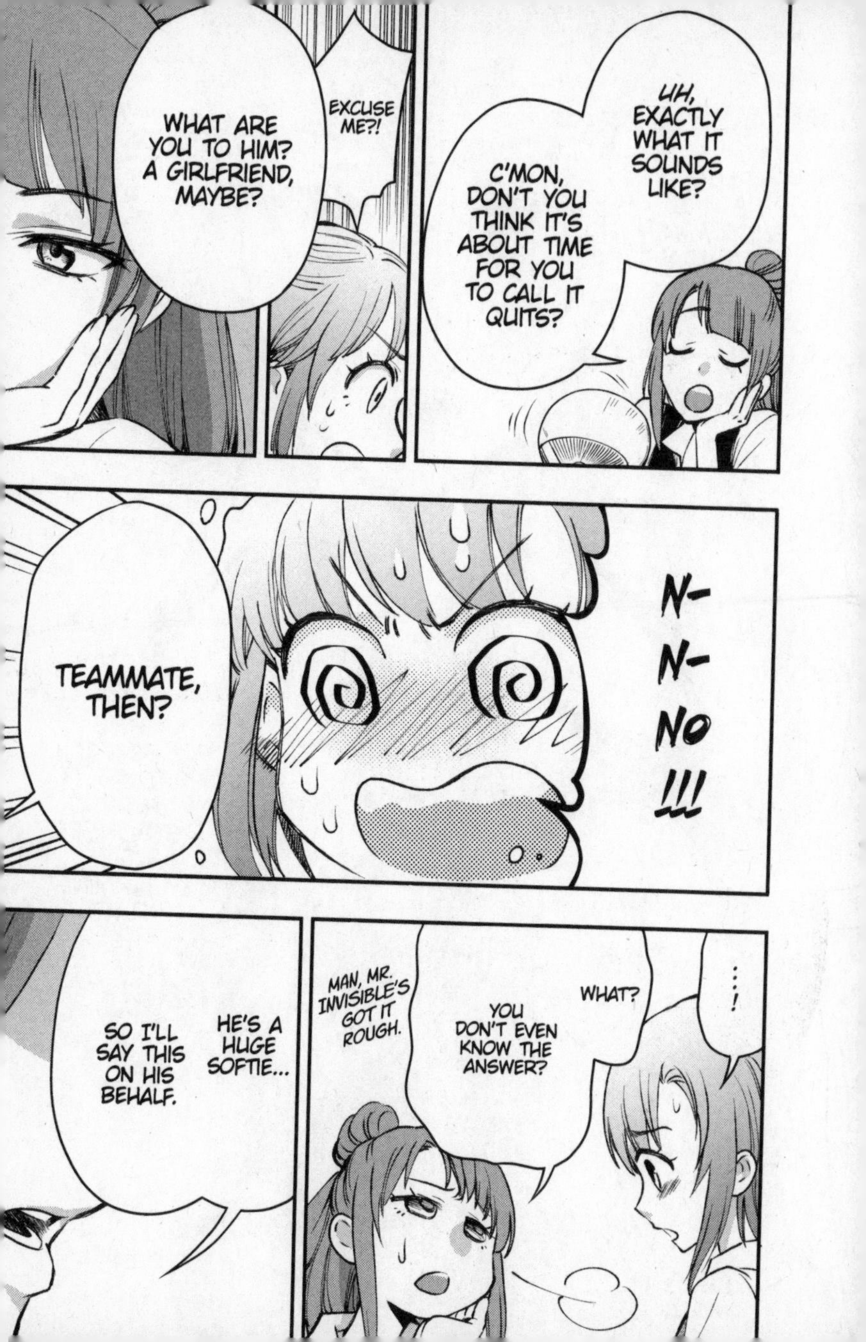
UH, EXACTLY WHAT IT SOUNDS LIKE?
C'MON, DON'T YOU THINK IT'S ABOUT TIME FOR YOU TO CALL IT QUITS?
EXCUSE ME?!
WHAT ARE YOU TO HIM? A GIRLFRIEND, MAYBE?
N-N-NO!!!
TEAMMATE, THEN?
...!
WHAT?
YOU DON'T EVEN KNOW THE ANSWER?
MAN, MR. INVISIBLE'S GOT IT ROUGH.
HE'S A HUGE SOFTIE...
SO I'LL SAY THIS ON HIS BEHALF.

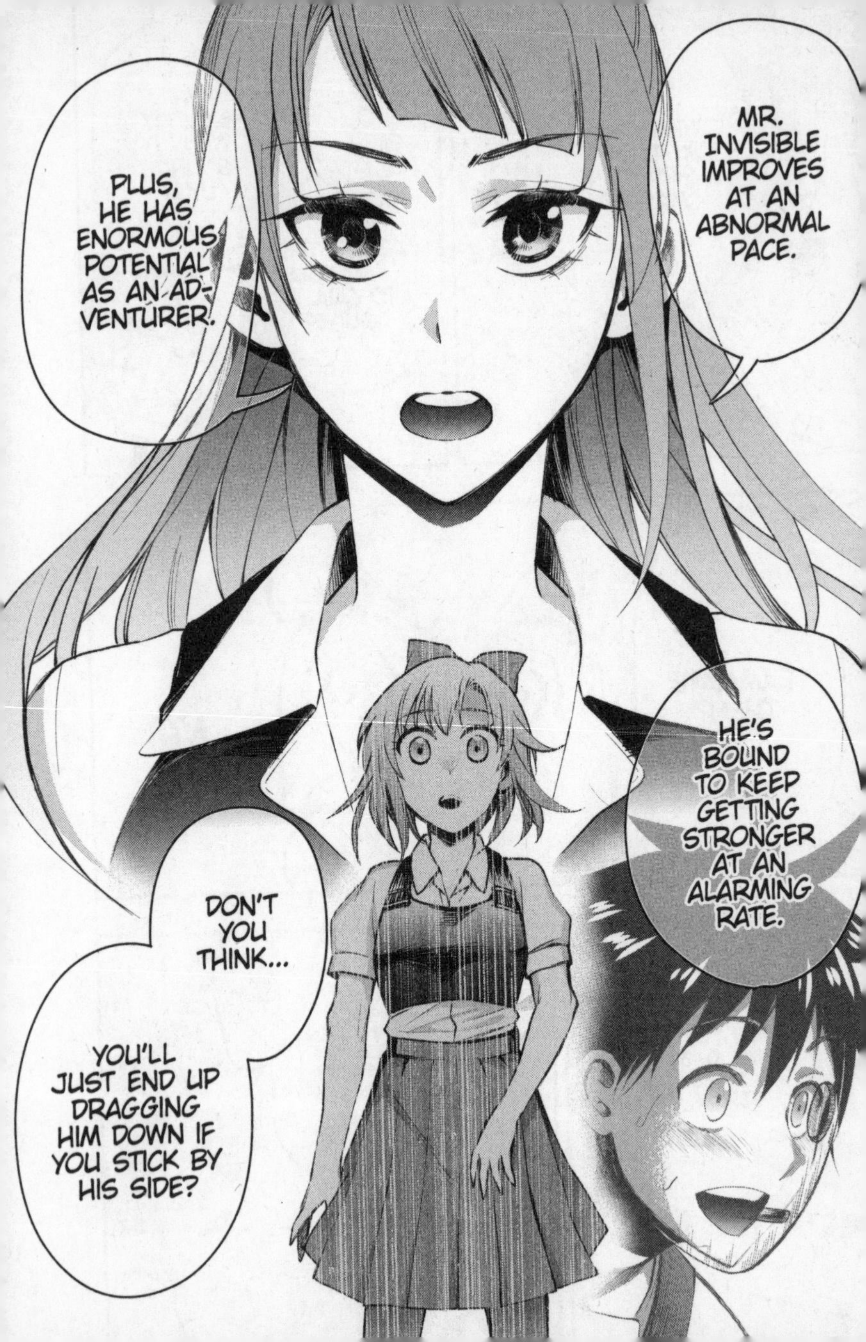
MR. INVISIBLE IMPROVES AT AN ABNORMAL PACE.
PLUS, HE HAS ENORMOUS POTENTIAL AS AN AD-VENTURER.
HE'S BOUND TO KEEP GETTING STRONGER AT AN ALARMING RATE.
DON'T YOU THINK...
YOU'LL JUST END UP DRAGGING HIM DOWN IF YOU STICK BY HIS SIDE?

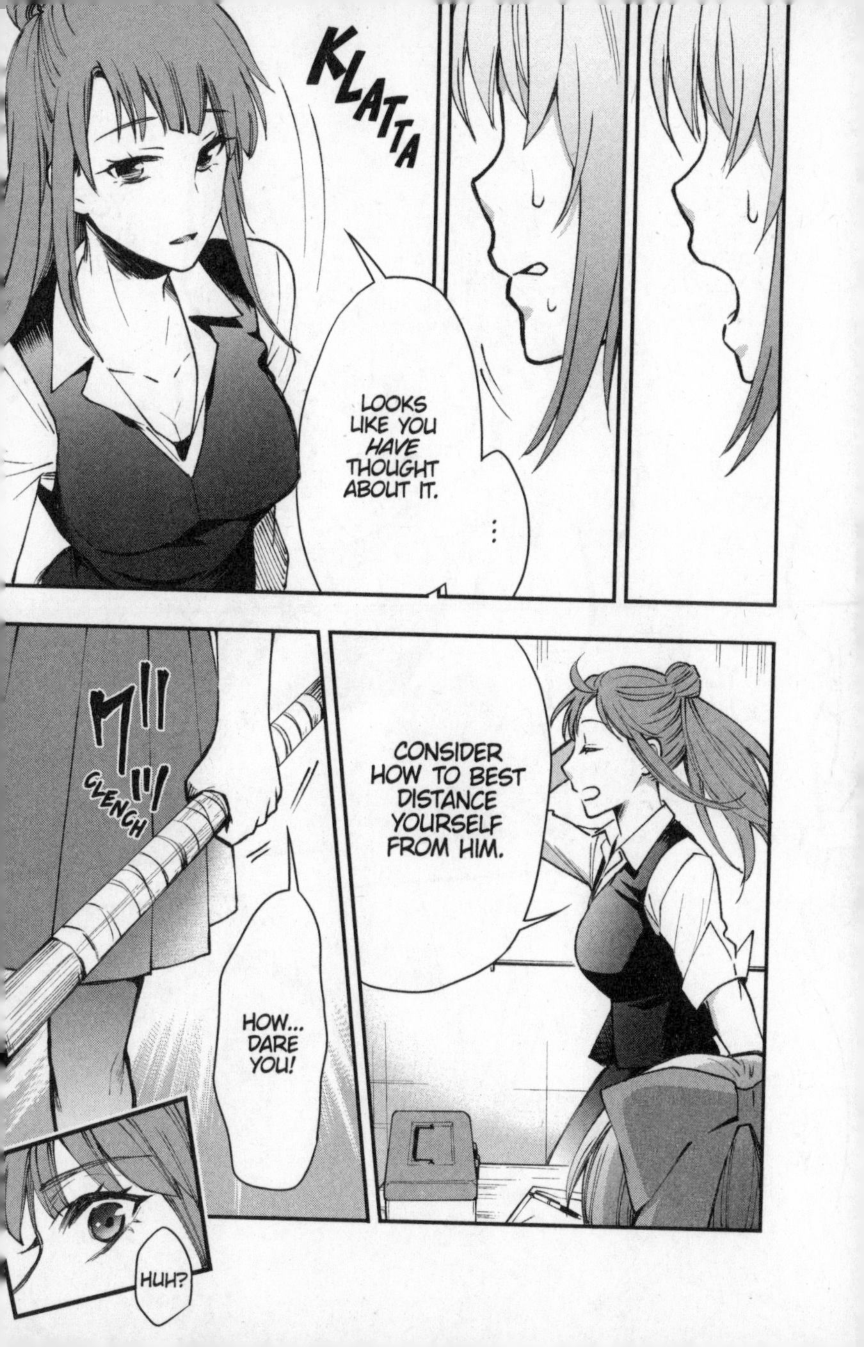
KLATTA
LOOKS LIKE YOU *HAVE* THOUGHT ABOUT IT.
…
CONSIDER HOW TO BEST DISTANCE YOURSELF FROM HIM.
CLENCH
HOW... DARE YOU!
HUH?

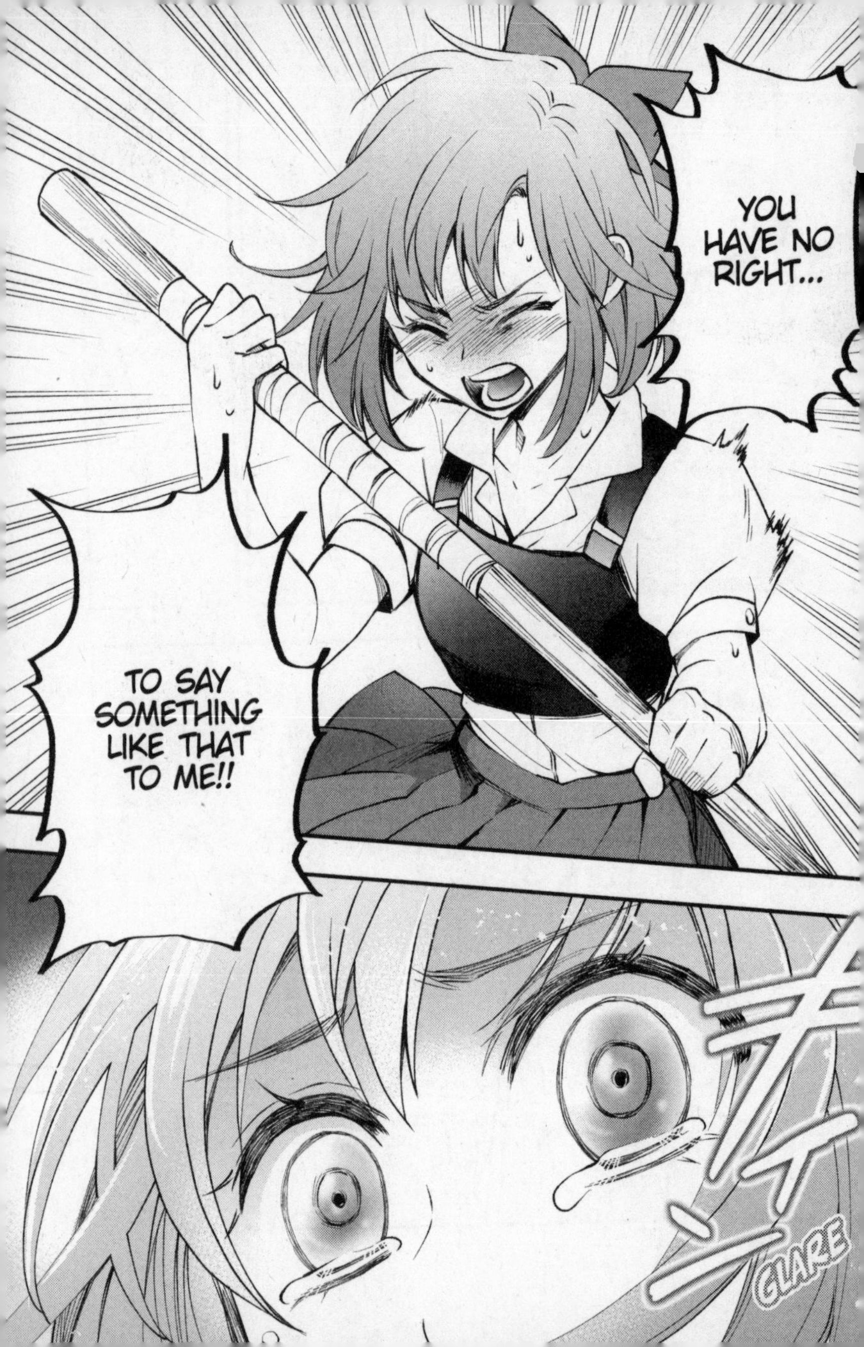
YOU HAVE NO RIGHT...
TO SAY SOMETHING LIKE THAT TO ME!!
GLARE

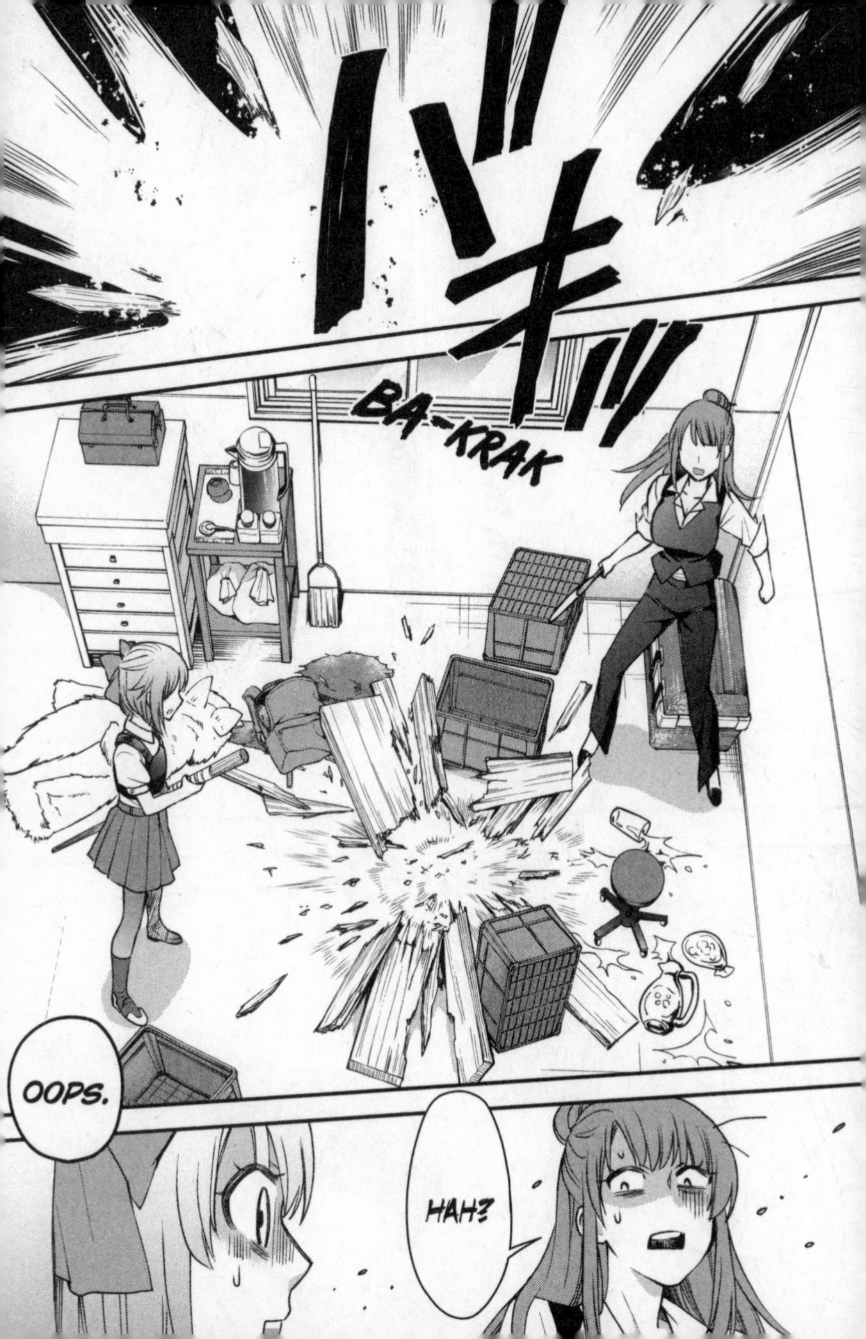
BA-KRAK
OOPS.
HAH?

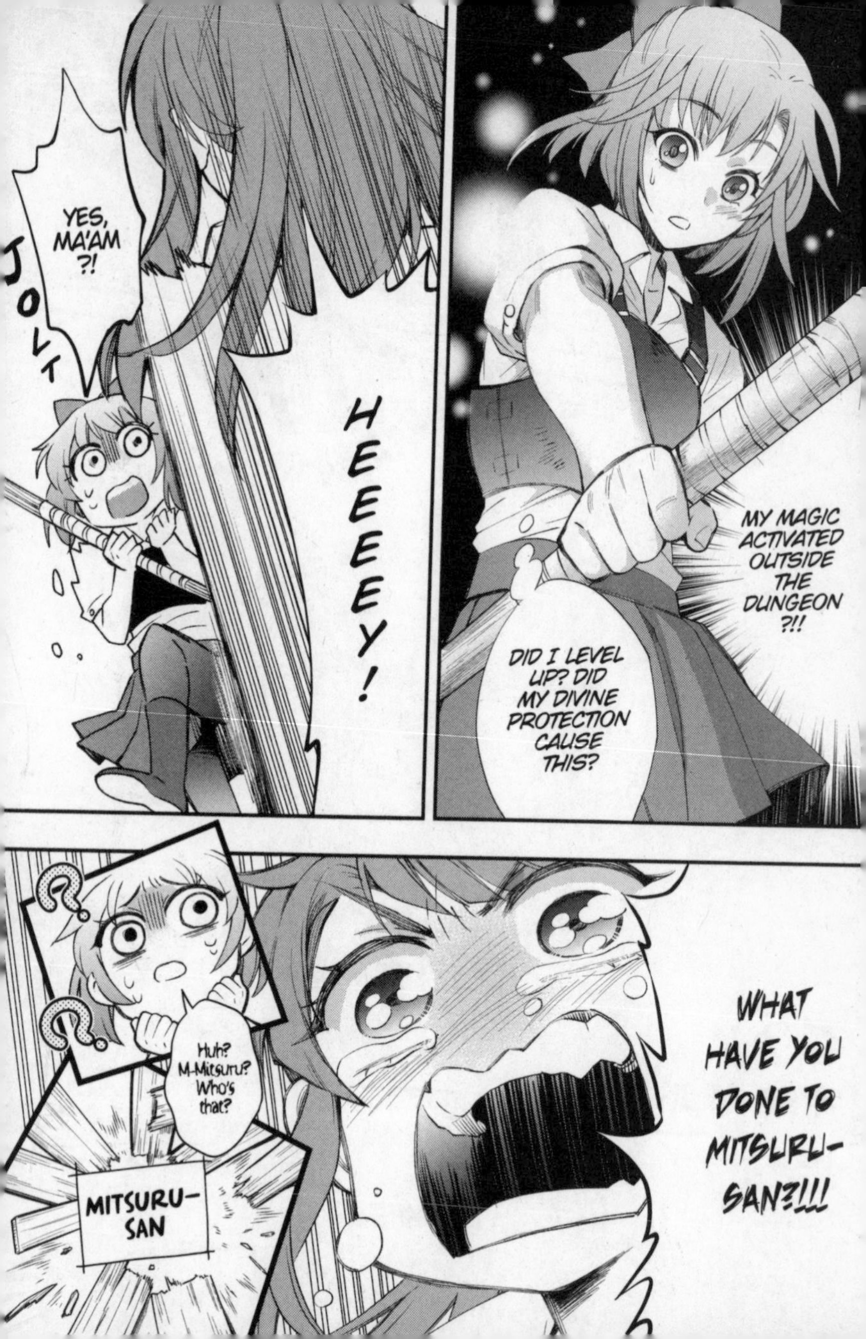
MY MAGIC ACTIVATED OUTSIDE THE DUNGEON ?!!
DID I LEVEL UP? DID MY DIVINE PROTECTION CAUSE THIS?
HEEEEEY!
YES, MA'AM ?!
JOLT
WHAT HAVE YOU DONE TO MITSURU-SAN?!!!
Huh? M-Mitsuru? Who's that?
MITSURU-SAN

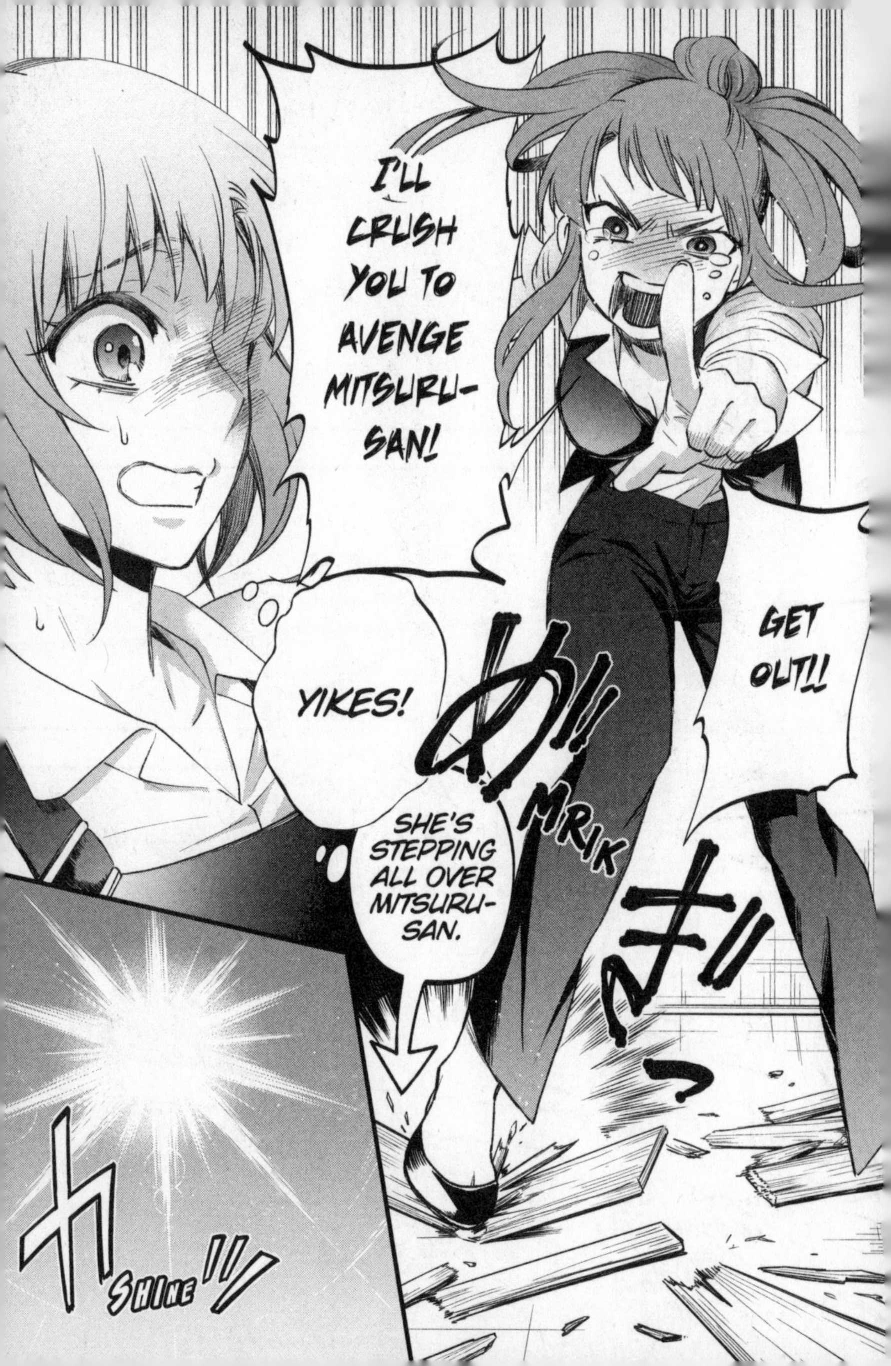
I'LL CRUSH YOU TO AVENGE MITSURU-SAN!
GET OUT!!
YIKES!
MRIK
SHE'S STEPPING ALL OVER MITSURU-SAN.
SHINE

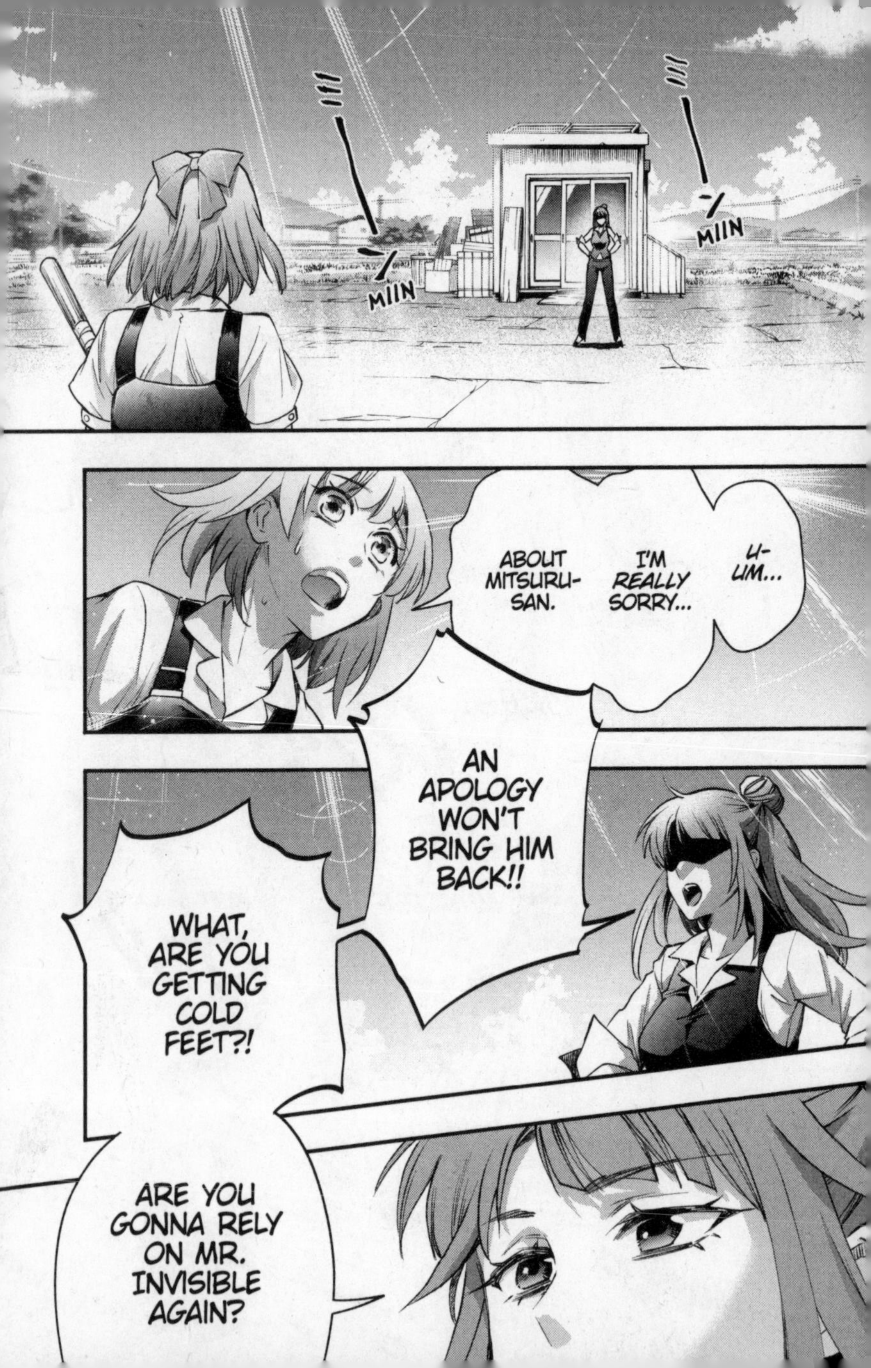
MIIN
MIIN
U-UM...
I'M REALLY SORRY...
ABOUT MITSURU-SAN.
AN APOLOGY WON'T BRING HIM BACK!!
WHAT, ARE YOU GETTING COLD FEET?!
ARE YOU GONNA RELY ON MR. INVISIBLE AGAIN?

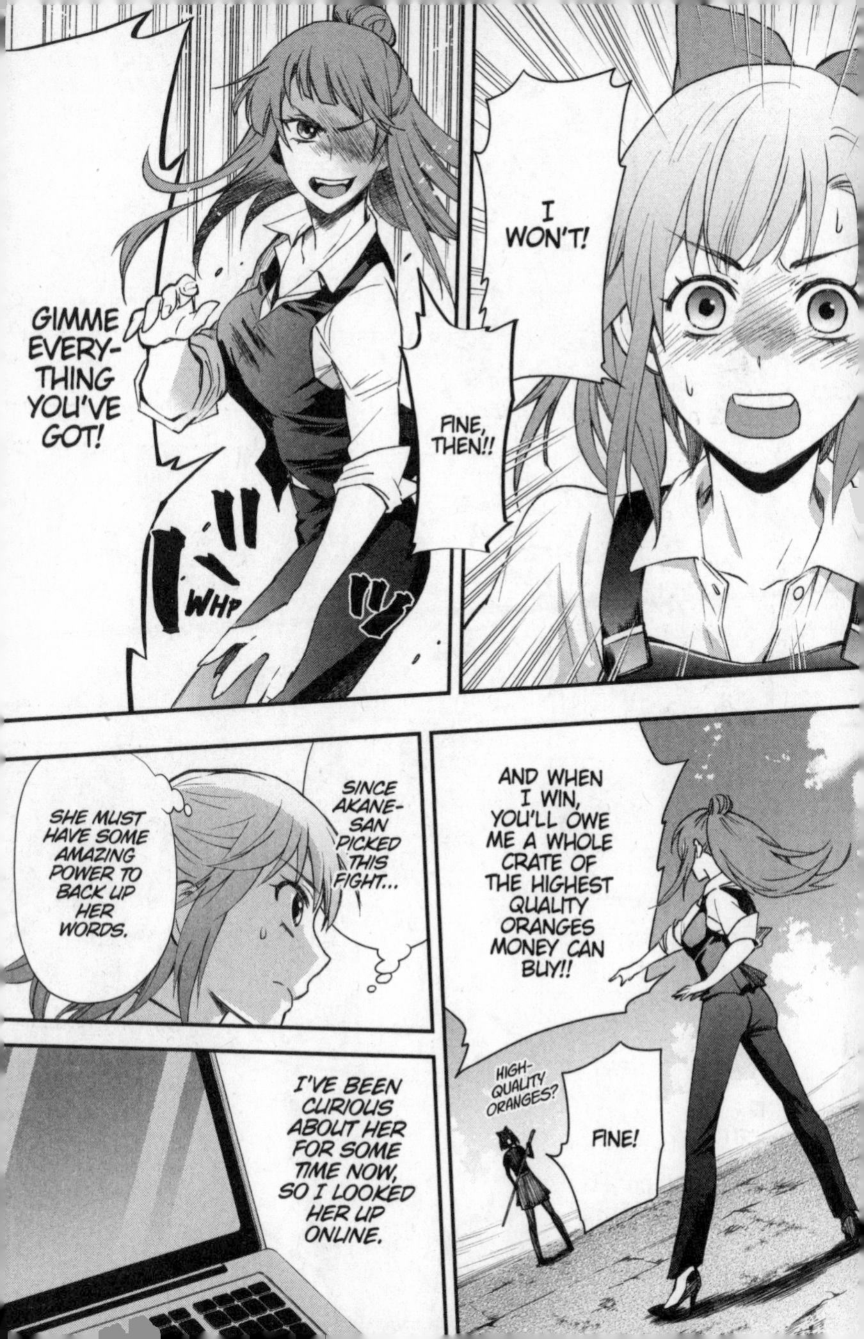
I WON'T!
FINE, THEN!!
GIMME EVERY-THING YOU'VE GOT!
WHP
AND WHEN I WIN, YOU'LL OWE ME A WHOLE CRATE OF THE HIGHEST QUALITY ORANGES MONEY CAN BUY!!
HIGH-QUALITY ORANGES?
FINE!
SINCE AKANE-SAN PICKED THIS FIGHT...
SHE MUST HAVE SOME AMAZING POWER TO BACK UP HER WORDS.
I'VE BEEN CURIOUS ABOUT HER FOR SOME TIME NOW, SO I LOOKED HER UP ONLINE.

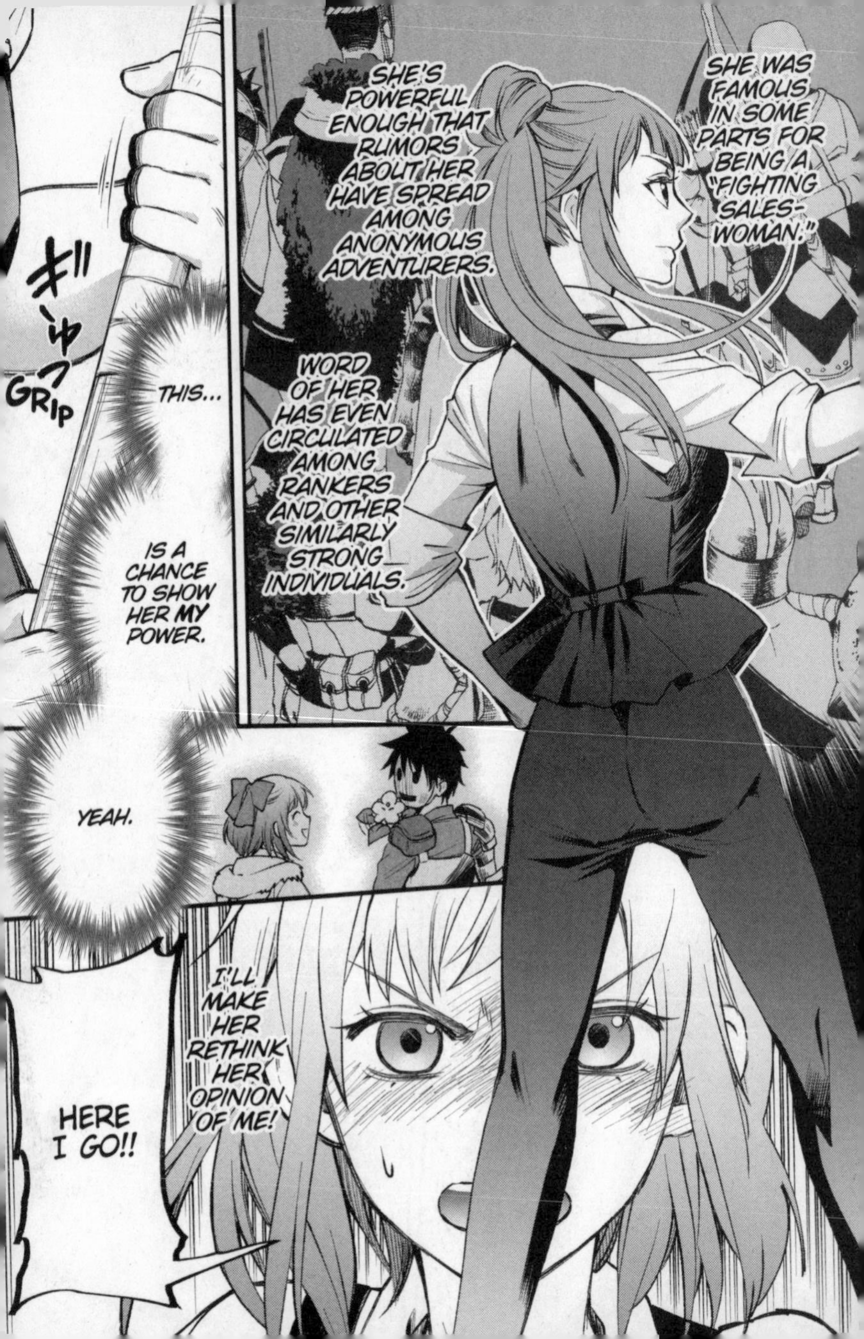

SHE WAS FAMOUS IN SOME PARTS FOR BEING A "FIGHTING SALES-WOMAN."
SHE'S POWERFUL ENOUGH THAT RUMORS ABOUT HER HAVE SPREAD AMONG ANONYMOUS ADVENTURERS.
WORD OF HER HAS EVEN CIRCULATED AMONG RANKERS AND OTHER SIMILARLY STRONG INDIVIDUALS.
I'LL MAKE HER RETHINK HER OPINION OF ME!
ギュッ
GRIP
THIS...
IS A CHANCE TO SHOW HER MY POWER.
YEAH.
HERE I GO!!

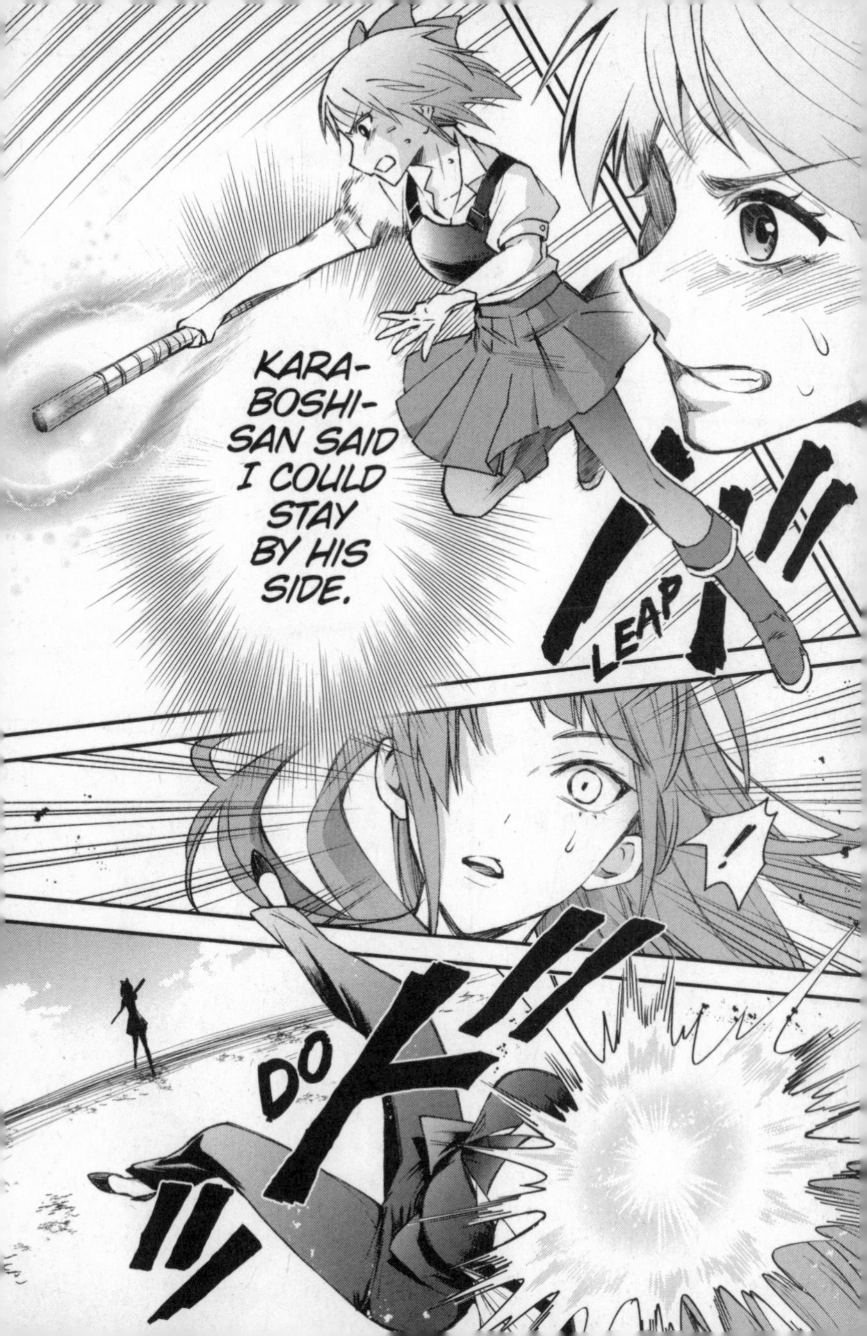
KARA-BOSHI-SAN SAID I COULD STAY BY HIS SIDE.
LEAP
!
DO

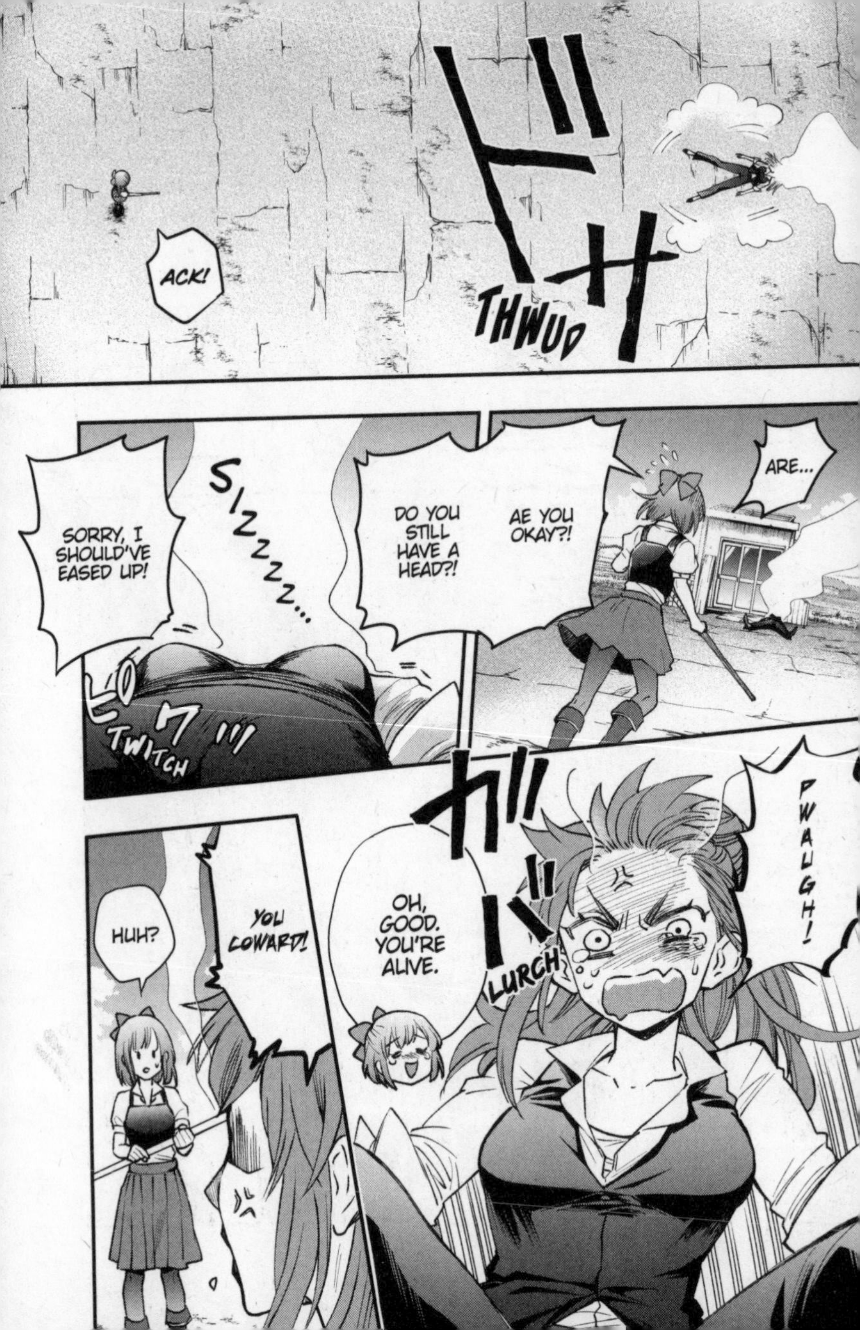
THWUD
ACK!
ARE...
AE YOU OKAY?!
DO YOU STILL HAVE A HEAD?!
SIZZZZZ...
SORRY, I SHOULD'VE EASED UP!
TWITCH
PWAUGH!
LURCH
OH, GOOD. YOU'RE ALIVE.
YOU COWARD!
HUH?

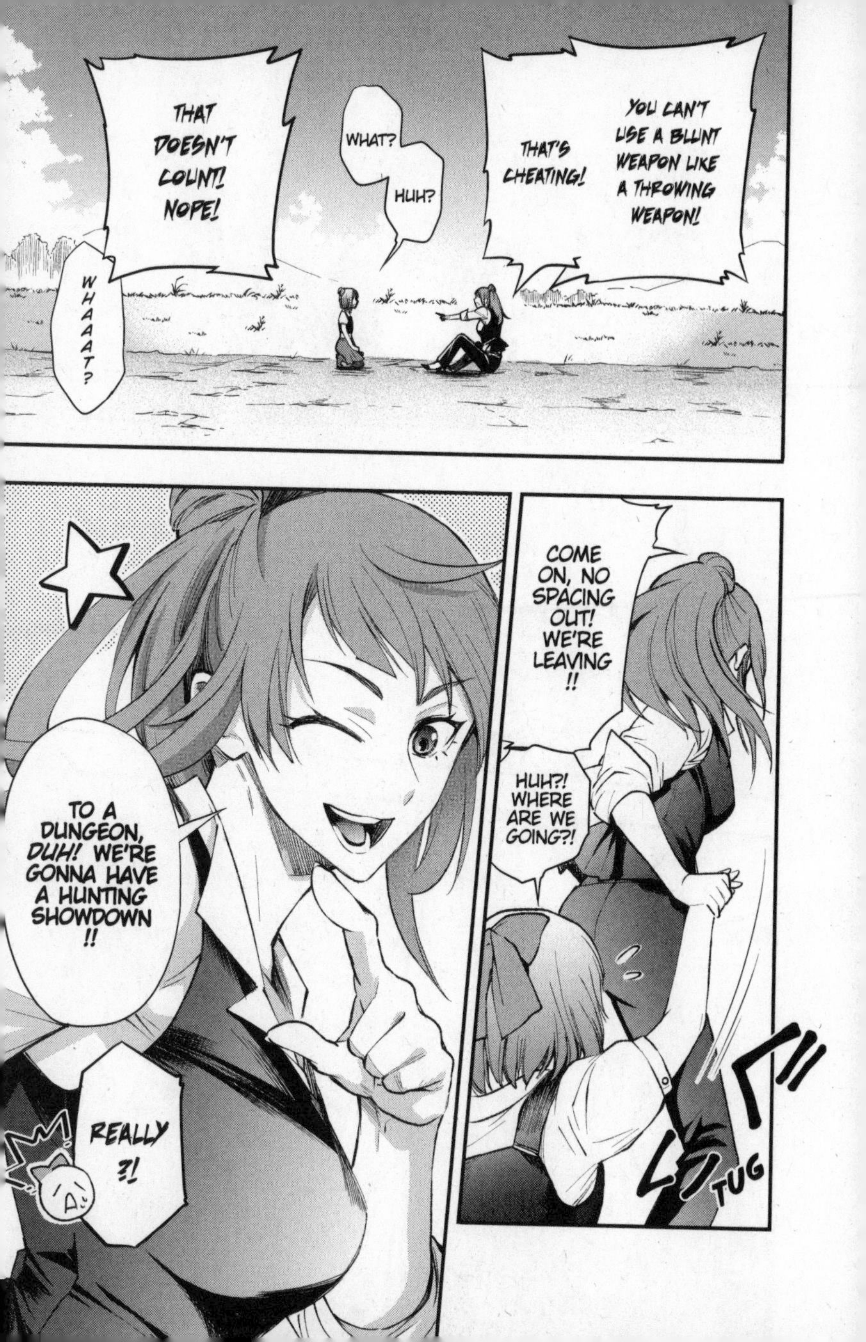
YOU CAN'T USE A BLUNT WEAPON LIKE A THROWING WEAPON!
THAT'S CHEATING!
WHAT?
HUH?
THAT DOESN'T COUNT! NOPE!
WHAAAT?
COME ON, NO SPACING OUT! WE'RE LEAVING!!
HUH?! WHERE ARE WE GOING?!
TUG
TO A DUNGEON, DUH! WE'RE GONNA HAVE A HUNTING SHOWDOWN!!
REALLY?!

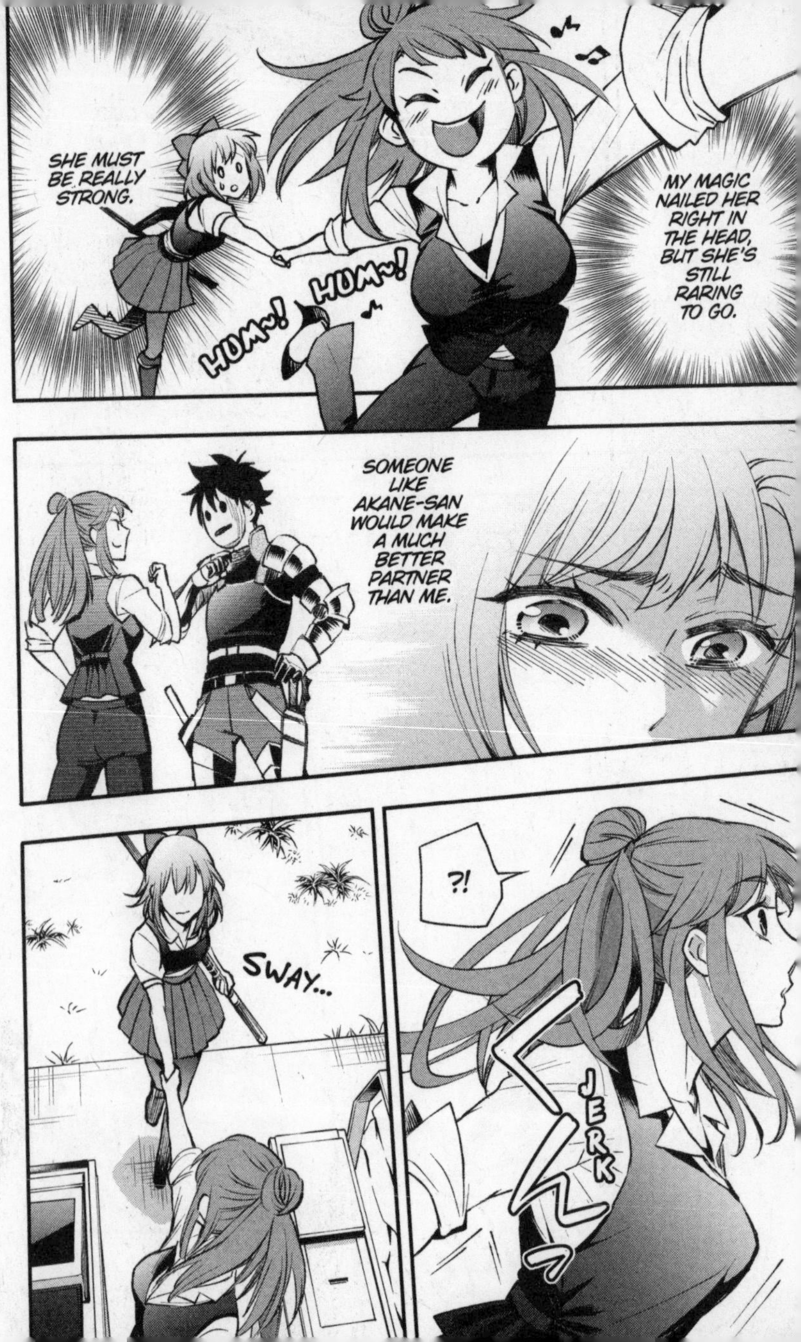

MY MAGIC NAILED HER RIGHT IN THE HEAD, BUT SHE'S STILL RARING TO GO.
HUM~! HUM~!
SHE MUST BE REALLY STRONG.
SOMEONE LIKE AKANE-SAN WOULD MAKE A MUCH BETTER PARTNER THAN ME.
?!
JERK
SWAY...

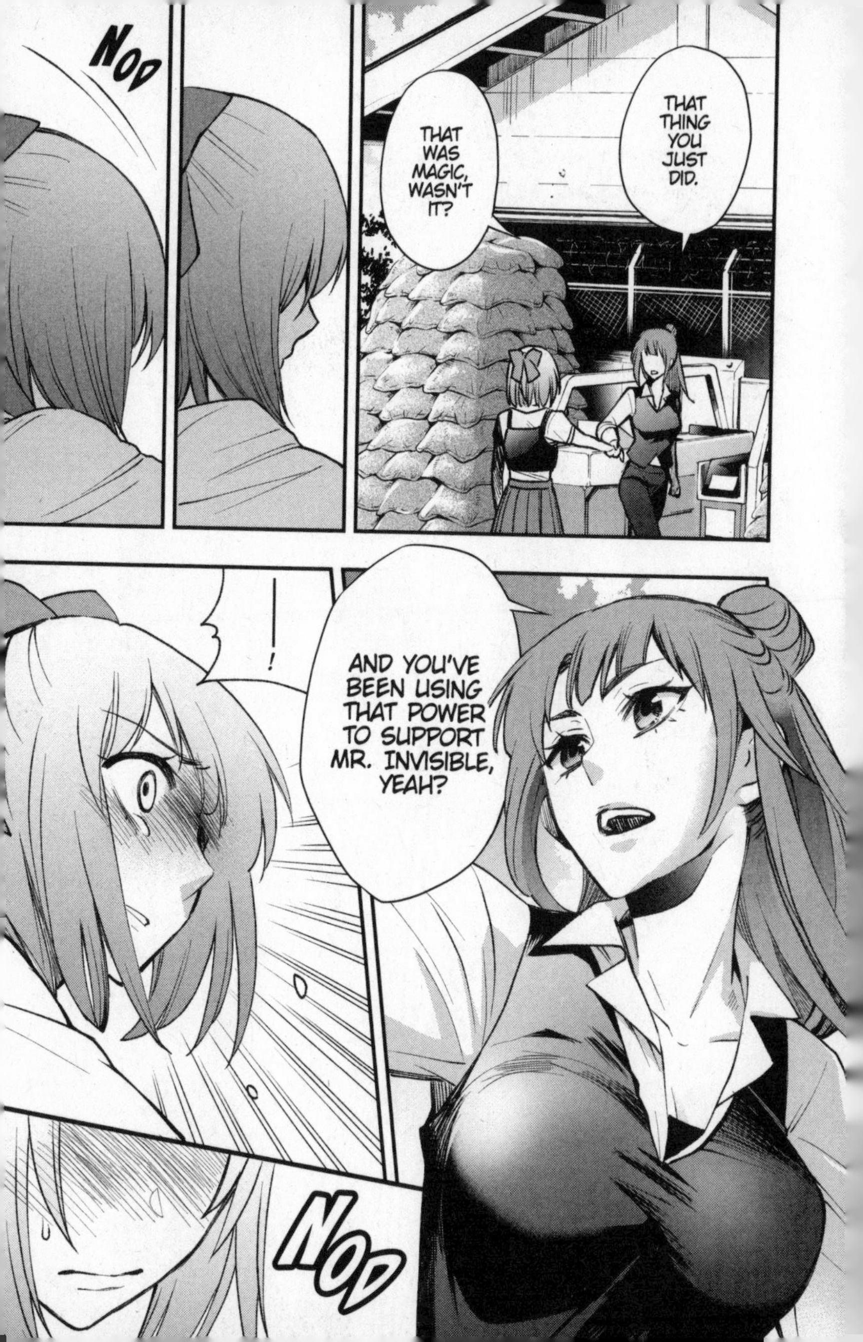
THAT THING YOU JUST DID.
THAT WAS MAGIC, WASN'T IT?
NOD
AND YOU'VE BEEN USING THAT POWER TO SUPPORT MR. INVISIBLE, YEAH?
!
NOD

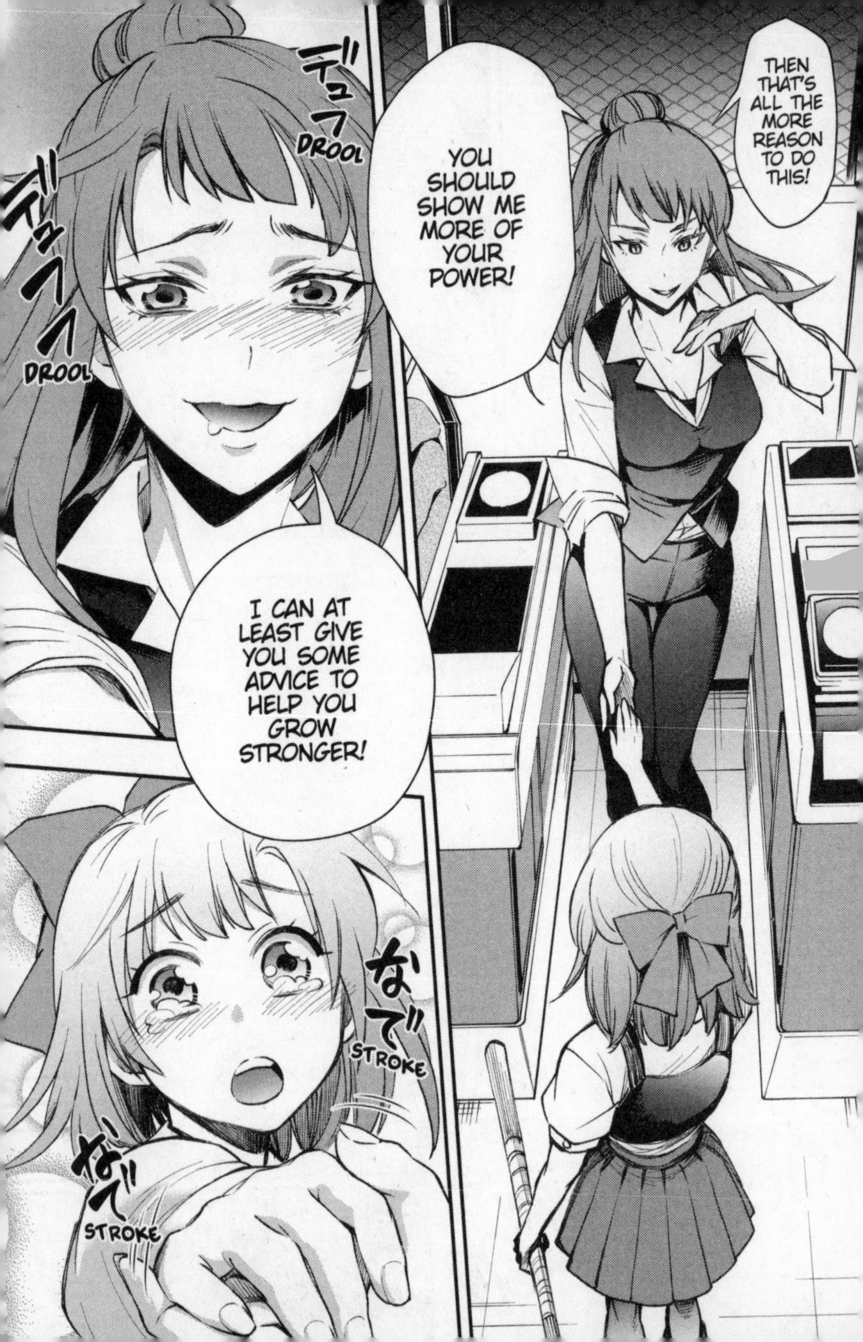
THEN THAT'S ALL THE MORE REASON TO DO THIS!
YOU SHOULD SHOW ME MORE OF YOUR POWER!
デュフ
DROOL
デュフフ
DROOL
I CAN AT LEAST GIVE YOU SOME ADVICE TO HELP YOU GROW STRONGER!
なで
STROKE
なで
STROKE

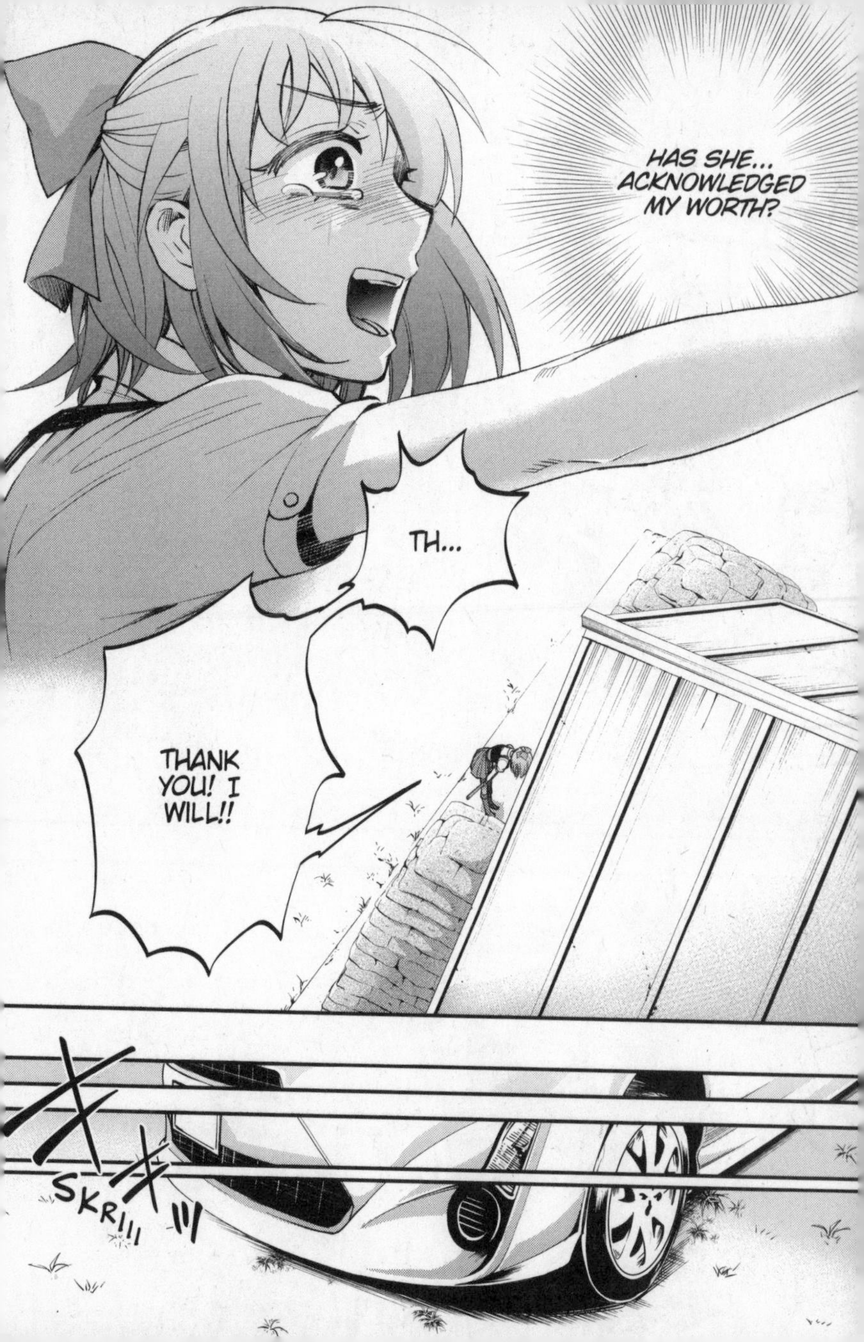
HAS SHE... ACKNOWLEDGED MY WORTH?
TH...
THANK YOU! I WILL!!
SKRI!!!

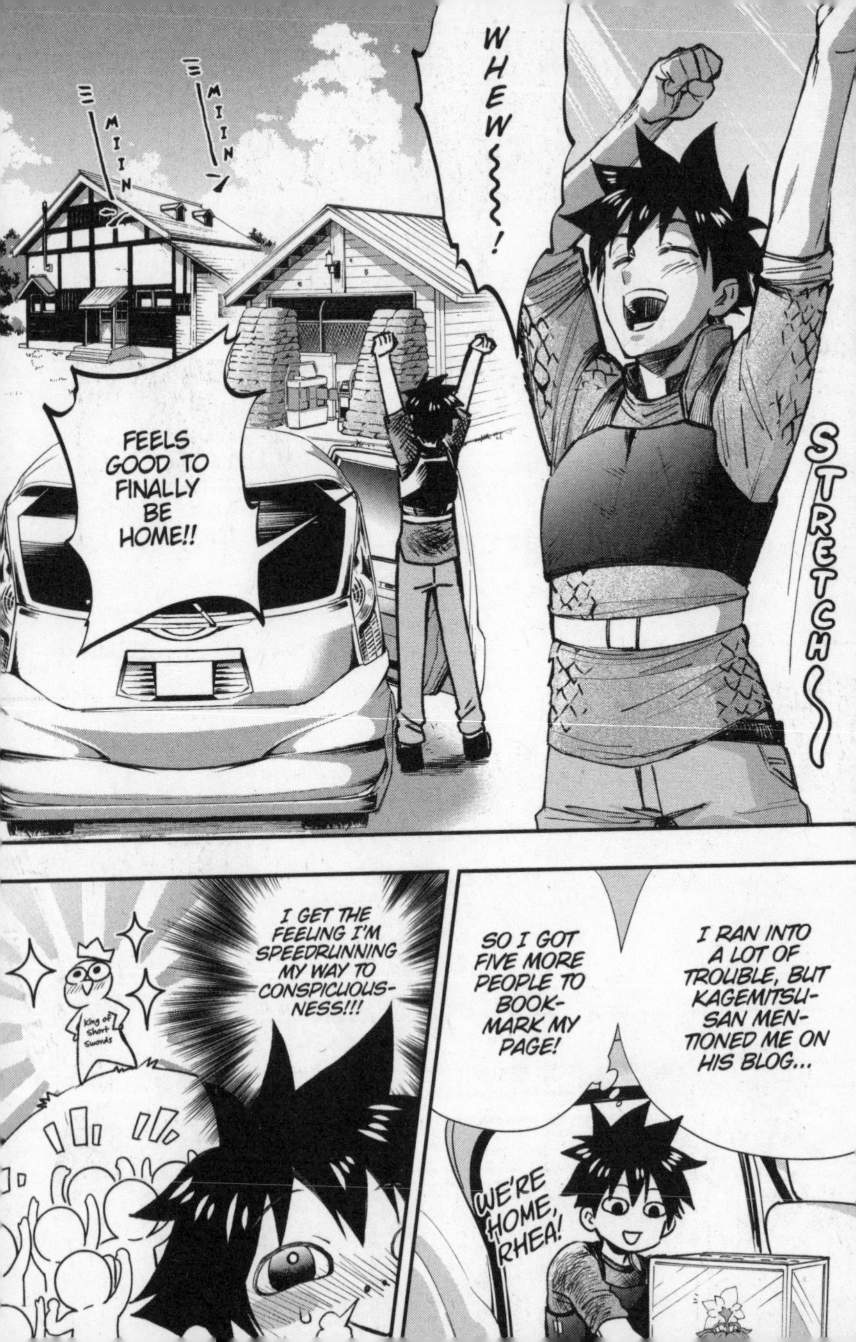
WHEW~~!
STRETCH~
MIIN
MIIN
FEELS GOOD TO FINALLY BE HOME!!
I RAN INTO A LOT OF TROUBLE, BUT KAGEMITSU-SAN MENTIONED ME ON HIS BLOG...
SO I GOT FIVE MORE PEOPLE TO BOOKMARK MY PAGE!
WE'RE HOME, RHEA!
I GET THE FEELING I'M SPEEDRUNNING MY WAY TO CONSPICUOUSNESS!!!
King of Short Swords

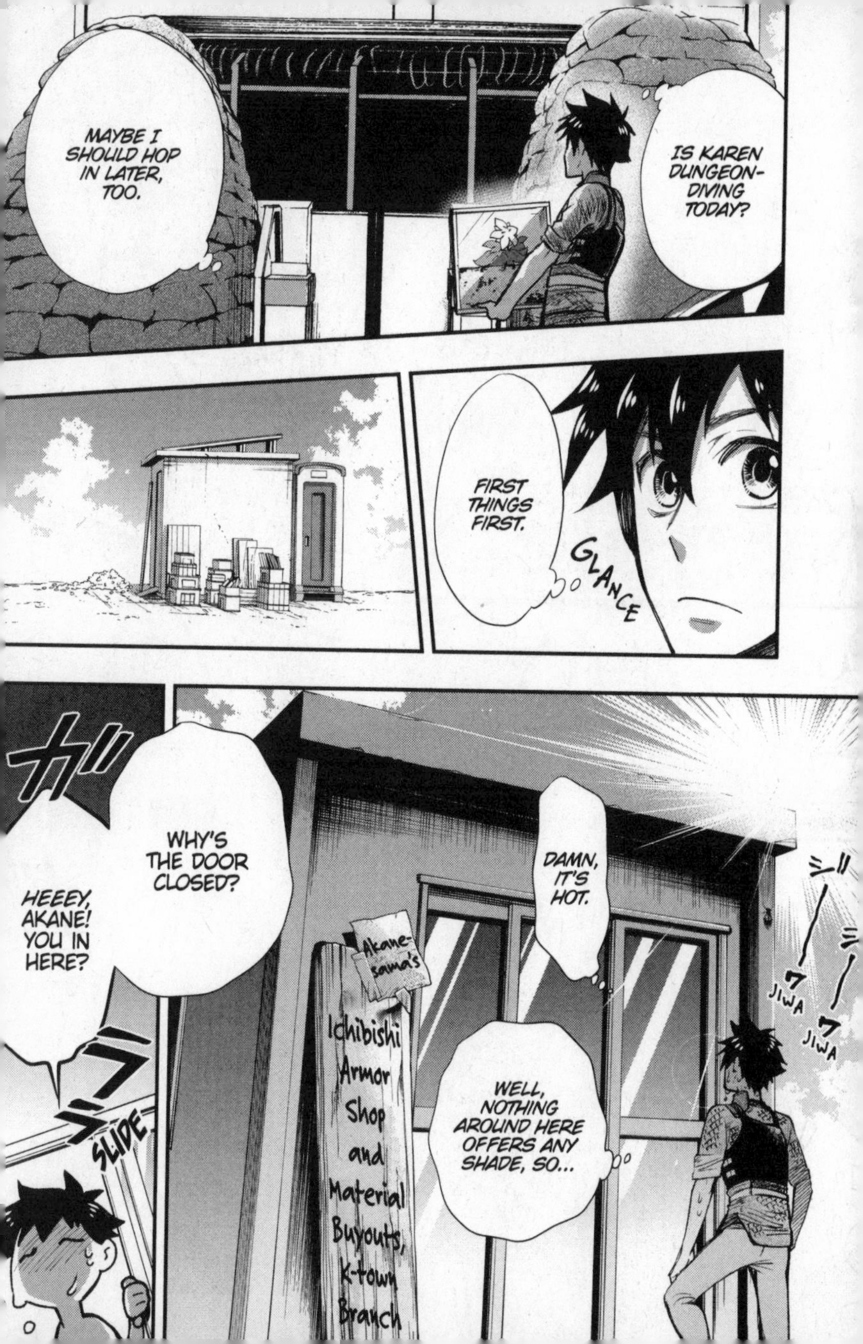
IS KAREN DUNGEON-DIVING TODAY?
MAYBE I SHOULD HOP IN LATER, TOO.
FIRST THINGS FIRST.
GLANCE
JIWA
JIWA
DAMN, IT'S HOT.
WELL, NOTHING AROUND HERE OFFERS ANY SHADE, SO...
Akane-sama's
Ichibishi Armor Shop and Material Buyouts, K-town Branch
WHY'S THE DOOR CLOSED?
HEEEY, AKANE! YOU IN HERE?
SLIDE

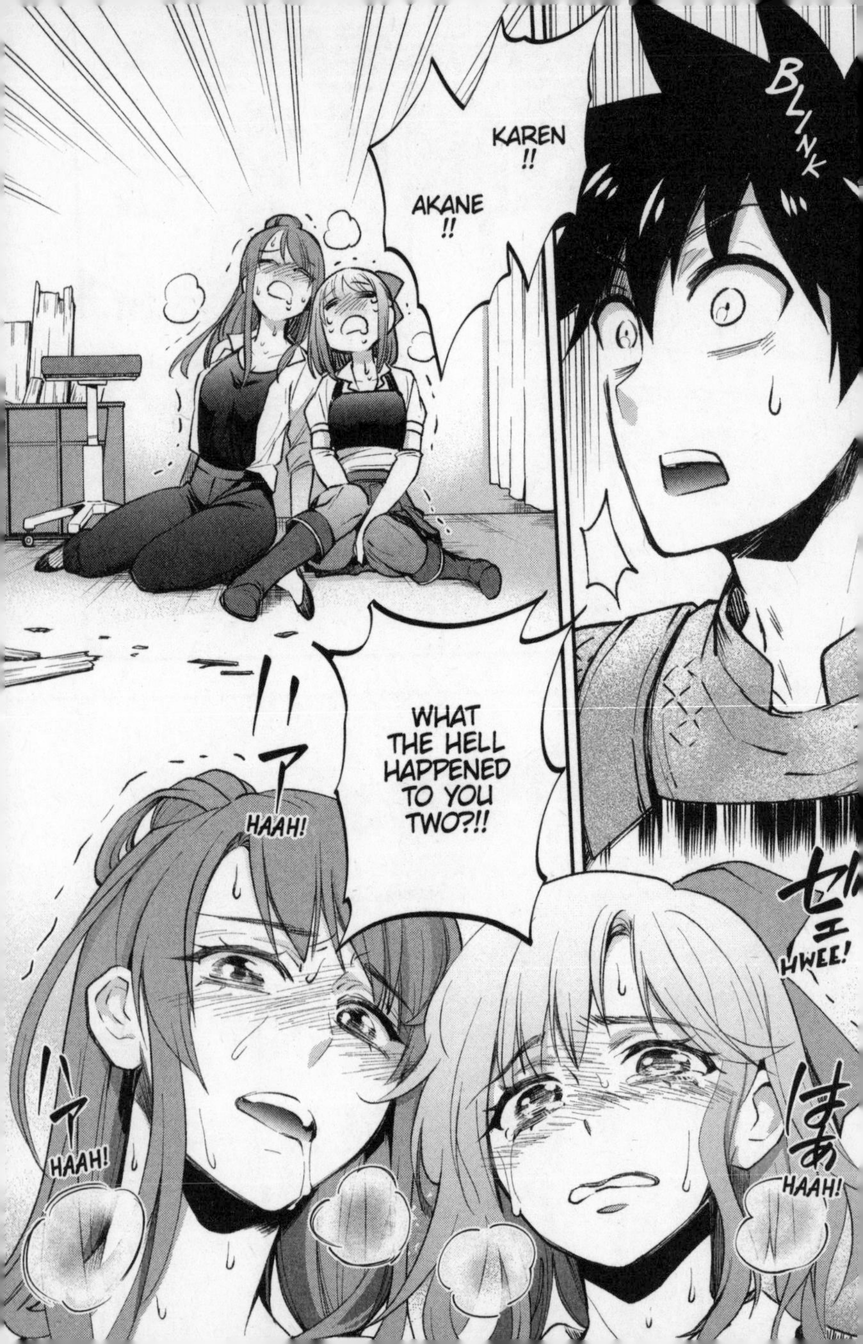
BLINK
KAREN !!
AKANE !!
WHAT THE HELL HAPPENED TO YOU TWO?!!
セェ HWEE!
はぁ HAAH!
ハァ HAAH!
ハァ HAAH!

CALL TO ADVENTURE!

DEFEATING DUNGEONS WITH A SKILL BOARD

5

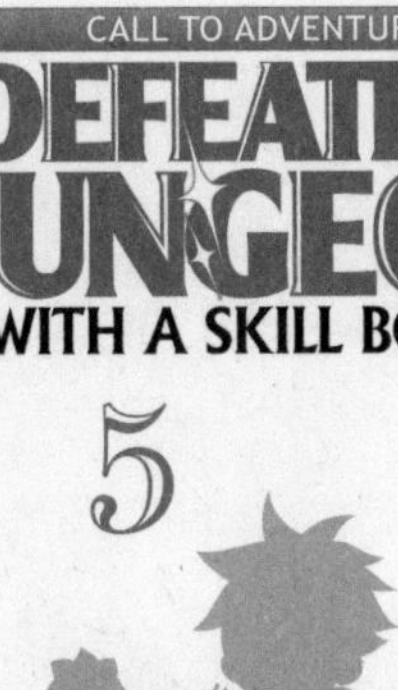

CALL TO ADVENTURE!

DEFEATING DUNGEONS

WITH A SKILL BOARD

5

Chapter 25

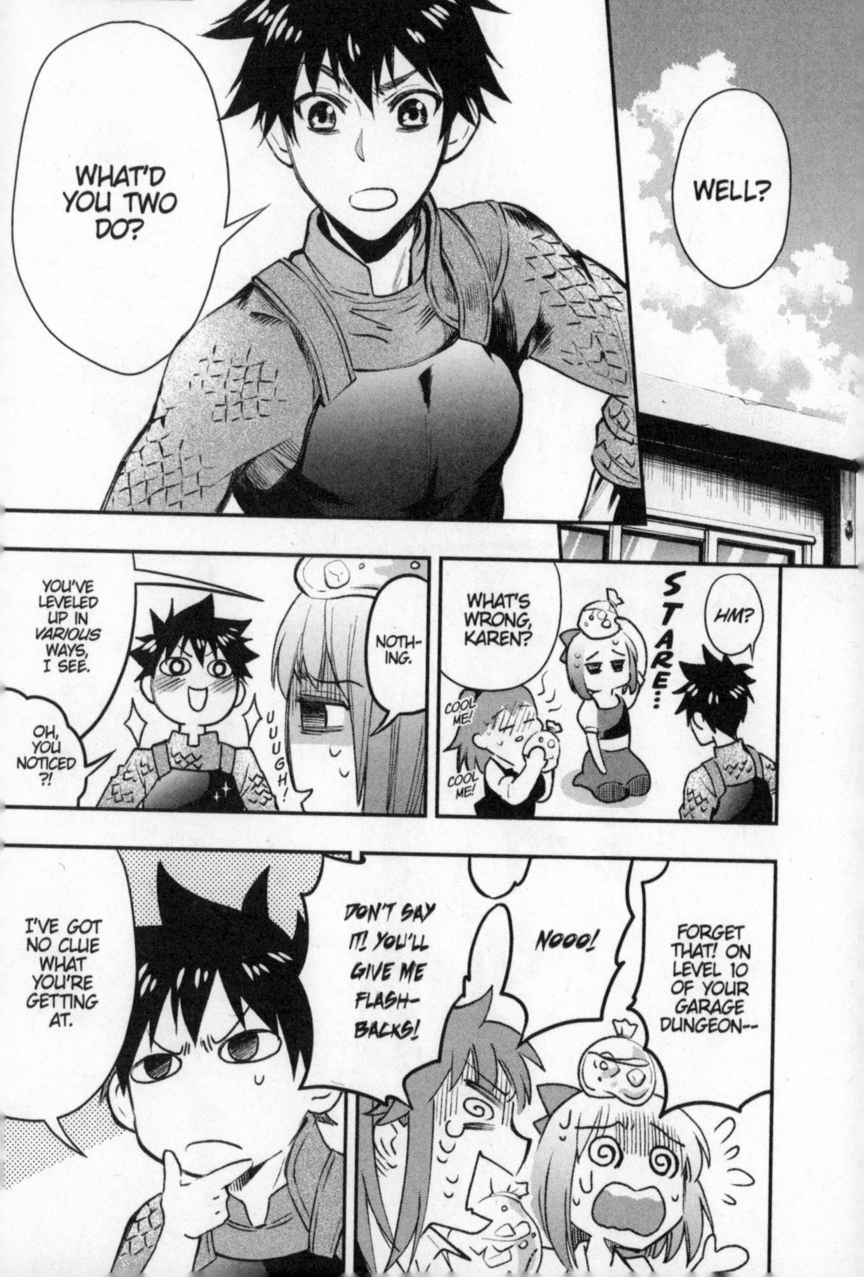
WELL?
WHAT'D YOU TWO DO?
HM?
STARE...
WHAT'S WRONG, KAREN?
COOL ME!
COOL ME!
NOTHING.
UUUGH!
YOU'VE LEVELED UP IN VARIOUS WAYS, I SEE.
OH, YOU NOTICED?!
FORGET THAT! ON LEVEL 10 OF YOUR GARAGE DUNGEON--
NOOO!
DON'T SAY IT! YOU'LL GIVE ME FLASHBACKS!
I'VE GOT NO CLUE WHAT YOU'RE GETTING AT.

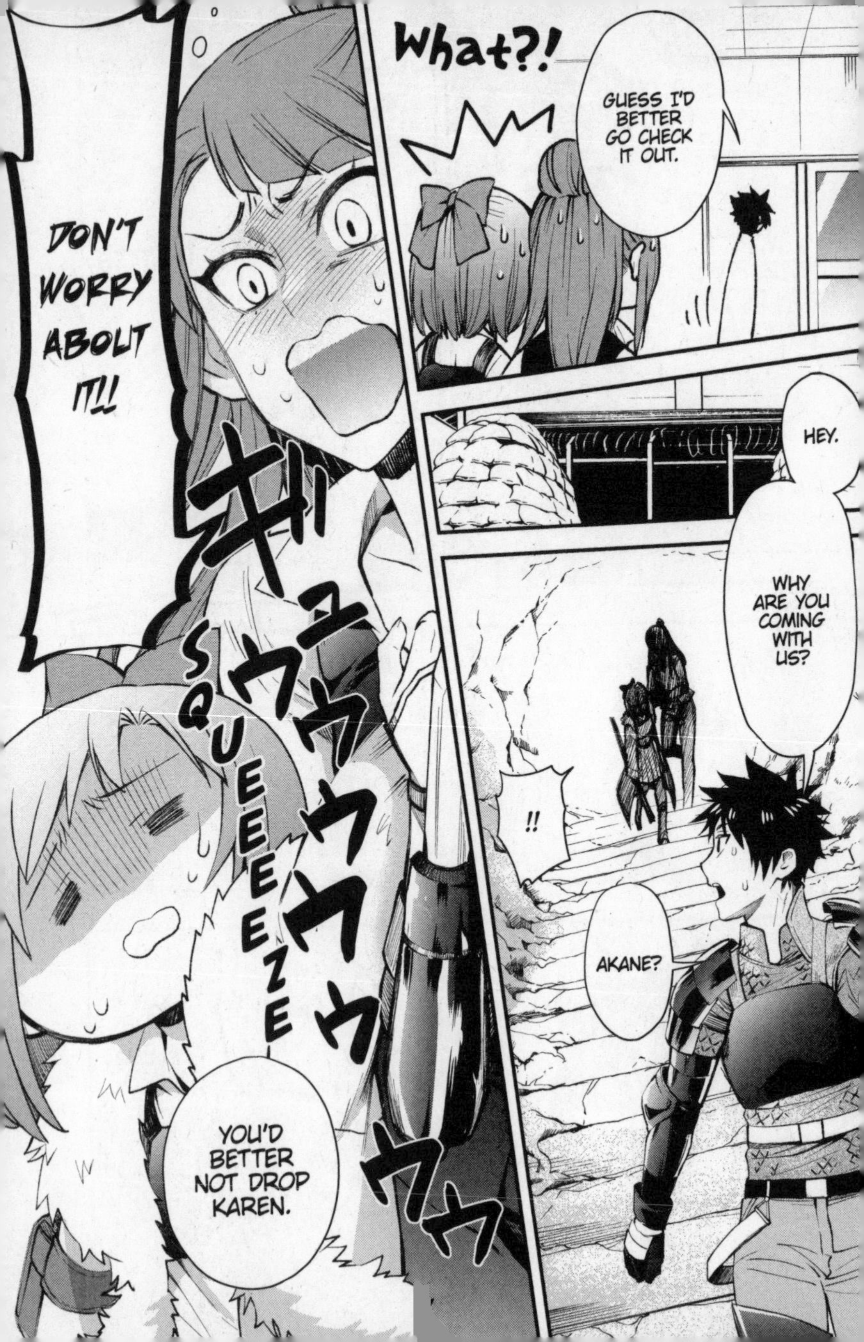

GUESS I'D BETTER GO CHECK IT OUT.
What?!
HEY.
WHY ARE YOU COMING WITH US?
!!
AKANE?
DON'T WORRY ABOUT IT!!
SQUEEEEZE
YOU'D BETTER NOT DROP KAREN.

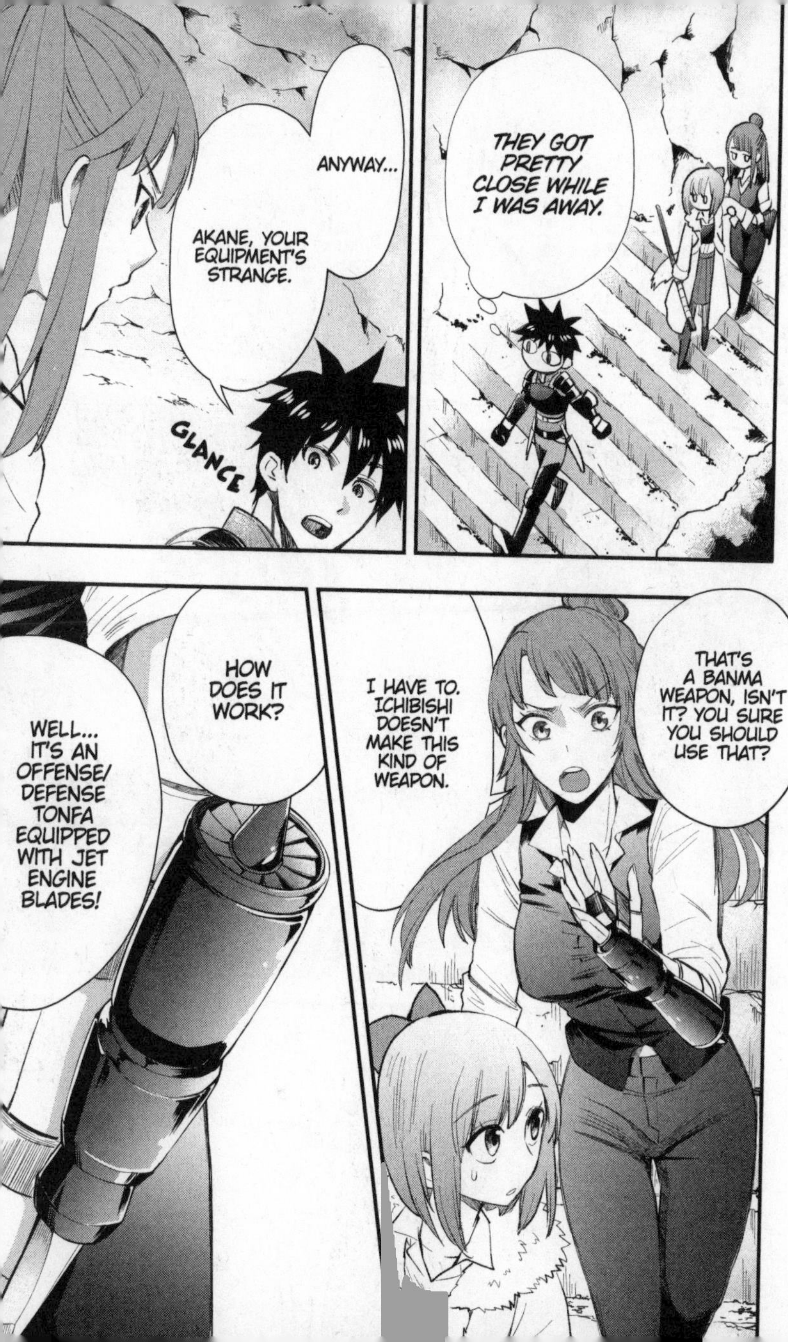
THEY GOT PRETTY CLOSE WHILE I WAS AWAY.
ANYWAY...
AKANE, YOUR EQUIPMENT'S STRANGE.
GLANCE
THAT'S A BANMA WEAPON, ISN'T IT? YOU SURE YOU SHOULD USE THAT?
I HAVE TO. ICHIBISHI DOESN'T MAKE THIS KIND OF WEAPON.
HOW DOES IT WORK?
WELL... IT'S AN OFFENSE/ DEFENSE TONFA EQUIPPED WITH JET ENGINE BLADES!

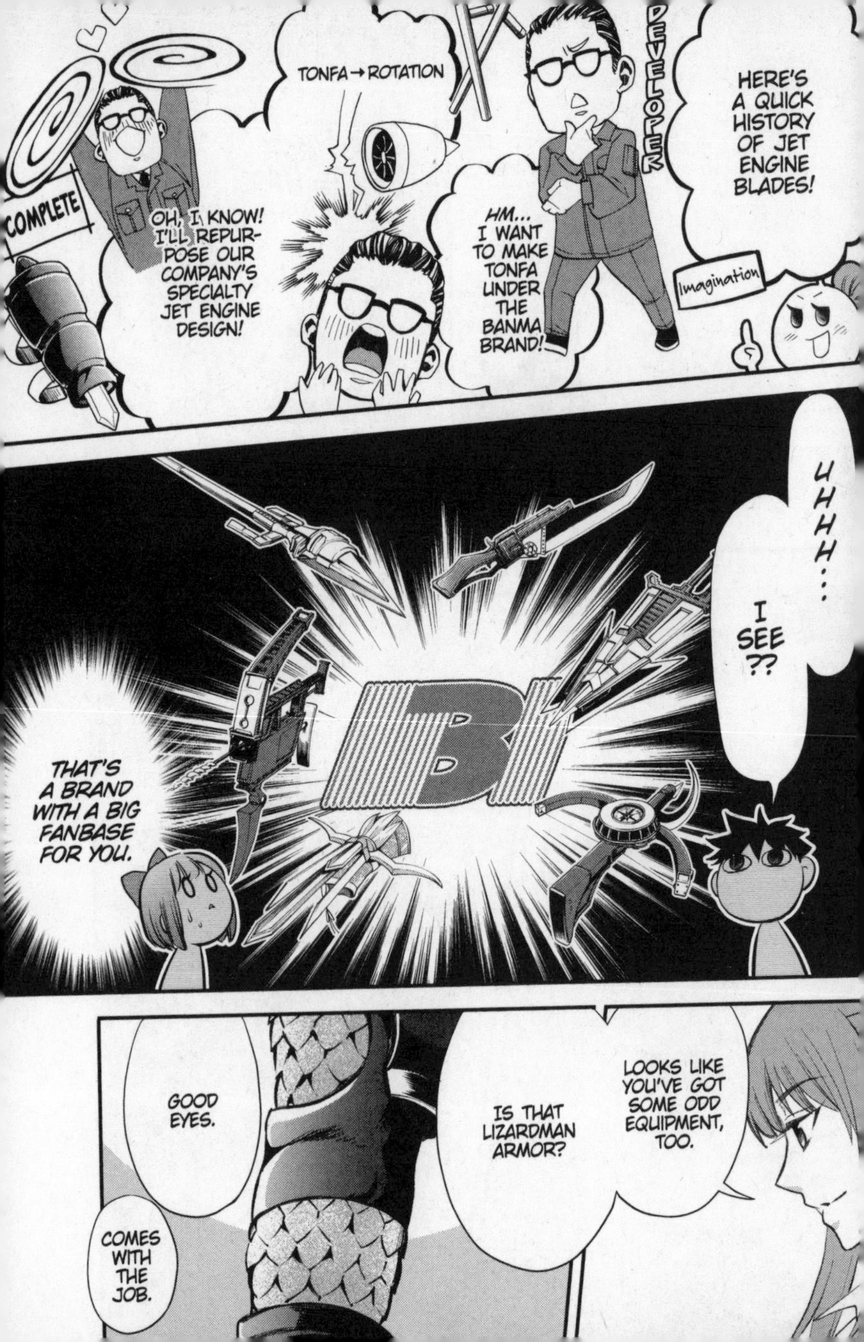
HERE'S A QUICK HISTORY OF JET ENGINE BLADES!
Imagination
DEVELOPER
HM... I WANT TO MAKE TONFA UNDER THE BANMA BRAND!
TONFA → ROTATION
OH, I KNOW! I'LL REPURPOSE OUR COMPANY'S SPECIALTY JET ENGINE DESIGN!
COMPLETE
UHHHH...
I SEE??
THAT'S A BRAND WITH A BIG FANBASE FOR YOU.
LOOKS LIKE YOU'VE GOT SOME ODD EQUIPMENT, TOO.
IS THAT LIZARDMAN ARMOR?
GOOD EYES.
COMES WITH THE JOB.

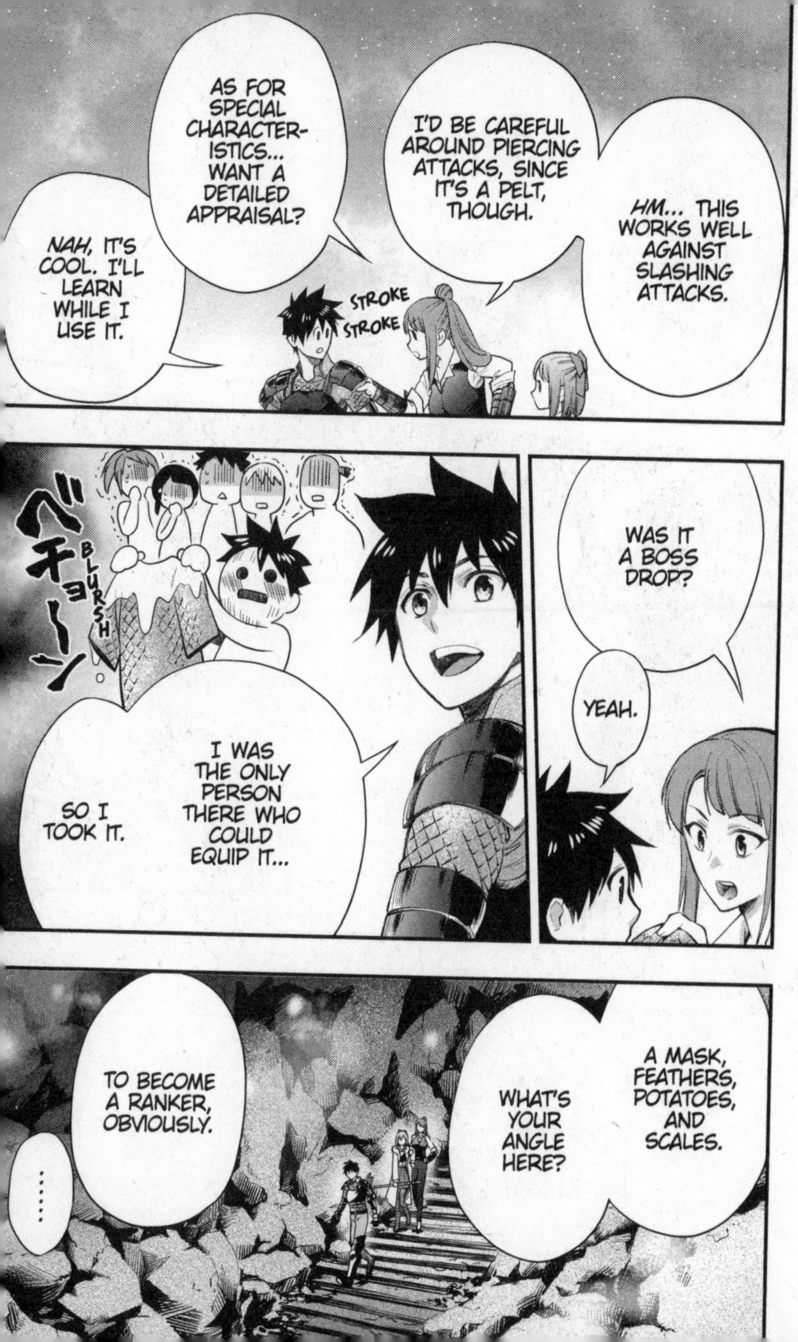
HM... THIS WORKS WELL AGAINST SLASHING ATTACKS.
I'D BE CAREFUL AROUND PIERCING ATTACKS, SINCE IT'S A PELT, THOUGH.
STROKE STROKE
AS FOR SPECIAL CHARACTER-ISTICS... WANT A DETAILED APPRAISAL?
NAH, IT'S COOL. I'LL LEARN WHILE I USE IT.
WAS IT A BOSS DROP?
YEAH.
I WAS THE ONLY PERSON THERE WHO COULD EQUIP IT...
SO I TOOK IT.
ベチョーン
BLURSH
A MASK, FEATHERS, POTATOES, AND SCALES.
WHAT'S YOUR ANGLE HERE?
TO BECOME A RANKER, OBVIOUSLY.
......

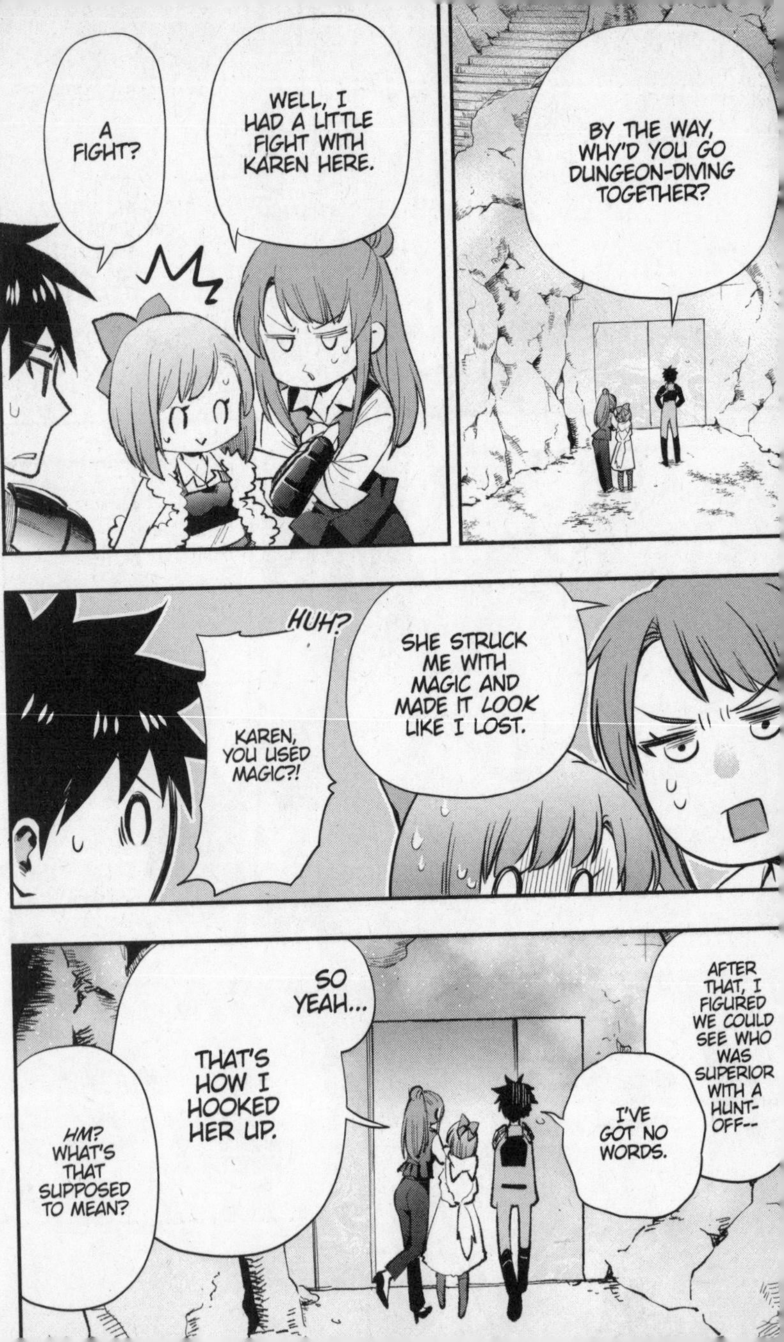
BY THE WAY, WHY'D YOU GO DUNGEON-DIVING TOGETHER?
WELL, I HAD A LITTLE FIGHT WITH KAREN HERE.
A FIGHT?
SHE STRUCK ME WITH MAGIC AND MADE IT *LOOK* LIKE I LOST.
HUH?
KAREN, YOU USED MAGIC?!
AFTER THAT, I FIGURED WE COULD SEE WHO WAS SUPERIOR WITH A HUNT-OFF--
I'VE GOT NO WORDS.
SO YEAH...
THAT'S HOW I HOOKED HER UP.
HM? WHAT'S THAT SUPPOSED TO MEAN?

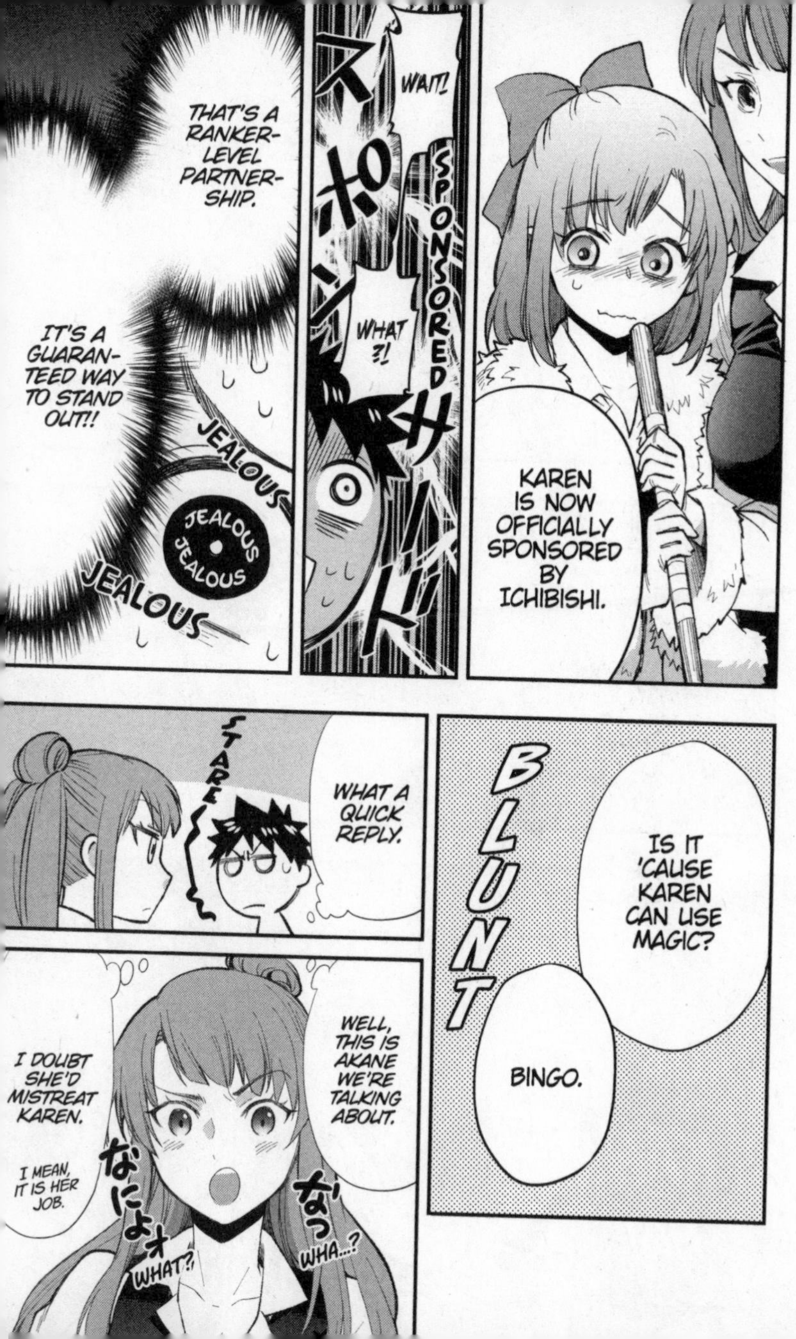
KAREN IS NOW OFFICIALLY SPONSORED BY ICHIBISHI.
WAIT!
SPONSORED
WHAT?!
THAT'S A RANKER-LEVEL PARTNERSHIP.
IT'S A GUARANTEED WAY TO STAND OUT!!
JEALOUS
JEALOUS JEALOUS
JEALOUS
BLUNT
IS IT 'CAUSE KAREN CAN USE MAGIC?
BINGO.
STARE
WHAT A QUICK REPLY.
WELL, THIS IS AKANE WE'RE TALKING ABOUT.
I DOUBT SHE'D MISTREAT KAREN.
I MEAN, IT IS HER JOB.
WHA...?
WHAT?!

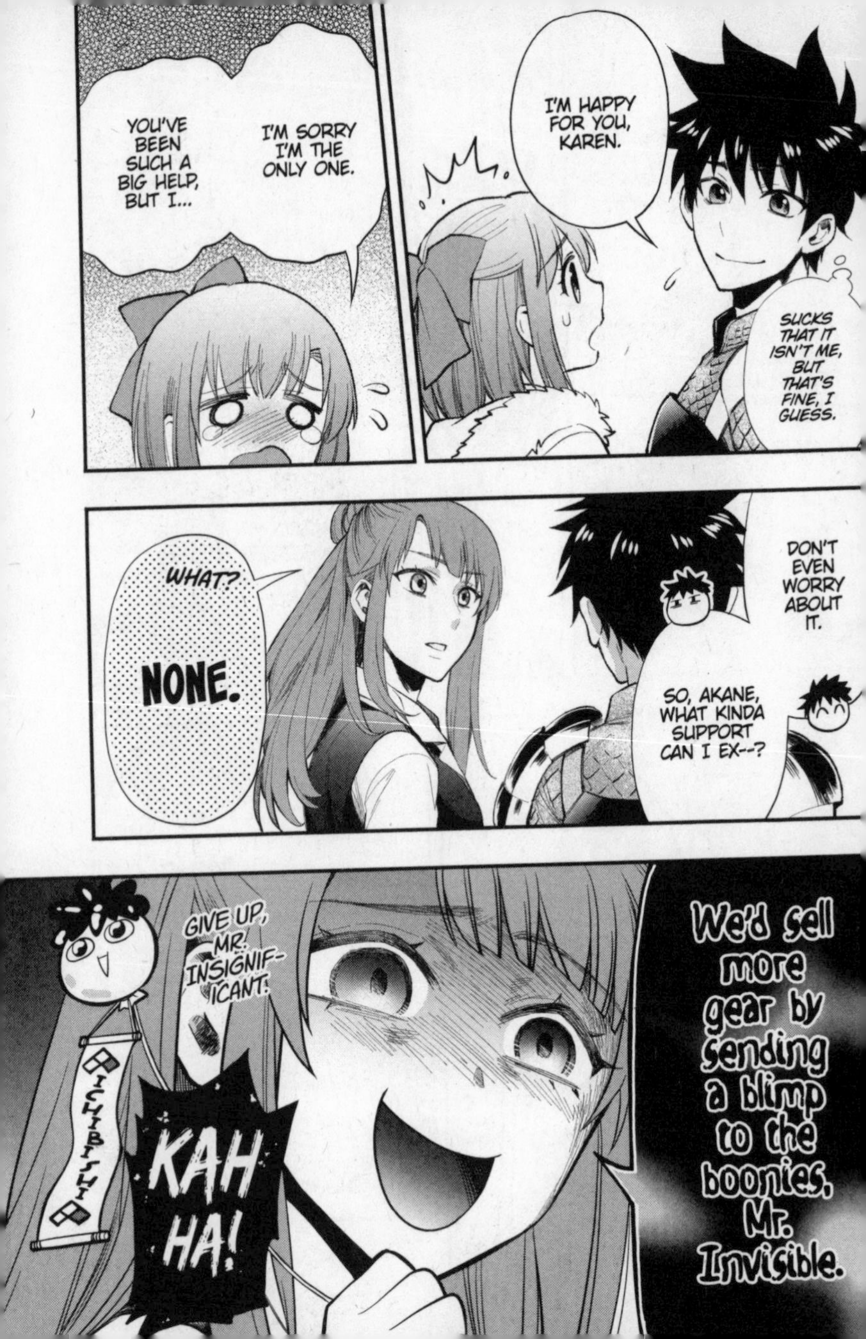
I'M HAPPY FOR YOU, KAREN.
SUCKS THAT IT ISN'T ME, BUT THAT'S FINE, I GUESS.
I'M SORRY I'M THE ONLY ONE.
YOU'VE BEEN SUCH A BIG HELP, BUT I...
DON'T EVEN WORRY ABOUT IT.
SO, AKANE, WHAT KINDA SUPPORT CAN I EX--?
WHAT? NONE.
We'd sell more gear by sending a blimp to the boonies, Mr. Invisible.
GIVE UP, MR. INSIGNIF-ICANT!
KAH HA!
ICHIBISHI

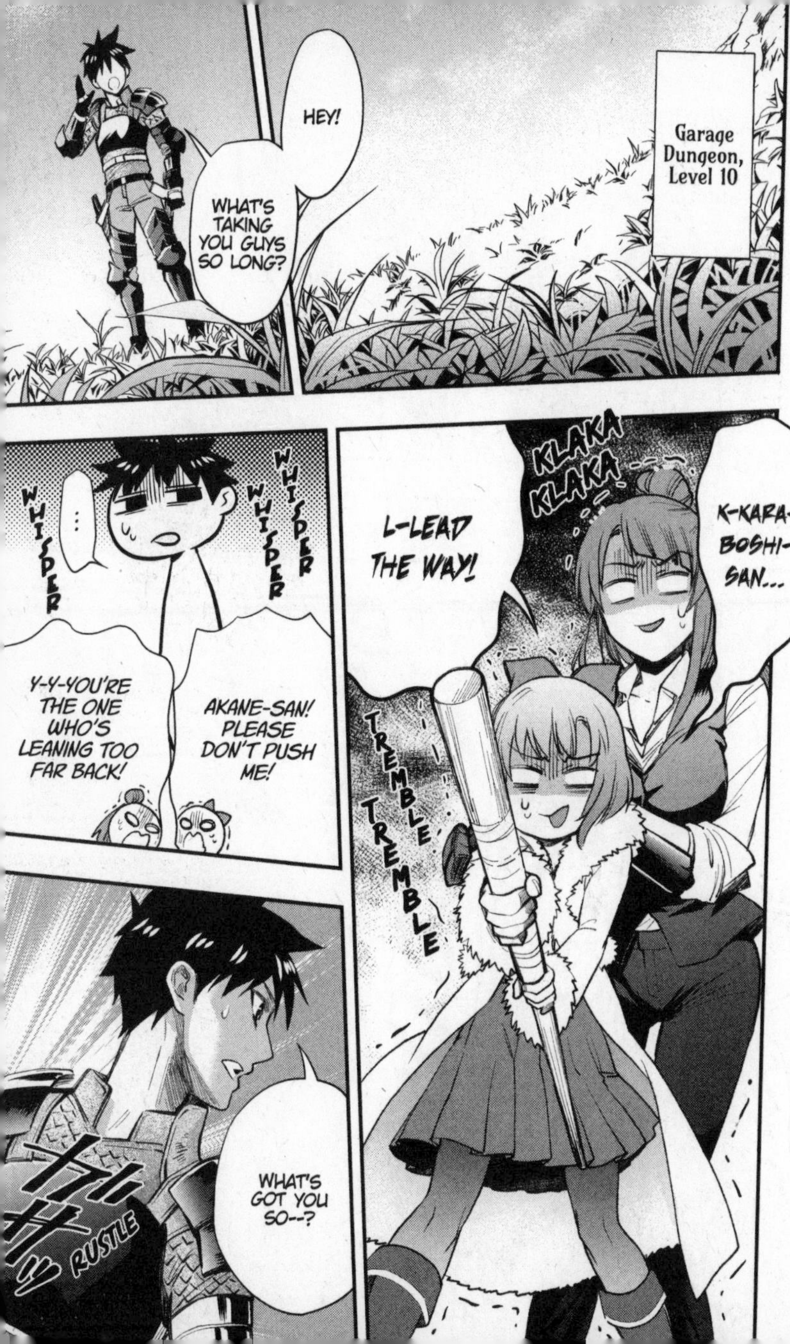
Garage Dungeon, Level 10
HEY!
WHAT'S TAKING YOU GUYS SO LONG?
K-KARA-BOSHI-SAN...
KLAKA KLAKA
L-LEAD THE WAY!
TREMBLE TREMBLE
WHISPER WHISPER
...
WHISPER
AKANE-SAN! PLEASE DON'T PUSH ME!
Y-Y-YOU'RE THE ONE WHO'S LEANING TOO FAR BACK!
WHAT'S GOT YOU SO--?
RUSTLE

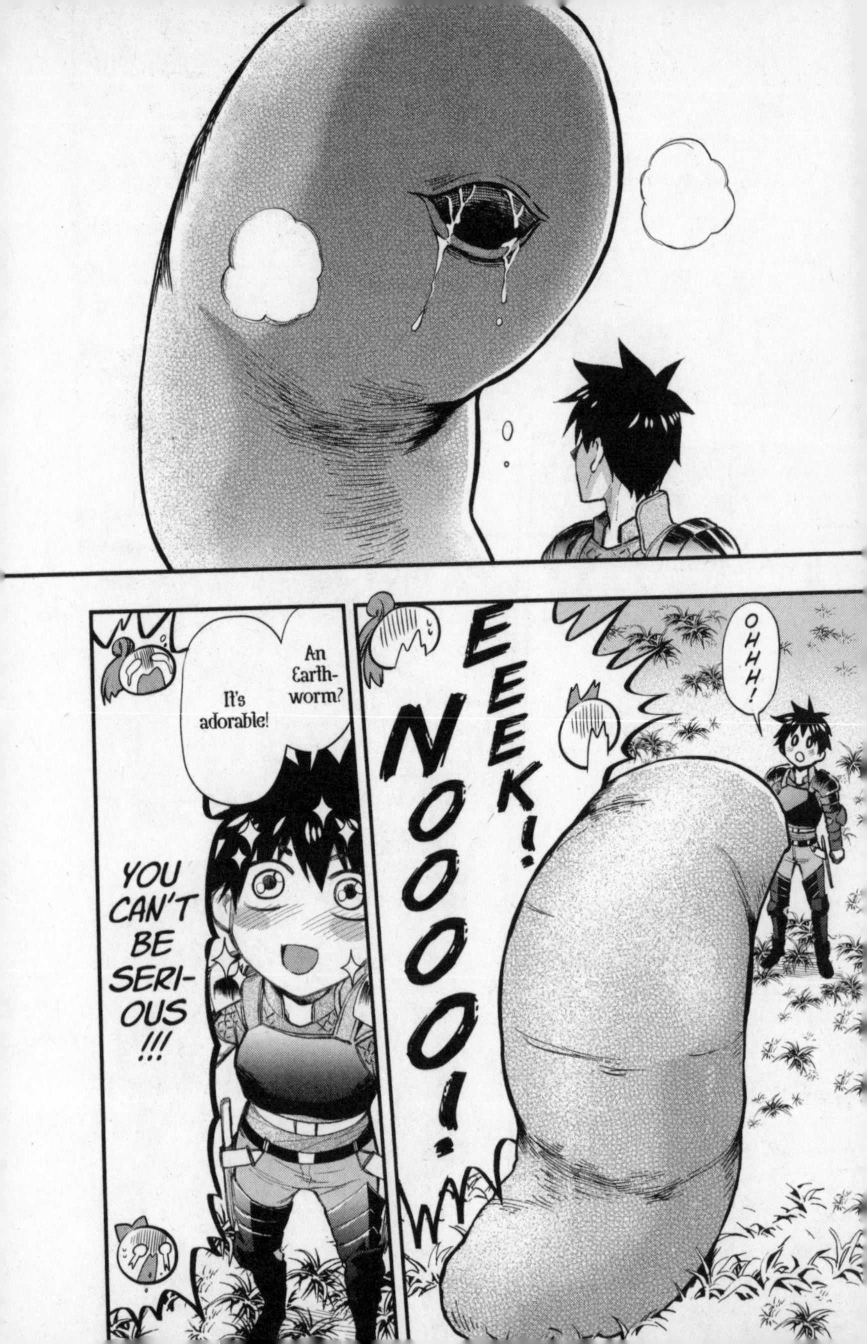
OHHH!
EEEEK! NOOOOO!
An Earth-worm? It's adorable!
YOU CAN'T BE SERI-OUS!!!

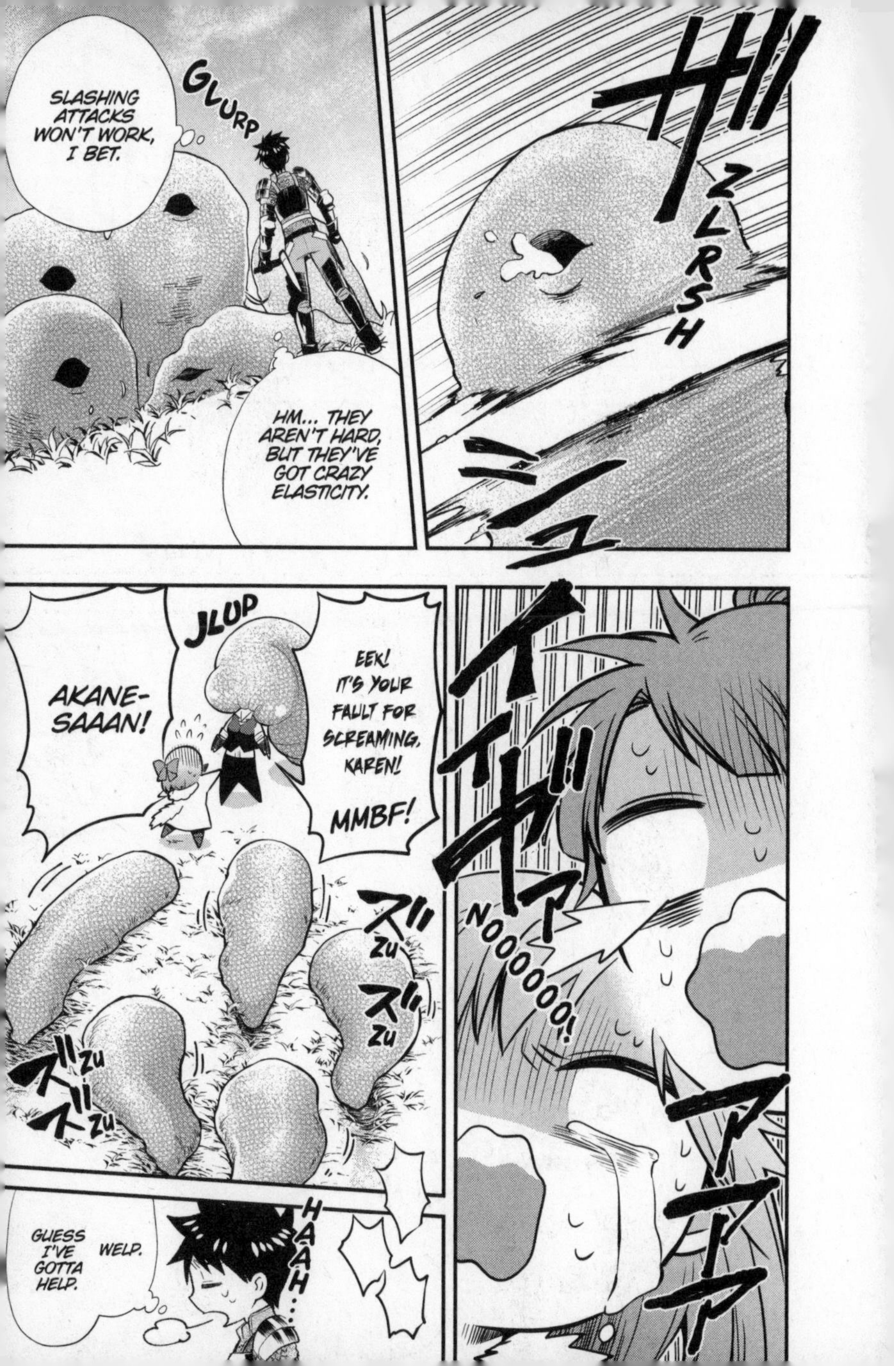

ZLRSH
GLURP
SLASHING ATTACKS WON'T WORK, I BET.
HM... THEY AREN'T HARD, BUT THEY'VE GOT CRAZY ELASTICITY.
NOOOOOOO!!
JLUP
EEK! IT'S YOUR FAULT FOR SCREAMING, KAREN!
MMBF!
AKANE-SAAAN!
ZU
ZU
ZU
ZU
HAAAH...
WELP.
GUESS I'VE GOTTA HELP.

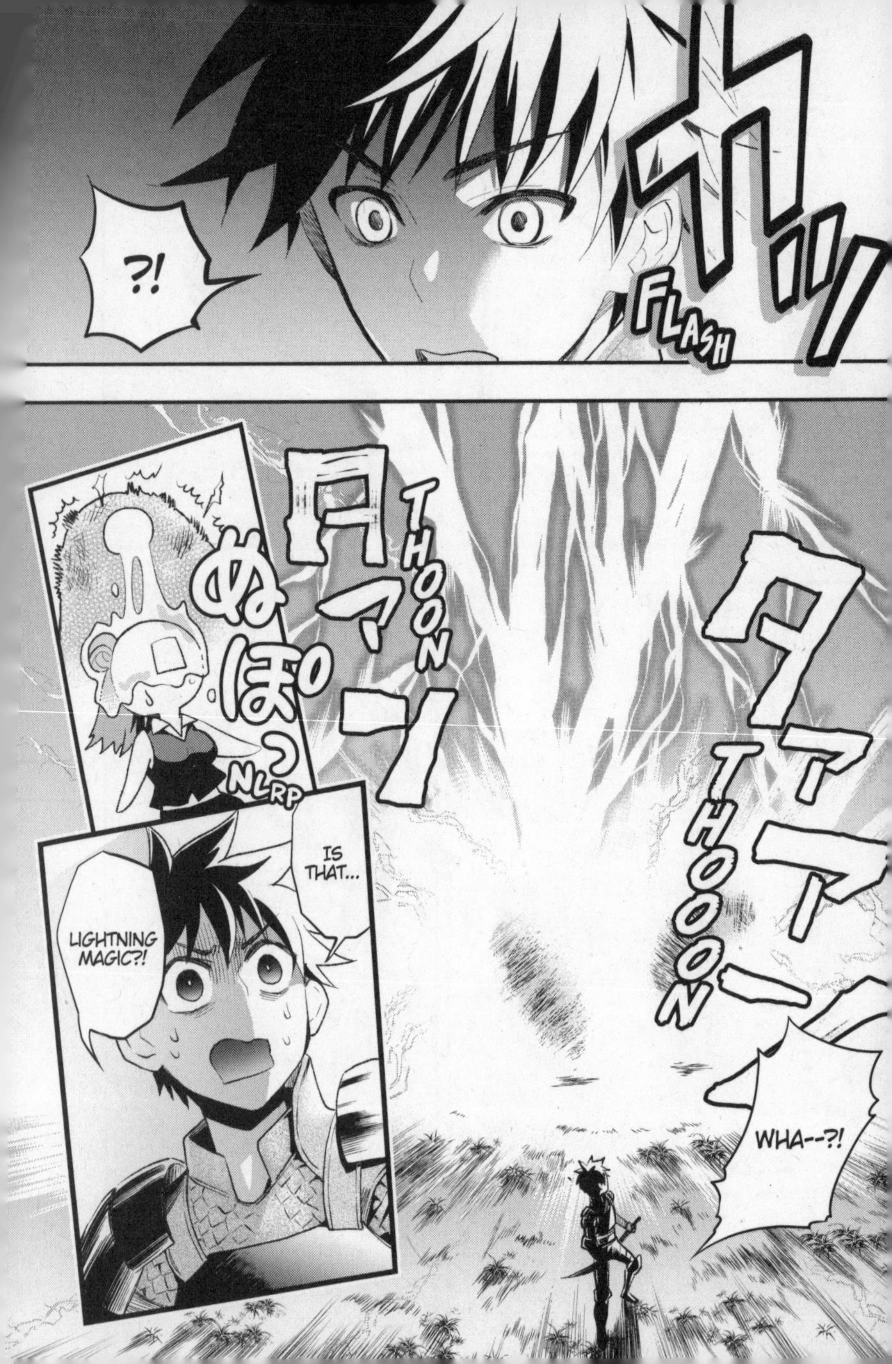
FLASH
?!
THOOOON
WHA--?!
THOON
NLRP
IS THAT...
LIGHTNING MAGIC?!

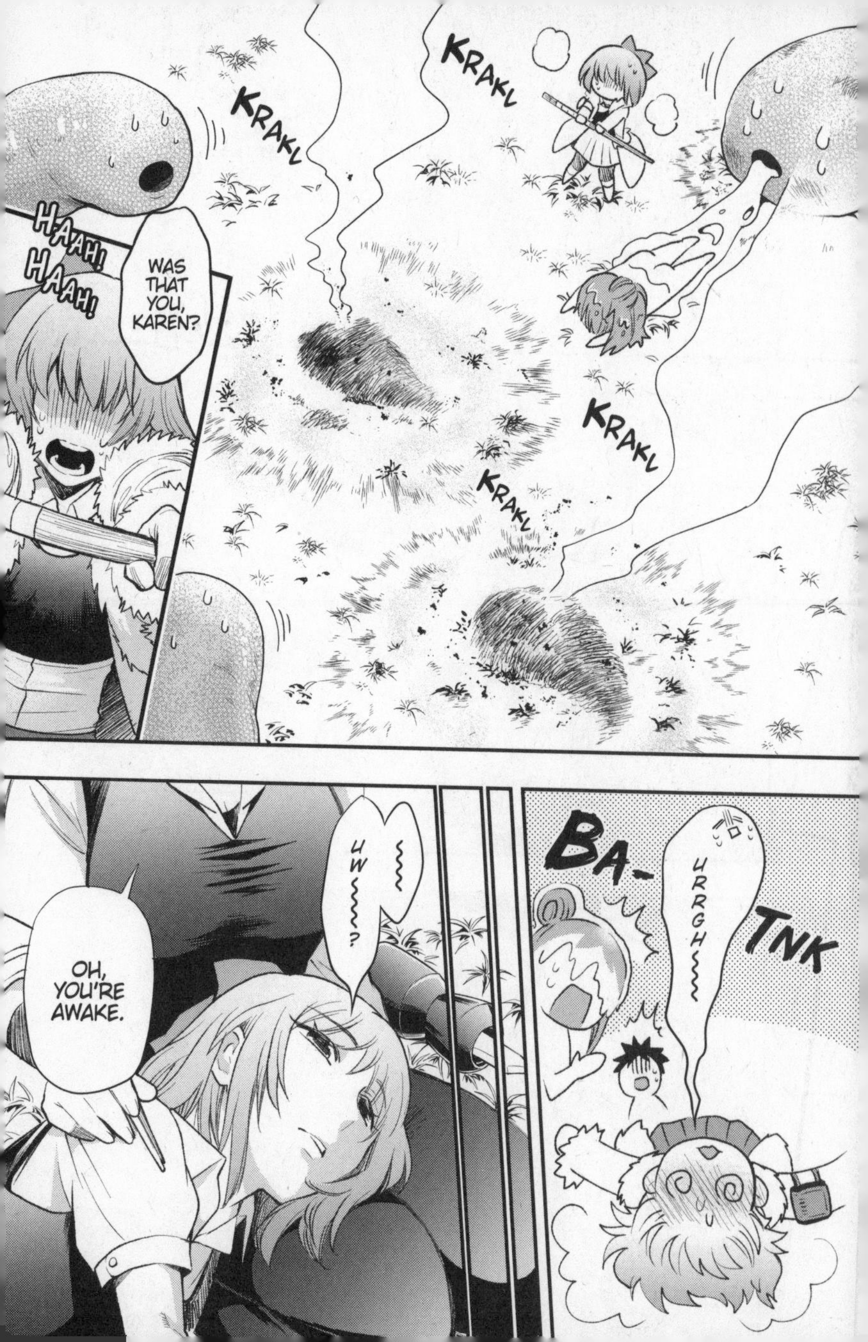
KRAKL
KRAKL
KRAKL
KRAKL
HAAAH! HAAAH!
WAS THAT YOU, KAREN?
BA-TNK
URRGH~~~
~~~ UW~~~?
OH, YOU'RE AWAKE.
~~~

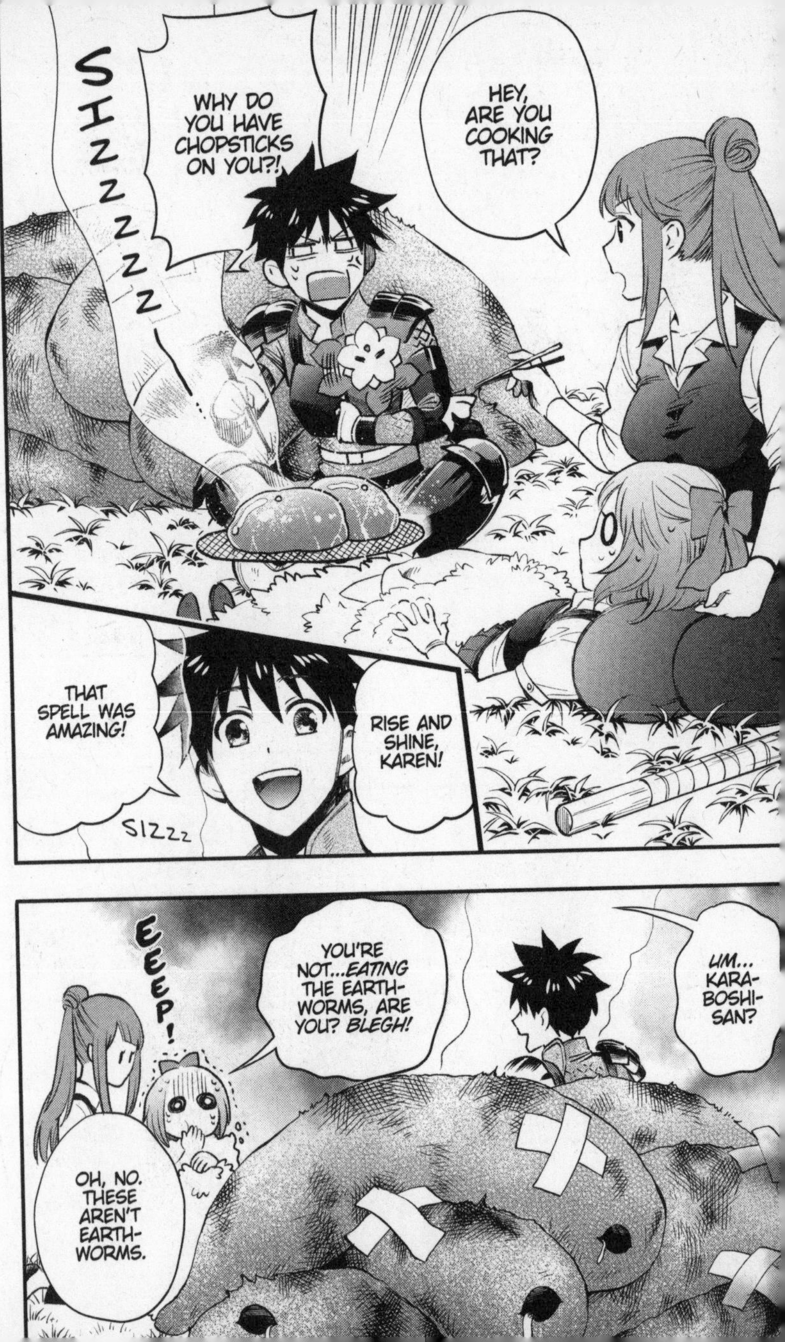
HEY, ARE YOU COOKING THAT?
WHY DO YOU HAVE CHOPSTICKS ON YOU?!
SIZZZZZZZ—
RISE AND SHINE, KAREN!
THAT SPELL WAS AMAZING!
SIZZzz
UM... KARA-BOSHI-SAN?
YOU'RE NOT...*EATING* THE EARTH-WORMS, ARE YOU? *BLEGH!*
EEEP!
OH, NO. THESE AREN'T EARTH-WORMS.

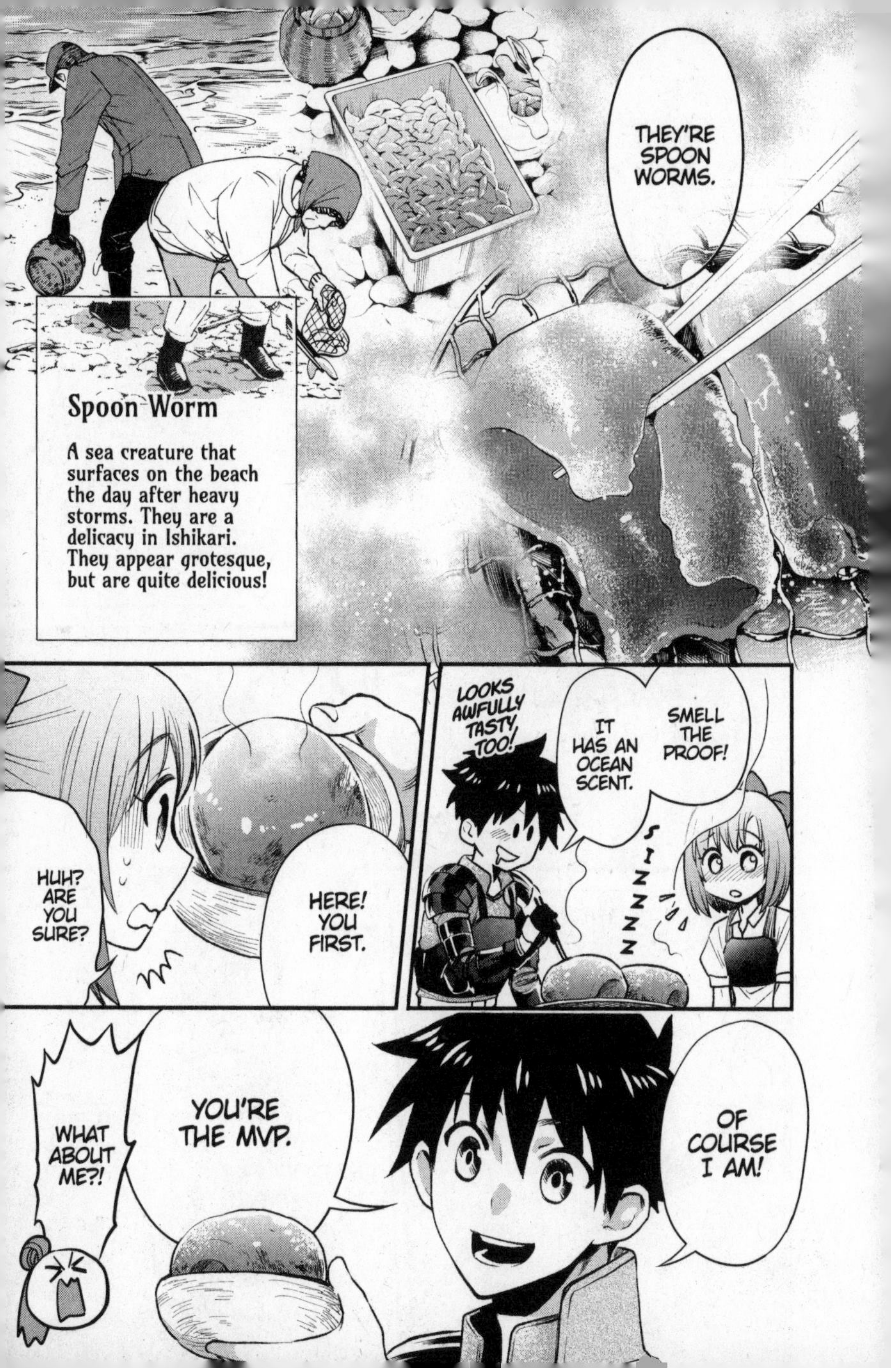
THEY'RE SPOON WORMS.
Spoon Worm
A sea creature that surfaces on the beach the day after heavy storms. They are a delicacy in Ishikari. They appear grotesque, but are quite delicious!
SMELL THE PROOF!
IT HAS AN OCEAN SCENT.
LOOKS AWFULLY TASTY TOO!
SIZZZZ
HERE! YOU FIRST.
HUH? ARE YOU SURE?
OF COURSE I AM!
YOU'RE THE MVP.
WHAT ABOUT ME?!

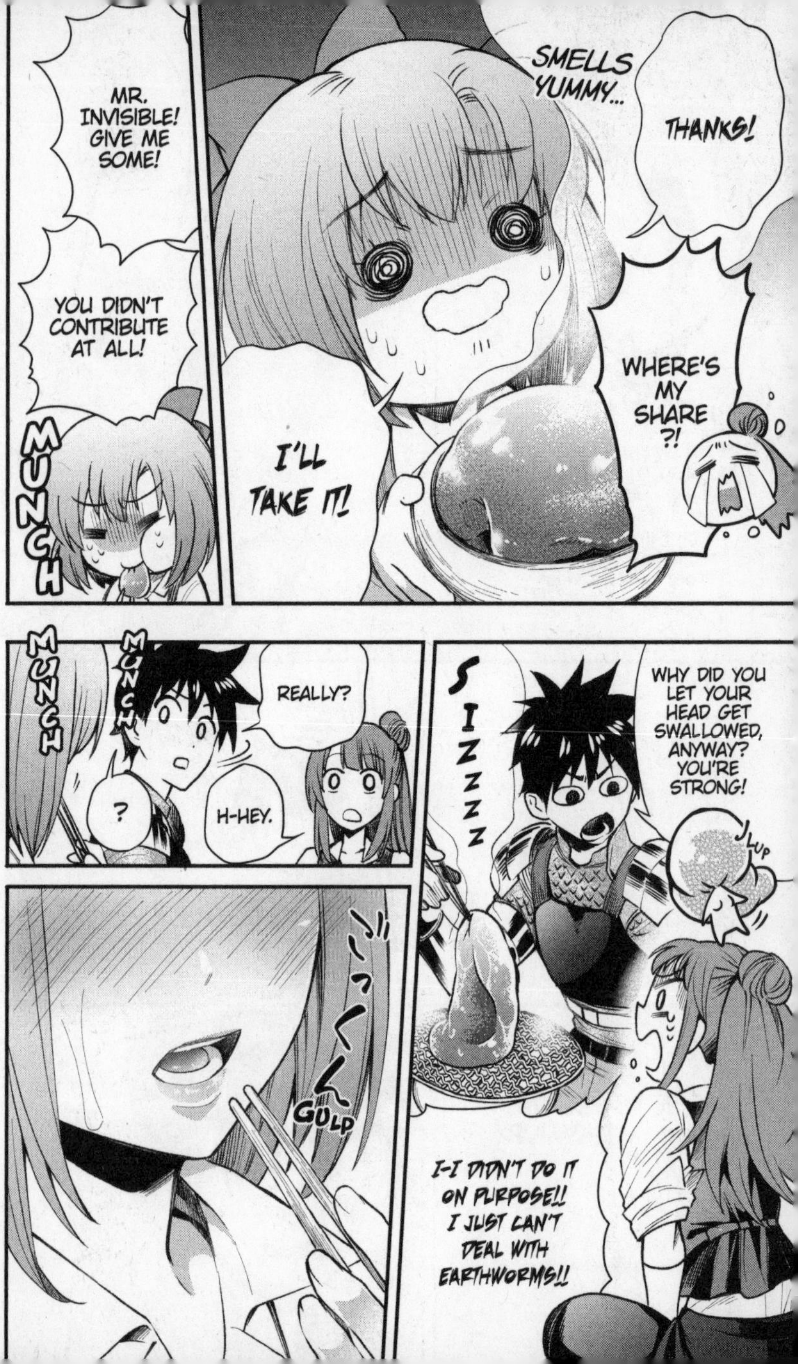

SMELLS YUMMY...
THANKS!
WHERE'S MY SHARE?!
I'LL TAKE IT!
MR. INVISIBLE! GIVE ME SOME!
YOU DIDN'T CONTRIBUTE AT ALL!
MUNCH
WHY DID YOU LET YOUR HEAD GET SWALLOWED, ANYWAY? YOU'RE STRONG!
SIZZZZ
JLUP
I-I DIDN'T DO IT ON PURPOSE!! I JUST CAN'T DEAL WITH EARTHWORMS!!
REALLY?
MUNCH
MUNCH
H-HEY.
?
GULP

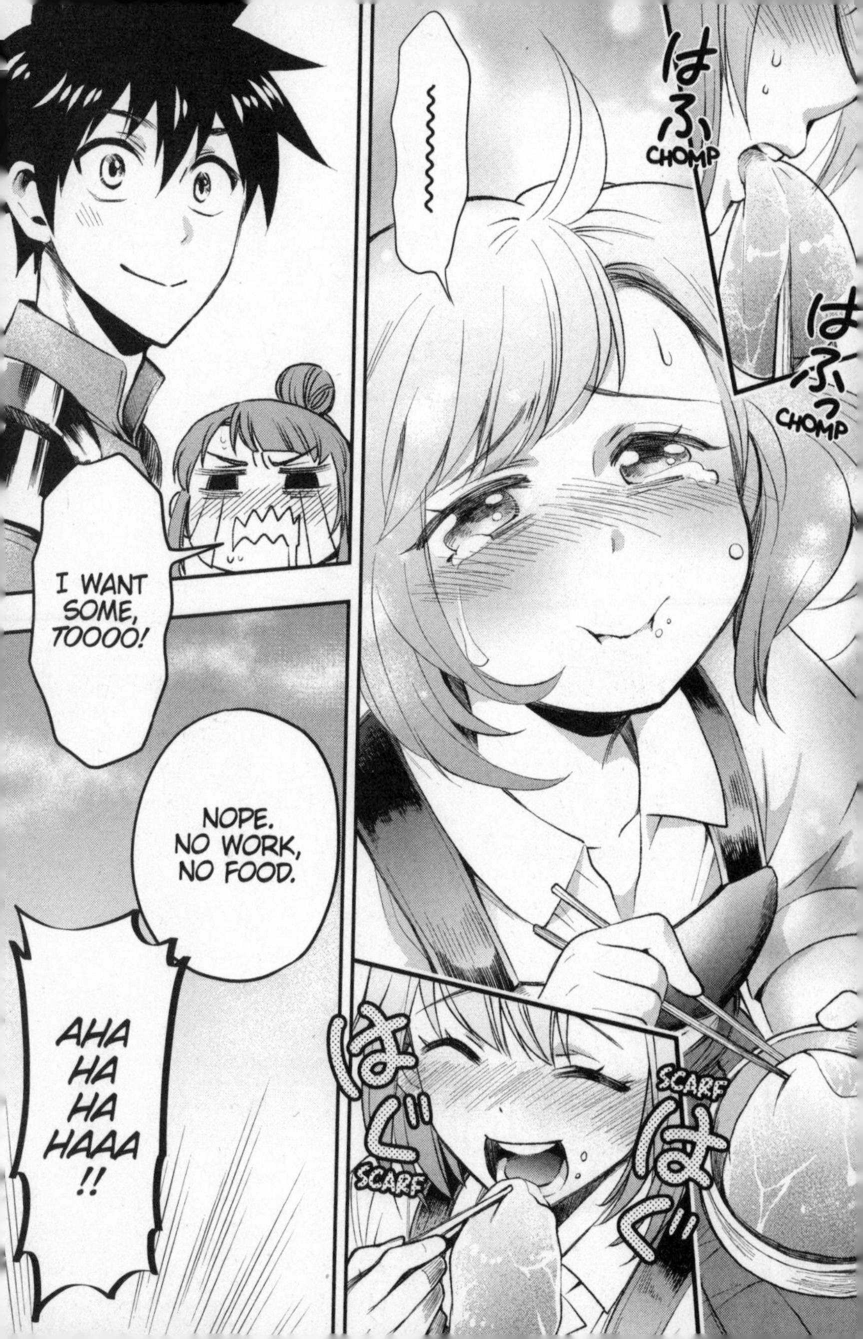
はふ
CHOMP
はふっ
CHOMP
~
はぐ
SCARF
はぐ
SCARF
I WANT SOME, TOOOO!
NOPE. NO WORK, NO FOOD.
AHA HA HA HAAAA!!

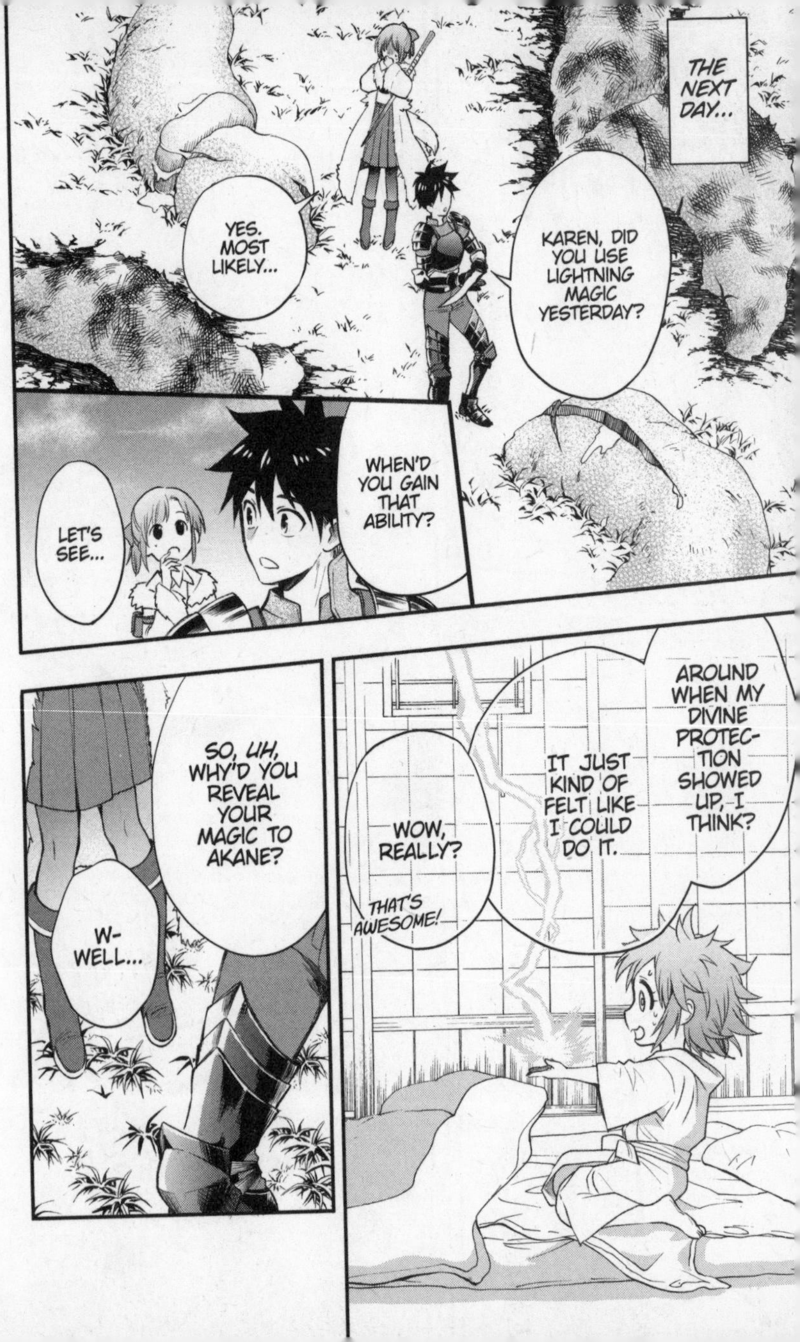
THE NEXT DAY...
KAREN, DID YOU USE LIGHTNING MAGIC YESTERDAY?
YES. MOST LIKELY...
WHEN'D YOU GAIN THAT ABILITY?
LET'S SEE...
AROUND WHEN MY DIVINE PROTECTION SHOWED UP, I THINK?
IT JUST KIND OF FELT LIKE I COULD DO IT.
WOW, REALLY?
THAT'S AWESOME!
SO, UH, WHY'D YOU REVEAL YOUR MAGIC TO AKANE?
W-WELL...

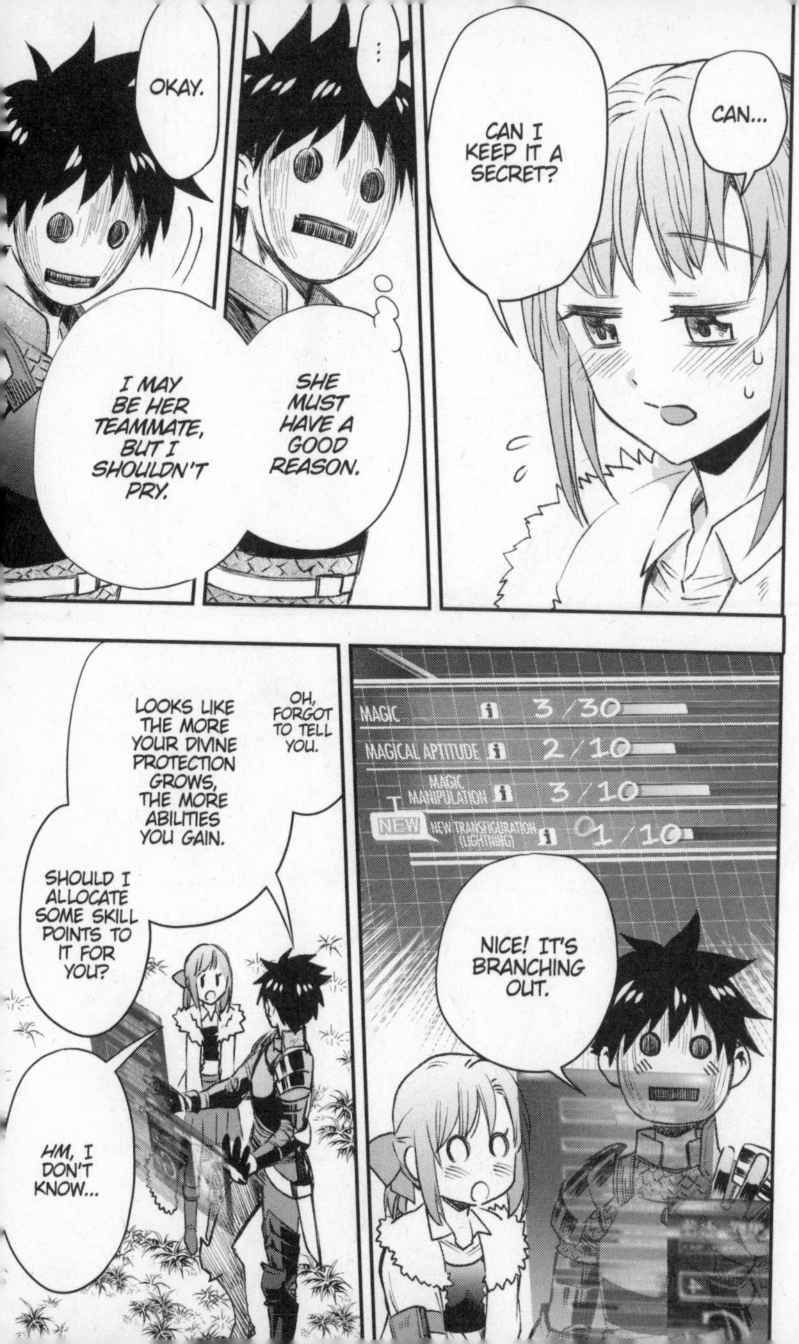
CAN...
CAN I KEEP IT A SECRET?
...
SHE MUST HAVE A GOOD REASON.
OKAY.
I MAY BE HER TEAMMATE, BUT I SHOULDN'T PRY.
MAGIC 3/30
MAGICAL APTITUDE 2/10
MAGIC MANIPULATION 3/10
NEW
NEW TRANSFIGURATION (LIGHTNING) 0 1/10
NICE! IT'S BRANCHING OUT.
OH, FORGOT TO TELL YOU.
LOOKS LIKE THE MORE YOUR DIVINE PROTECTION GROWS, THE MORE ABILITIES YOU GAIN.
SHOULD I ALLOCATE SOME SKILL POINTS TO IT FOR YOU?
HM, I DON'T KNOW...

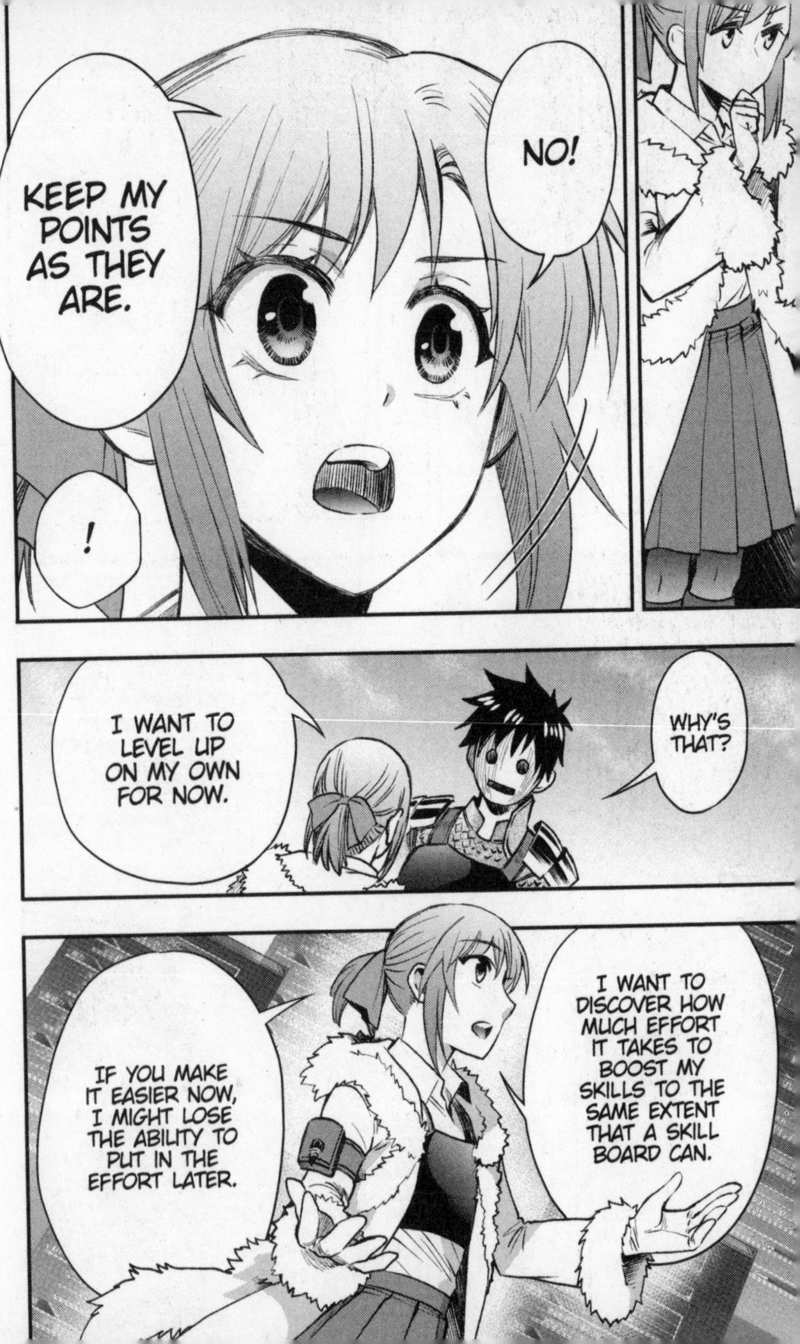
NO!
KEEP MY POINTS AS THEY ARE.
!
WHY'S THAT?
I WANT TO LEVEL UP ON MY OWN FOR NOW.
I WANT TO DISCOVER HOW MUCH EFFORT IT TAKES TO BOOST MY SKILLS TO THE SAME EXTENT THAT A SKILL BOARD CAN.
IF YOU MAKE IT EASIER NOW, I MIGHT LOSE THE ABILITY TO PUT IN THE EFFORT LATER.

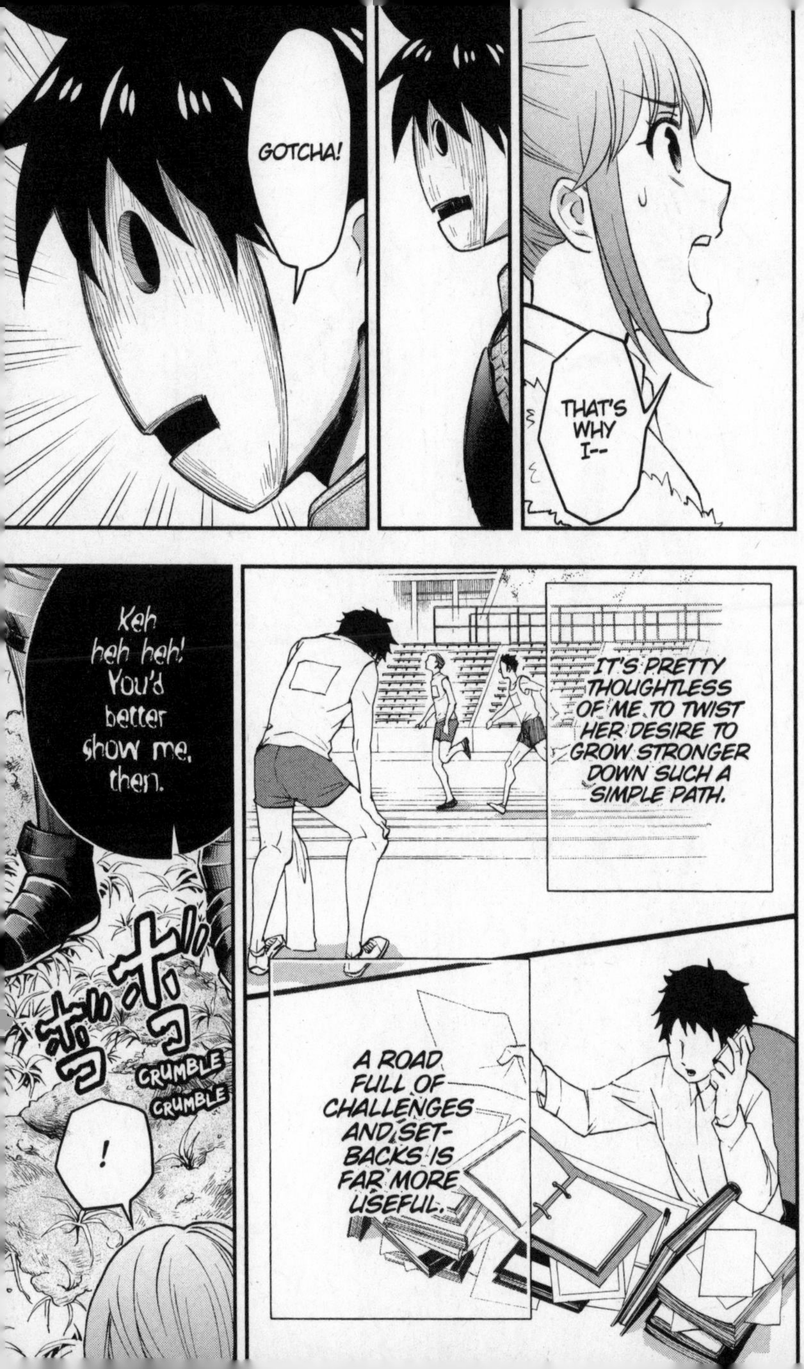
THAT'S WHY I--
GOTCHA!
IT'S PRETTY THOUGHTLESS OF ME TO TWIST HER DESIRE TO GROW STRONGER DOWN SUCH A SIMPLE PATH.
A ROAD FULL OF CHALLENGES AND SET-BACKS IS FAR MORE USEFUL.
Keh heh heh! You'd better show me, then.
CRUMBLE CRUMBLE
!

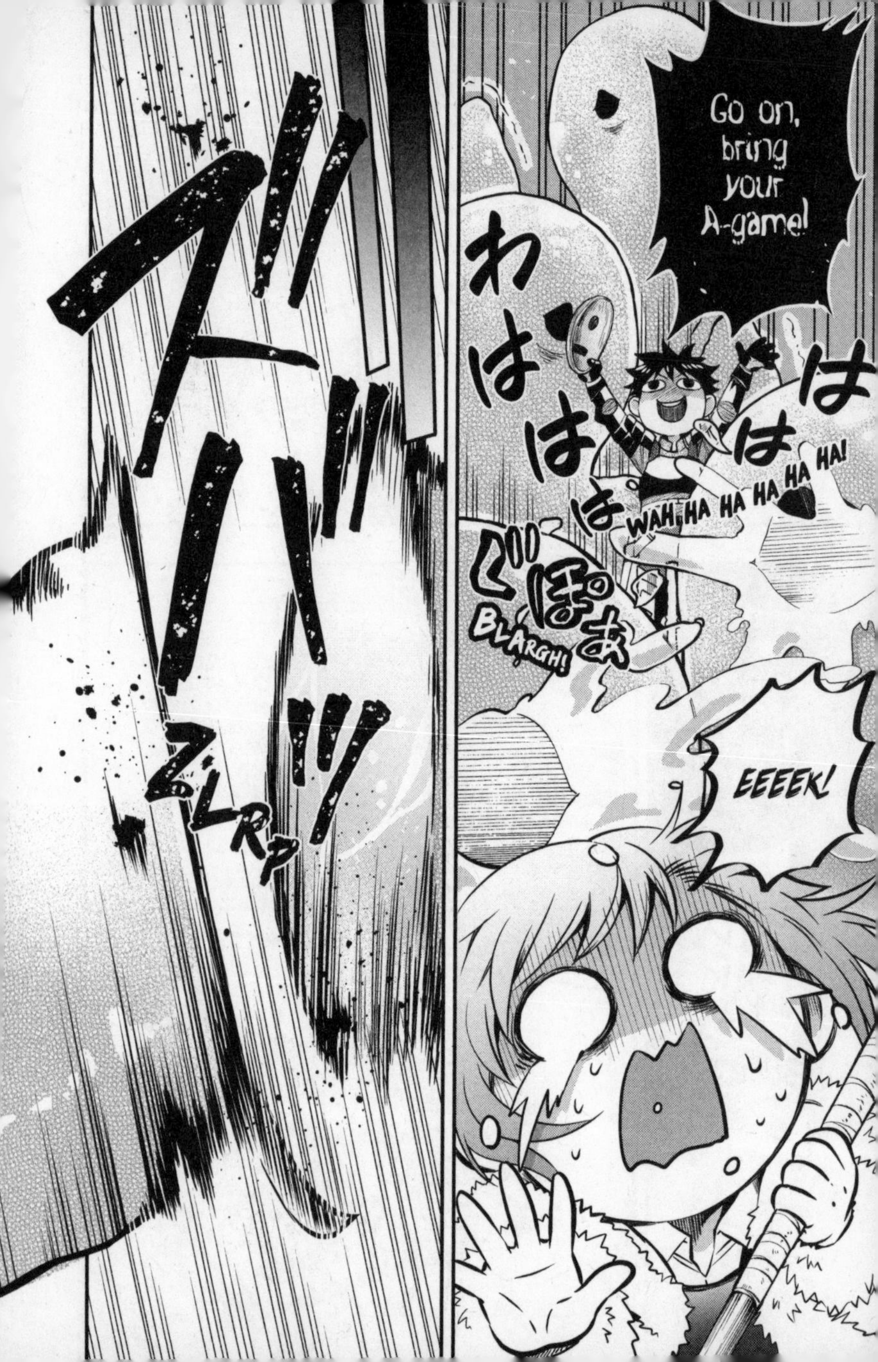
Go on, bring your A-game!
わははははは
WAH HA HA HA HA HA!
ぐぽぁ
BLARGH!
EEEEK!
ZLRP

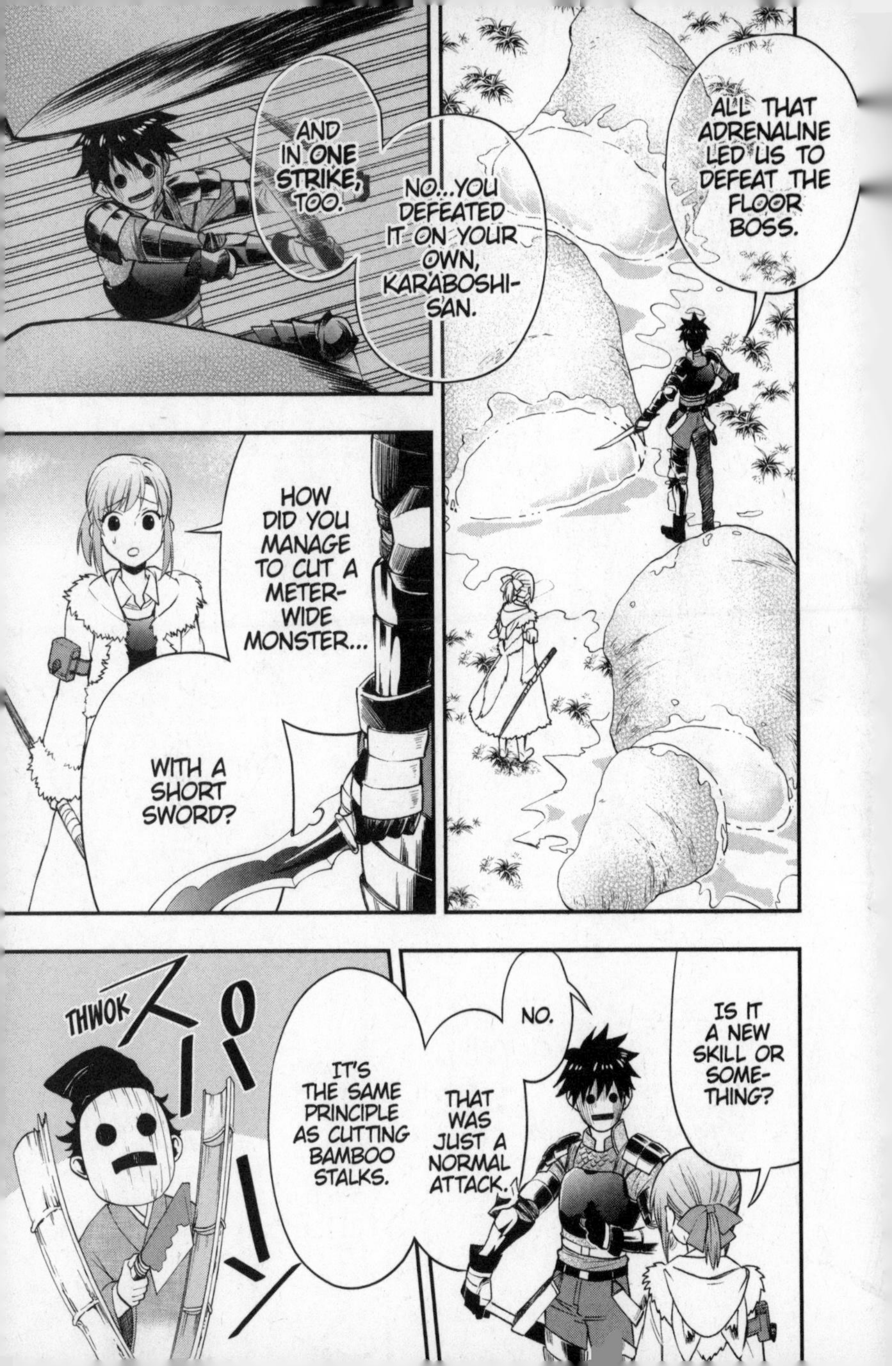

ALL THAT ADRENALINE LED US TO DEFEAT THE FLOOR BOSS.
NO...YOU DEFEATED IT ON YOUR OWN, KARABOSHI-SAN.
AND IN ONE STRIKE, TOO.
HOW DID YOU MANAGE TO CUT A METER-WIDE MONSTER...
WITH A SHORT SWORD?
IS IT A NEW SKILL OR SOME-THING?
NO.
THAT WAS JUST A NORMAL ATTACK.
IT'S THE SAME PRINCIPLE AS CUTTING BAMBOO STALKS.
THWOK

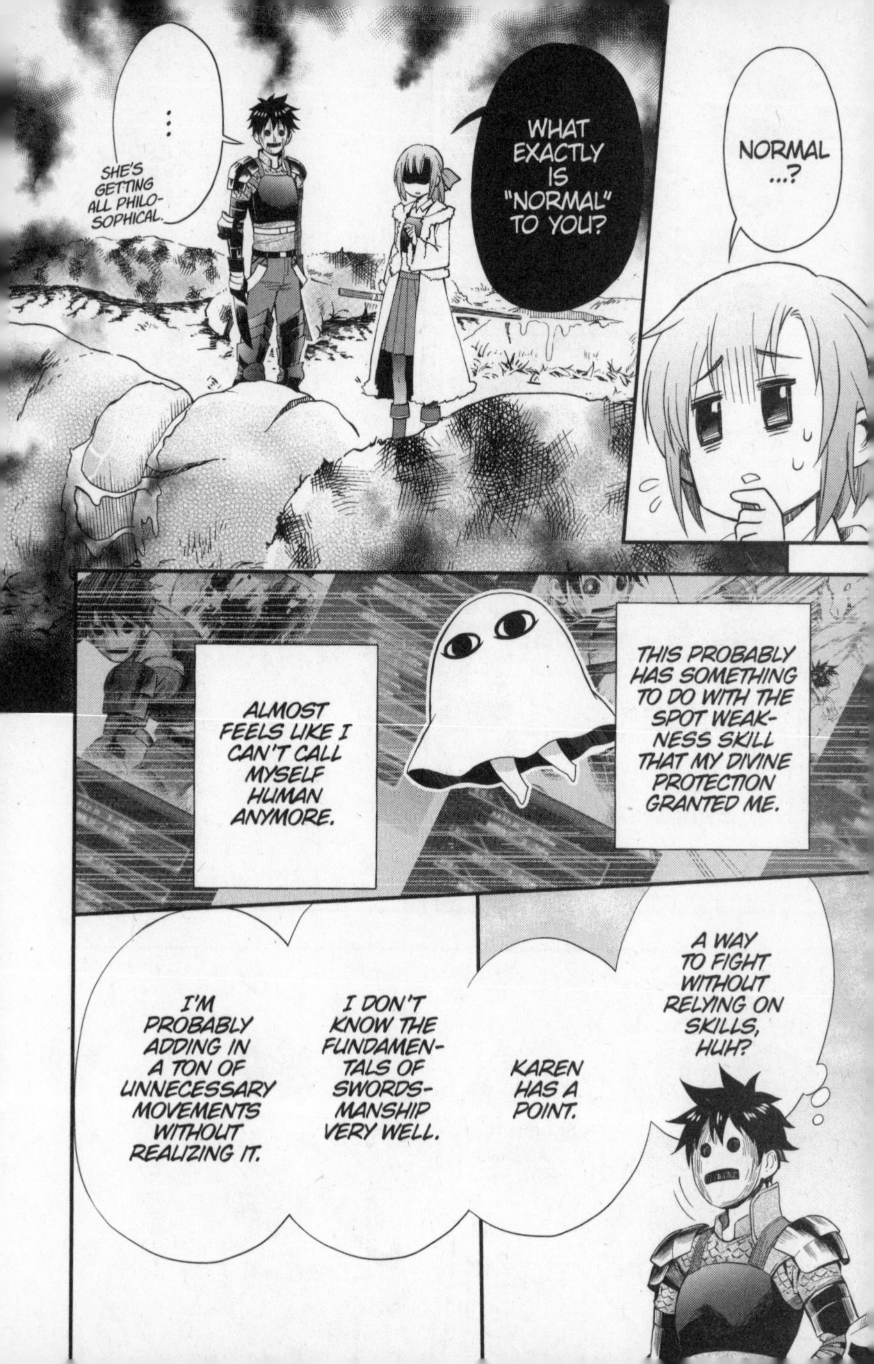
NORMAL ...?
WHAT EXACTLY IS "NORMAL" TO YOU?
...
SHE'S GETTING ALL PHILO-SOPHICAL.
THIS PROBABLY HAS SOMETHING TO DO WITH THE SPOT WEAK-NESS SKILL THAT MY DIVINE PROTECTION GRANTED ME.
ALMOST FEELS LIKE I CAN'T CALL MYSELF HUMAN ANYMORE.
A WAY TO FIGHT WITHOUT RELYING ON SKILLS, HUH?
KAREN HAS A POINT.
I DON'T KNOW THE FUNDAMEN-TALS OF SWORDS-MANSHIP VERY WELL.
I'M PROBABLY ADDING IN A TON OF UNNECESSARY MOVEMENTS WITHOUT REALIZING IT.

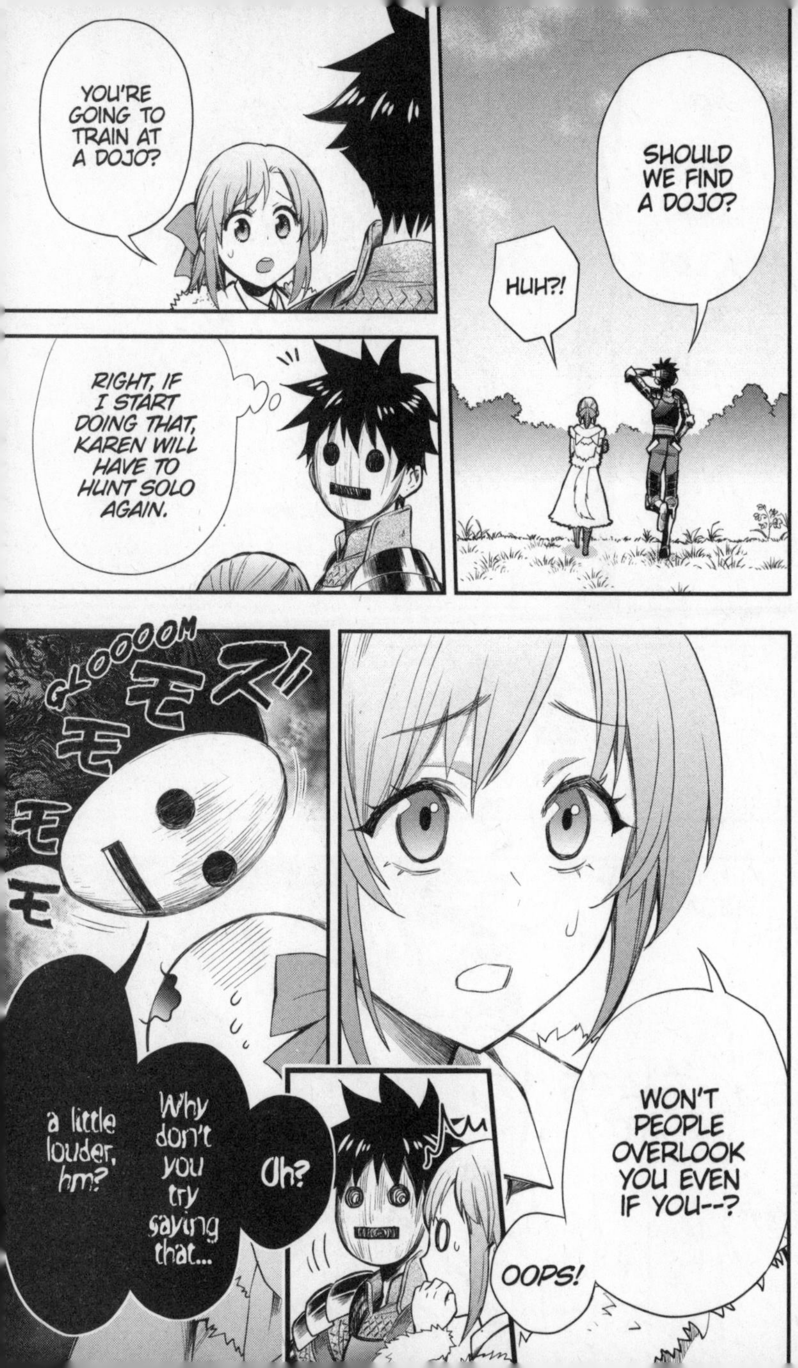
SHOULD WE FIND A DOJO?
HUH?!
YOU'RE GOING TO TRAIN AT A DOJO?
RIGHT, IF I START DOING THAT, KAREN WILL HAVE TO HUNT SOLO AGAIN.
WON'T PEOPLE OVERLOOK YOU EVEN IF YOU--?
OOPS!
GLOOOOOM
モモモモス
Oh?
Why don't you try saying that...
a little louder, hm?

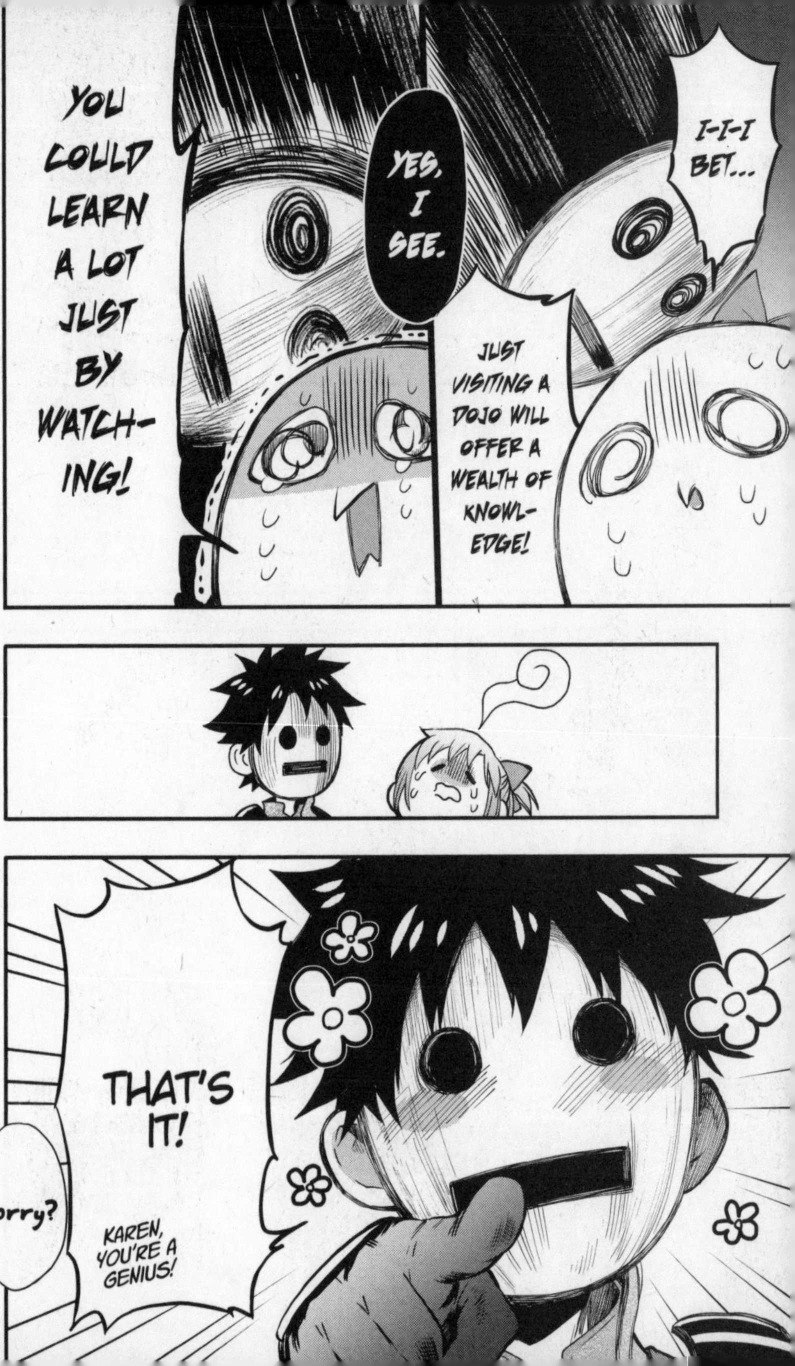
I-I-I BET...
JUST VISITING A DOJO WILL OFFER A WEALTH OF KNOWL-EDGE!
YES, I SEE.
YOU COULD LEARN A LOT JUST BY WATCH-ING!
THAT'S IT!
KAREN, YOU'RE A GENIUS!
Sorry?

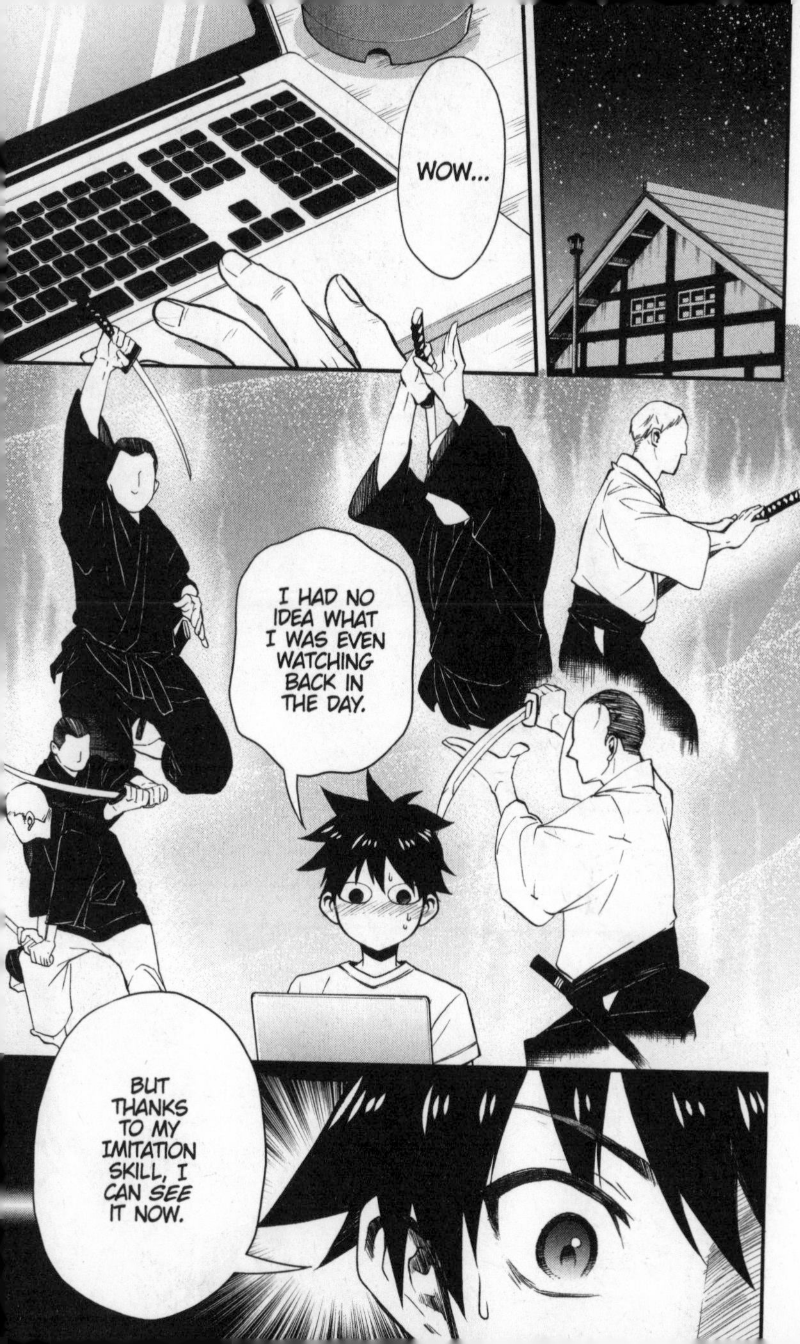
WOW...
I HAD NO IDEA WHAT I WAS EVEN WATCHING BACK IN THE DAY.
BUT THANKS TO MY IMITATION SKILL, I CAN SEE IT NOW.

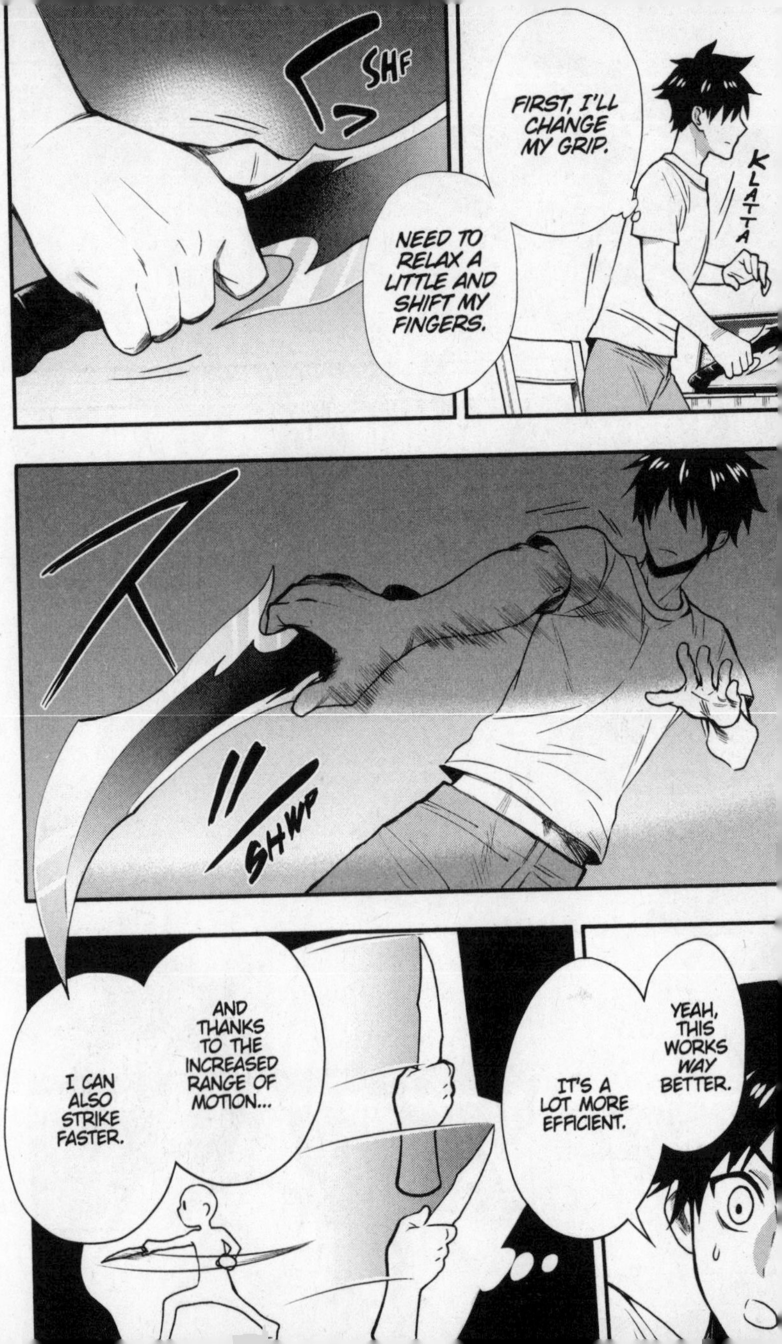
FIRST, I'LL CHANGE MY GRIP.
KLATTA
NEED TO RELAX A LITTLE AND SHIFT MY FINGERS.
SHF
SHWP
YEAH, THIS WORKS WAY BETTER.
IT'S A LOT MORE EFFICIENT.
...
AND THANKS TO THE INCREASED RANGE OF MOTION...
I CAN ALSO STRIKE FASTER.

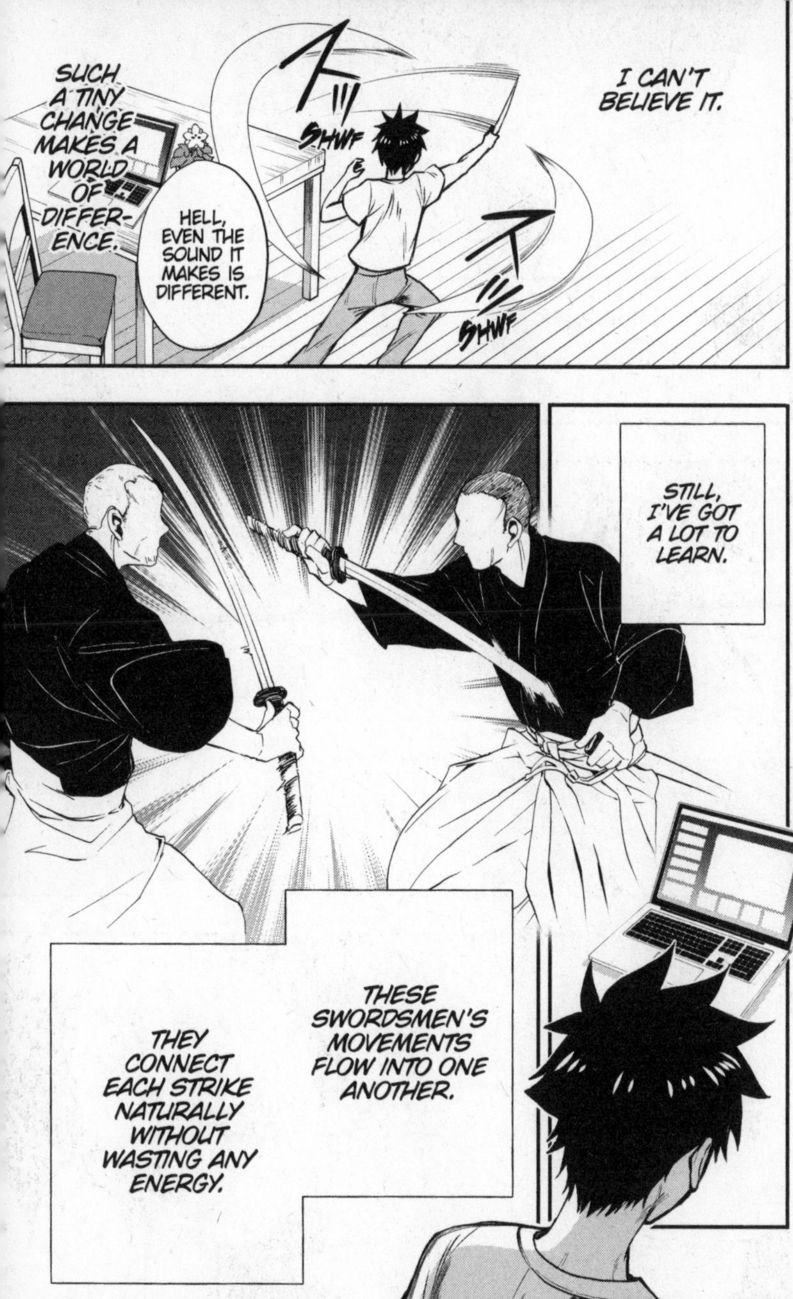
I CAN'T BELIEVE IT.
SHWF
SHWF
HELL, EVEN THE SOUND IT MAKES IS DIFFERENT.
SUCH A TINY CHANGE MAKES A WORLD OF DIFFER-ENCE.
STILL, I'VE GOT A LOT TO LEARN.
THESE SWORDSMEN'S MOVEMENTS FLOW INTO ONE ANOTHER.
THEY CONNECT EACH STRIKE NATURALLY WITHOUT WASTING ANY ENERGY.

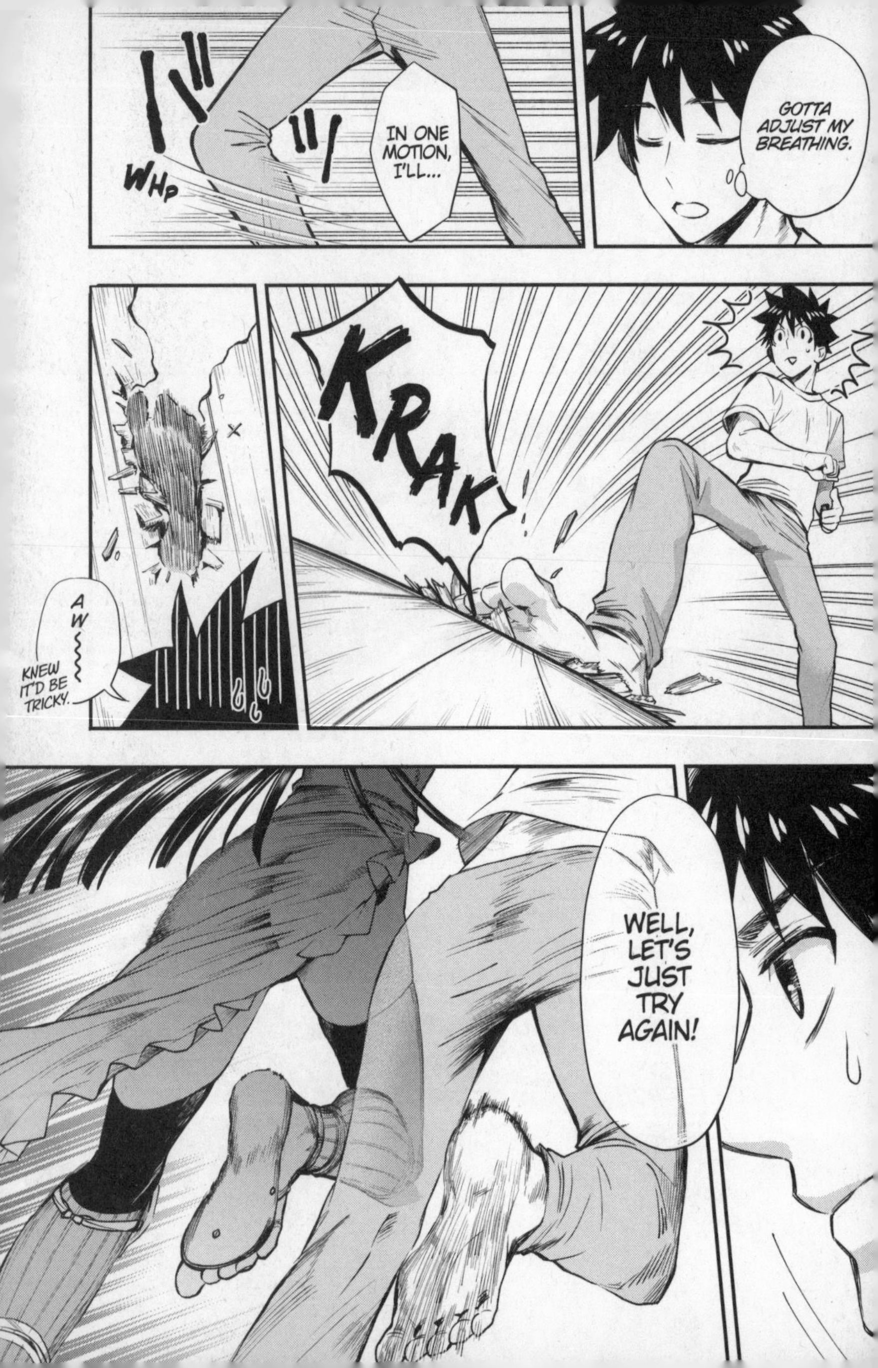
GOTTA ADJUST MY BREATHING.
IN ONE MOTION, I'LL...
WHP
KRAK
AW~~~
KNEW IT'D BE TRICKY.
WELL, LET'S JUST TRY AGAIN!

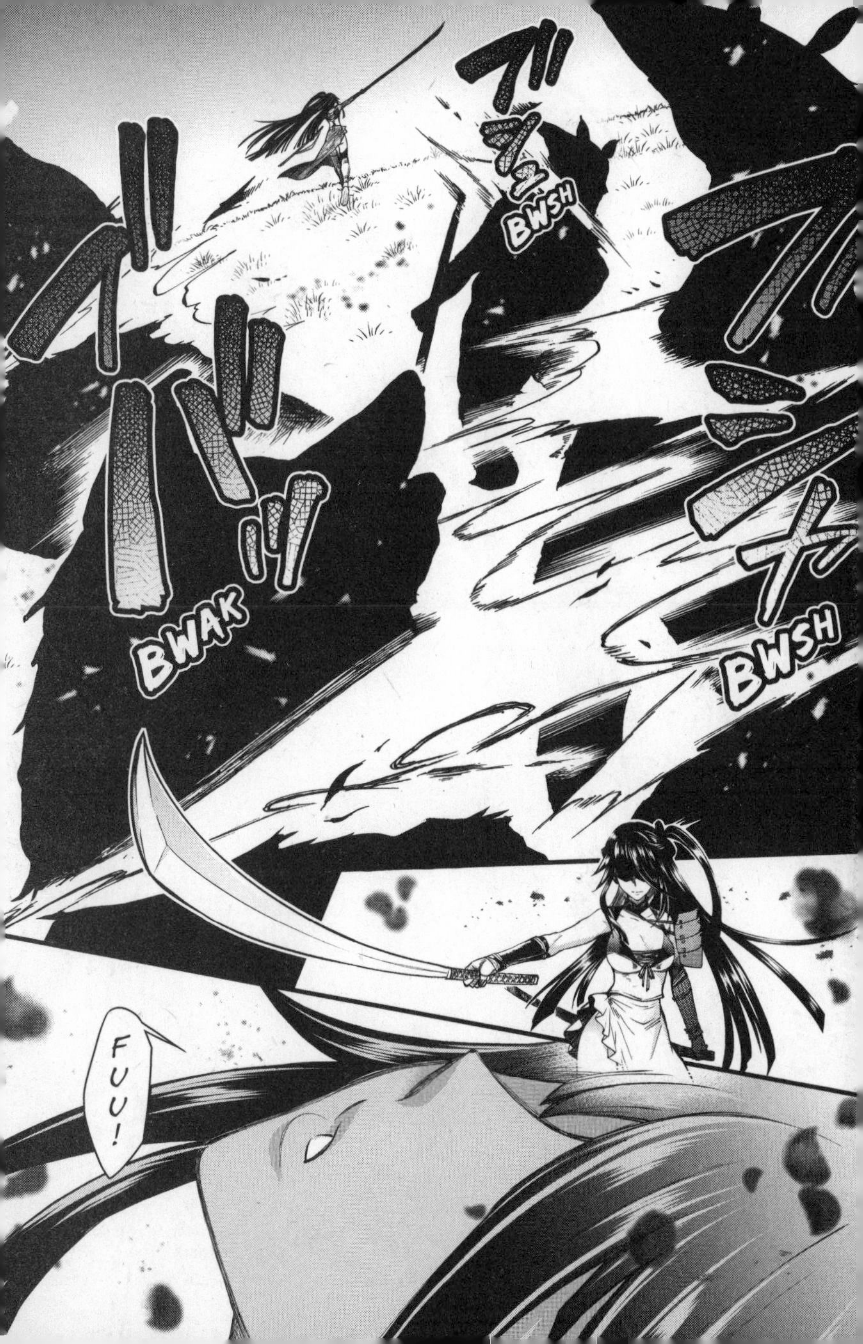
BWSH
BWSH
BWAK
FUU!

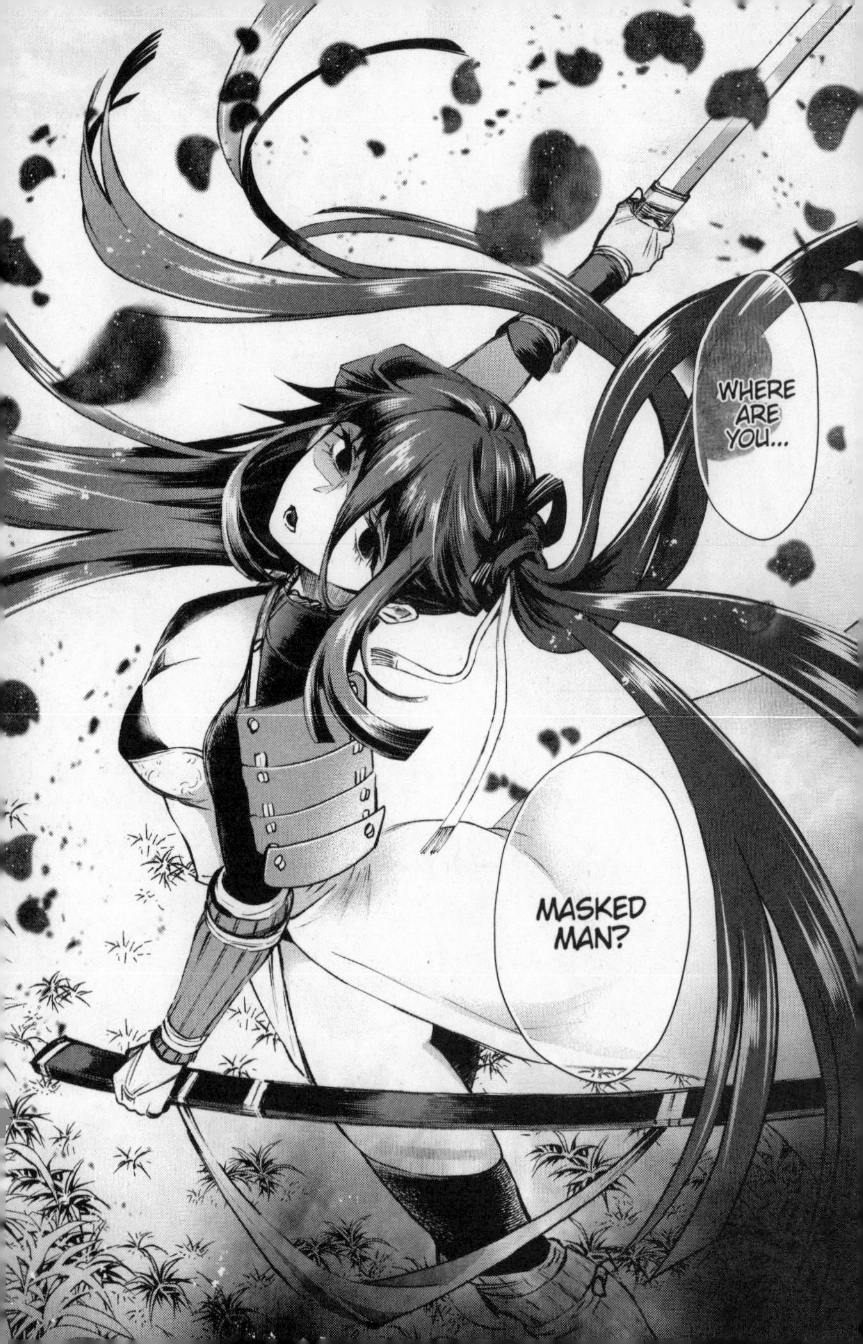
WHERE ARE YOU...
MASKED MAN?

CALL TO ADVENTURE!

DEFEATING DUNGEONS

WITH A SKILL BOARD

5

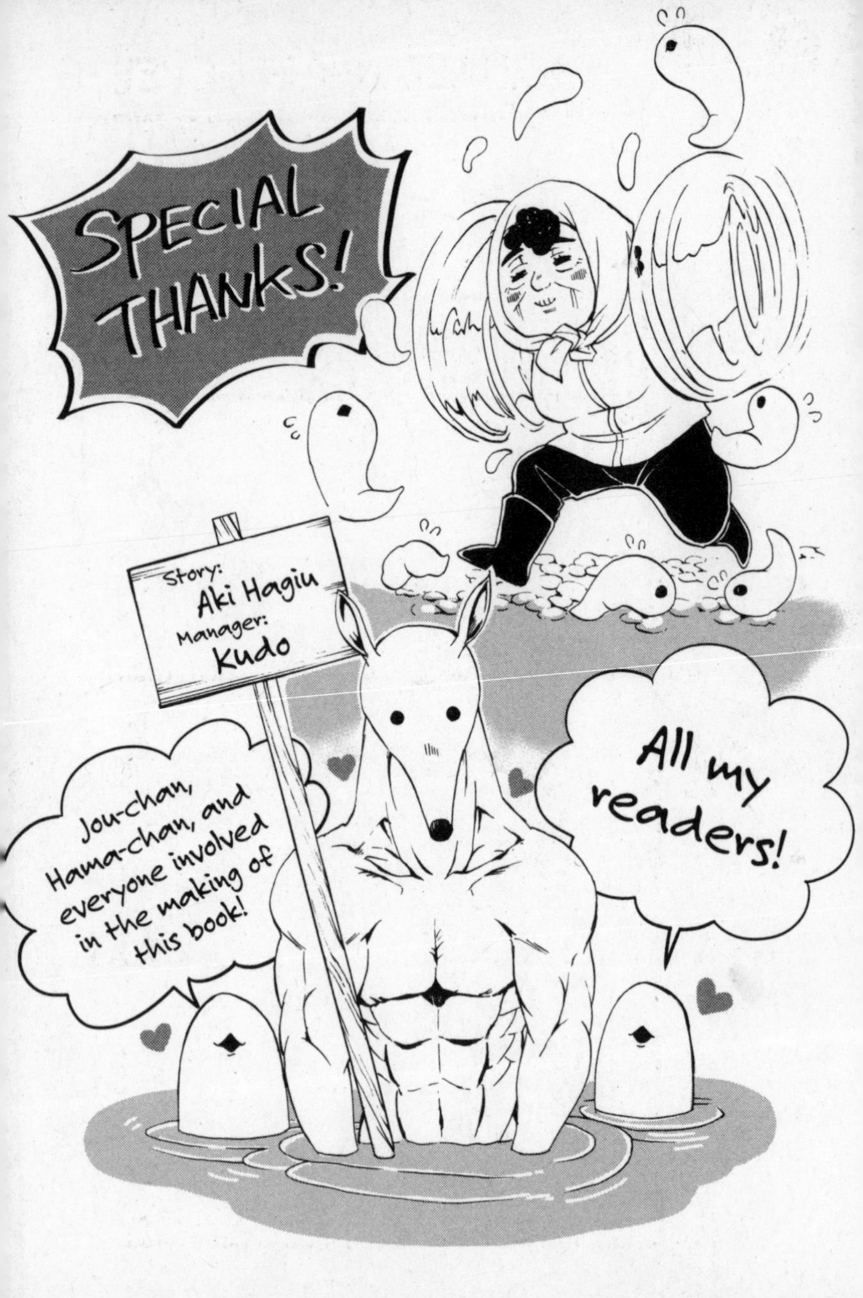
SPECIAL THANKS!
Story: Aki Hagiu
Manager: Kudo
All my readers!
Jou-chan, Hama-chan, and everyone involved in the making of this book!

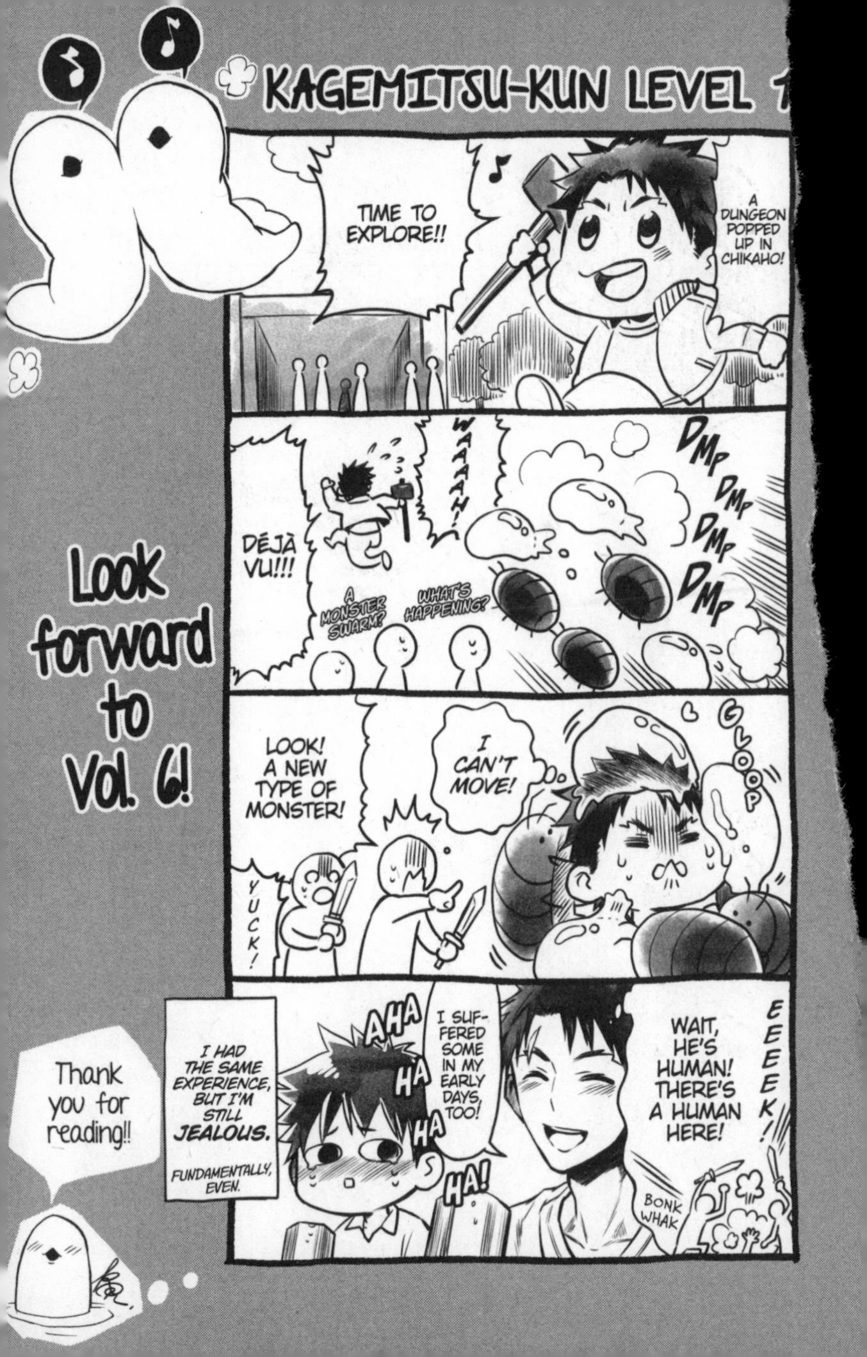
KAGEMITSU-KUN LEVEL 1
A DUNGEON POPPED UP IN CHIKAHO!
TIME TO EXPLORE!!
DMP DMP DMP DMP
WAAAAAH!
DÉJÀ VU!!!
WHAT'S HAPPENING?
A MONSTER SWARM?
GLOOP
I CAN'T MOVE!
LOOK! A NEW TYPE OF MONSTER!
YUCK!
EEEEEK!
WAIT, HE'S HUMAN! THERE'S A HUMAN HERE!
BONK WHAK
I SUFFERED SOME IN MY EARLY DAYS, TOO!
AHAHAHAHA!
I HAD THE SAME EXPERIENCE, BUT I'M STILL JEALOUS.
FUNDAMENTALLY, EVEN.
Look forward to Vol. 6!
Thank you for reading!!

SEVEN SEAS ENTERTAINMENT PRESENTS

CALL TO ADVENTURE! DEFEATING DUNGEONS WITH A SKILL BOARD Vol. 5

by **AKI HAGIU**   art by **RENJI KURIYAMA**   character design by **TEDDY**

TRANSLATION
Morgan Watchorn

ADAPTATION
Maneesh Maganti

LETTERING
Ochie Caraan

COVER DESIGN
H. Qi

LOGO DESIGN
George Panella

PROOFREADER
Kurestin Armada

COPY EDITOR
B. Lillian Martin

SENIOR EDITOR
Jenn Grunigen

PREPRESS TECHNICIAN
Jules Valera

PRINT MANAGER
Shannon Rasmussen-Silverstein

PRODUCTION DESIGNER
Christa Miesner

PRODUCTION MANAGER
Lissa Pattillo

EDITOR-IN-CHIEF
Julie Davis

ASSOCIATE PUBLISHER
Adam Arnold

PUBLISHER
Jason DeAngelis

CALL TO ADVENTURE! Defeating Dungeons with a Skill Board Vol. 5
© Renji Kuriyama, Aki Hagiu 2018
All rights reserved.
First published in Japan in 2021 by Futabasha Publishers Ltd., Tokyo.
English version published by Seven Seas Entertainment, LLC.
under license from Futabasha Publishers Ltd.

Seven Seas press and purchase enquiries can be sent to Marketing Manager Lianne Sentar at press@gomanga.com. Information about the distribution and purchase of digital editions is available from Digital Manager CK Russell at digital@gomanga.com.

Seven Seas and the Seven Seas logo are trademarks of Seven Seas Entertainment. All rights reserved.

ISBN: 978-1-63858-598-5
Printed in Canada
First Printing: February 2023
10 9 8 7 6 5 4 3 2 1

READING DIRECTIONS

This book reads from *right to left*, Japanese style. If this is your first time reading manga, you start reading from the top right panel on each page and take it from there. If you get lost, just follow the numbered diagram here. It may seem backwards at first, but you'll get the hang of it! Have fun!!

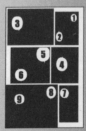

Follow us online: www.SevenSeasEntertainment.com